The Housekeeper: Love, Death, and Prizefighting

By Josh Samman

*Either write something worth reading, or
be something worth writing."*
-Benjamin Franklin

*For her
& mom*

"I just want to scream, 'Hello! My God, it's been so long. Never dreamed you'd return.' Now here you are, and here I am."

-Eddie Vedder

"Crack!"

I was woken from my daydream by the sound of a cue ball breaking a rack on the table behind me. It wasn't so much of a daydream as it was an evening one, awake but my mind somewhere other than Pockets, the shitty pool hall we were in.

The cigarette smoke was thick, and I wondered why we were still there. I hated the stuff, cigarette smoke. It aggravated my asthma and left me smelling like an ashtray. My bar stool was wobbling slightly, and every so often the same loud crack would send a soundwave through the building. My drinking companion for the night sat next to me as we ordered another round from the minimal beer selection.

Matt was my roommate and had been my closest friend for years. He was an outdoorsman, a meat and potatoes kind of guy that made his living doing tree removal. We'd both grown up in Tallahassee our whole lives, and per usual, the topic of conversation was the plot of our escape; when we would leave our beloved hometown, and where we'd go when we finally got out. We were always discussing ambitions of bigger and better things, and I tried to convince him that the time was past due. I was 24 years old, and beginning to finally get a grasp on how vast the world was, what it had to offer.

If there was one city I loved more than any, it was Tallahassee, but I felt stunted. The roots of my plant had outgrown the pot, and I yearned for more than the golden handcuffs that a cushy hometown provides. Too long I'd been inside my comfort zone, and I wanted change.

Tallahassee had its perks. It was by many accounts a young adult's playground. Leon County, where we lived, was named after Ponce de Leon, one of many Spanish explorers searching for the Fountain of Youth. If Ponce could see his county now, I think

HK

he'd agree it was a fitting title for the area. Nearly half the city's population were students, 18-24 years old, and the town was well known for its nightlife. A majority of the student body at the local university, FSU, hailed from around Miami, and much of the party atmosphere on the college side of town was influenced by sexy, but materialistic South Florida culture.

Often we saw friends get stuck spinning their wheels there. Either they were trying too hard to stick around and remain relevant with the rotation of young people coming in, or they were hanging with the same locals at the run-down hangouts like the one we were at.

That wasn't the case for everyone. Many stayed behind and began a nice life for themselves. Some were already starting families and settling into salaried nine to five careers. I felt destined for a different path though, and was determined to find out what it was.

"Corona with lime please," I called to my buddy behind the bar. "We're heading out after this one. What do I owe you?"

"You know you don't owe anything. Why out so soon? It's only midnight!" In Tallahassee, there is always time for one more.

"I have a client in the morning." I was doing personal training and private lessons at a gym I coached at, called Capital City Combat Club. I was a professional Mixed Martial Artist, "UFC fighting" as it was known to a casual fan, and I'd built a decent membership base of other fighters and clients looking to get in shape.

That's how Matt and I became attached in the first place, after he wandered in the gym one day seeking to learn how to fight. He was more of a friend now than he was a student, one of the few from the gym that I'd let seep into my personal life. We made an unlikely duo, having grown up hanging out with groups of friends that were much different. His rode pickup trucks, mine on skateboards. He was a year older than me, but I liked to big brother him.

I'm not sure why we decided to go to Pockets that evening. It wasn't a place we went often or enjoyed much. As a kid, it was the place my mom took me to play my first games of pool. Now it was a quick nightcap spot with cigarette-smoking locals, loose and worn out girls serving bad food and worse drinks. It was the side of town and sort of people that I was anxious to escape. It wasn't the type of place I expected anything life changing to happen.

I squeezed the lime in my cerveza before taking my first sip. Right as I set my bottle back on the bar I felt a pair of cold, small hands, wet with the froth of a beer, cover my eyes from behind.

A familiar voice whispered in my ear...

"Guess who?"

2.

II:II AM
March 14th, 1988,

I was born in Kissimmee, Florida, on my mother's 23rd birthday.

My first memory as a child was one of curiosity. I was five years old, and wandered out my front door and climbed onto my neighbor's motorcycle. It fell on top of me, and was the first of many signs that I was hell bent on self-destruction.

We lived in Orlando, near where I was born, for years before relocating to Florida's capital city of Tallahassee. My parents were divorced, and I stayed with my mother for the majority of my childhood, seeing my father only in bits and pieces over the years. They were so inexplicably different that I always struggled to imagine the two together. She was a tall blonde beauty, and him a short scruffy Middle Easterner.

There were brief periods when I saw small talk and short conversations between the two as they were dropping me off at each other's house, or meeting in the middle. He'd moved to Mobile, Alabama, around the same time we moved to Tallahassee.

My father was Palestinian and was born in Jerusalem. He came from a large family, went to a private school his whole life, and transferred to the states at 18 years old, eventually graduating from the University of Tennessee. He grew up in a Muslim family,

HK

but somewhere along the line decided that Muhammad and Allah weren't the doctrines for him, and began going to Christian churches shortly after moving to the states. He met my mother in a Pentecostal church in Arkansas. She joked that he'd gone there to try to pick up women.

My mom was born in Little Rock, where she lived with her brother, Mark, and my grandmother. She'd never met her father in person and was raised instead by my grandmother's new husband. They grew up in a small town, and there she stayed, playing in her school band and maintaining a 4.0 GPA, until at 18 she met my father, and got married that year.

They were divorced shortly after I was born, with my dad eventually finding another woman to build a family with, and my mom venturing in an opposite direction. For as long as I could remember, she'd always dated women, and made it clear that who she was with was not any of my father's business, and to keep her private life just that, should he ever get around to asking. I learned early that my dad equated being different with being bad.

My dad was 5'4", and what he lacked in height, he made up for with intensity. He was a conservative businessman, a buyer for department stores across the country. When he finally remarried, it was to another small town girl. This time it was a Southern Baptist from Lucedale, Mississippi, population 3,000. She was a nursing student, finishing up school in Mobile when they met. Frankie was her name, and where Frankie came from, everything revolved around church. My dad followed suit, and God became the theme of their household.

My mom had changed her last name and was a social worker for various projects in the Tallahassee area. Giving back was her passion, and she returned to school at FSU to get her Masters Degree in Social Work while I was still young, allowing her to hold leadership positions in her career. She acted as a coordinator for the local Health Department, worked for Veteran's Affairs, and was a Director for Homeless Shelters, before finally finding her niche in fundraising, becoming the director of a food drive called Second Harvest.

Growing up, I was an overly competitive kid, the one too

HK   4

concerned with winning to enjoy the game. If someone ever beat me in anything, I'd want to play them over and over until I'd won. I wanted the last word in every quibble, ever the combatant, and my mom told me I would grow up to be an attorney.

I was enrolled in our school's gifted program early, and took interests in things that many kids my age weren't into. I read at home as much as I did at school, and learned how to play chess. I was fascinated by tales of King Arthur and Camelot, enthralled with Luke Skywalker and Darth Vader. Star Wars was the first time I remember seeing good and evil reduced to something as simple as a red or blue lightsaber. My favorite color was red, and I wondered if that made me a bad guy.

I enjoyed times when I was challenged at school and had a healthy appetite for knowledge. My mom encouraged journal keeping from a young age. Eventually, I found a passion for athletics, which went hand in hand with my unhealthy competitive nature.

Running was the first form of competition I was introduced to. It felt beautiful, an instinctual thing that consisted only of being in the moment, making sure the person behind you didn't get ahead, and that the person in front of you was caught up with. It was also my first introduction to excess. I remember an occasion where the Phys Ed teacher offered an incentive for children to exercise on their own. "The 25 Mile Club," was the name of it, a challenge to kids to run over the semester. Parents would clock a distance in their neighborhood and verify their children's progress, should they partake in the challenge.

By the end of the semester, 20 or so children in the school had completed it. I'd decided I was going to run around my neighborhood until I'd reached 150 miles, making my own pointless club. I felt the urge to reach above others, over things as trivial as a few extra ribbons.

Besides jogging around my neighborhood, which I never grew out of, and being a nerd, I wanted to be in the military, to my mother's dismay. My uncle was in the army and used to take me to the shooting range to piss his sister off. If there was one thing she detested most, it was violence. As a child, I was not allowed to

HK

have toy guns, wasn't allowed to play football, and I damn sure wasn't allowed to watch anything with fighting.

She was adamant about it, but powerless as to what I did when I went to my dad's. Imagine his frustration, coming to pick me up and hearing from me all the manly shit my mom wouldn't let me do. My early memories of spending time with him are watching old Bruce Lee Kung Fu flicks and Clint Eastwood westerns, or playing fighting games that he bought for me on the Nintendo. Back and forth I would go between my two parents with conflicting ideologies, a confusing time for a young child.

I was nine years old when I returned home from one of these trips to my dad's that my mom sat me down on the couch to talk. I remember feeling frightened, that maybe I'd done something wrong and was getting disciplined.

We sat there for a moment in silence while I wondered what was going on. Her behavior was not the normal excited and jovial mother she usually was when I'd return home from a weekend away.

The lights were dim, yet bright enough for me to see her bluish green eyes were wet. I'd never seen my mom cry, and began to feel alarmed. She finally found the courage she was looking for.

"I have to tell you something honey, but I need you to know first that everything is going to be okay, no matter what."

3.

I played along, trying to guess who it was that had snuck up behind me. A girl, I just didn't know which one.

"Umm.. Give me a hint."

She let out a subtle giggle that I hadn't heard in years, and I was overcome by a flood of memories.

"Your worst nightmare," a playful whisper, and she took her hands off my eyes. I turned around. It was who I thought it was, and while she sounded the same, she didn't look it.

She was sporting an unusually pale complexion, wearing a thin Led Zeppelin t-shirt and jeans, the smell of cigarettes on her breath. She wasn't the girl I remembered, but my heartbeat rose as she stood in front of me and gave me a long embrace.

She sat to my right, doing her best to pick up where she left off years ago.

"Where have you been?" I asked her. My chest fluttered as I found eye contact.

"Don't act like you don't know where I've been." She was the only girl I knew without any social media accounts, and we'd been left to rumors for years.

"I've heard some things. How are you now?"

"Right now, with you, I'm doing good." Coy, with a weak attempt at charm, avoiding particulars. I understood but insisted.

"Besides this moment here and now, how are you?"

"I'm hanging in there." She interrupted our conversation and hailed the bartender for a drink.

"Whiskey soda?" I cut in. My dad had always warned me about girls that liked whiskey.

"You remembered," she smiled. I probably remembered a lot more than she thought.

She had her best friend, Anna, with her, who took a seat to the left of Matt. Anna was a wholesome girl, with a bold personality. They began a conversation of their own, and we decided to stick around a bit longer to catch up.

"We are going to go to the lady's room, don't run out on us while we're gone." They walked away, and Matt looked at me with a goofy smile. "So much for going home early, eh?"

"One more drink." He sensed something and was anxious to ask questions. The bartender began to chat it up, and the girls came back before he had the chance.

One drink turned into five, as we revisited old memories and stories from earlier in life. It became closing time, and a crossroads.

"We gonna take this to the house or what?" Matt said, trying to convince all three of us.

I looked at her to gauge her response. I wasn't sure, myself.

"How far do you live?" she replied.

HK

I don't know if it was intoxication or nostalgia that lured me in. I knew I hadn't seen her in too long, and wasn't sure when I would again.

4.

"Everything's going to be okay," my mom said again.

I sat there, curious, as I awaited what would be my first bit of real bad news in my life.

"Everything is going to be fine Josh, but what I need to tell you.." She paused again. "Is that I have breast cancer." She gazed me down, trying to get a glimpse into what I felt as she broke the news.

I wasn't old enough to have a grasp on the meaning. I didn't know what cancer did to people, or what it meant for us, but I knew that she looked nervous.

"Does that mean your hair is going to fall out?" I asked. My response garnered a look of relief from her, happy that I was worried about something as silly as her hair. I was young, but I understood the concept of terminal illnesses. I just didn't know what else to say at the time.

Being with my mom was my favorite thing as a kid, singing and dancing for her as she watched, smiling. I wondered for a second what life would be like without her. The thought frightened me, and I tried not to think about it again.

"Yes honey, my hair is probably going to fall out," she let out with a laugh of relief, still doing her best to hold back tears. In reality, the two of us would later buzz her hair off before it had a chance to fall out. She didn't tell me that then, though.

"I love you, sweetheart. Everything is going to be alright."

"I love you too." I struggled to show affection at that age. I thought it was too mushy to tell your mom you loved her, but I remember saying it that night. I believed her when she said everything was going to be alright.

One of her friends sat me down as the time for treatment

drew near, talking to me more candidly than my mom was willing to.

"Your mom is going to be very sick," she said. "At times she may not seem or look like the same person you're used to, but you need to be strong for her."

Tall order for a nine year old. At the time, I just sat and nodded, trying to take it in. It was the first time I'd been presented with any sort of heaviness, feeling the weight of a situation in a way children aren't used to.

"We are praying for you." I began to hear it often. It never gave me the comfort I think it was intended to. At this point in my life, even at nine, I had my suspicions about God. The more I went to Sunday school, the more I began to think that these stories in the bible weren't any different than the fairy tales I'd just grown out of hearing. Jonah and the Whale, Jack and the Beanstalk, Noah and the Ark, Alice in Wonderland, they might as well all have been the same. I tried to talk to Jesus, but I never heard anything back. I didn't know what everyone was praying for.

"God won't give you anything you can't handle," they said. The thought of someone controlling all of our destinies scared me. I struggled with the concept of an omnipotent being giving a person an illness, only to require everyone to pray for it to go away. I did my best to be strong for my mom like her friend told me to, and sometimes wondered if I should be praying too. The whole concept was puzzling, and I was a skeptic from the beginning.

5.

"All journeys have secret destinations of which the traveler is unaware."

- Martin Buber

We stumbled out of Pockets more inebriated than we'd planned, but my house was less than a mile away. They decided against leaving Anna's car, and followed us home in theirs.

HK

Matt got in the passenger seat and didn't waste time asking questions. He'd seen me with dozens of girls, and picked up on differences in behavior over the last hours. He had a knack for reading me and knew when something had my attention.

"What was all that about?" He grinned inquisitively.

The rock in my shoe.

"What was all 'what' about?" Poker face. He knew who she was, a local like us, he just had no context of our relationship. Matt had come into my life at the time that she'd last left it, and the brief minute or two home wasn't the time or place for that story. I promised I'd explain later.

Isabel was her name. Isabel Monroe, the crown jewel of the city. She was the youngest of four siblings, all brothers. Her father, Dallas, was a veterinarian and played in a popular band in Tallahassee. Their mom, Sue, was stunning herself. Her brothers, Owen, Wyatt, and Landon, were all heartbreakers in their own right. Growing up in Tallahassee, if you were a girl, you had a crush on the Monroe brothers, and if you were a guy you were in love with Isabel. It was like that for all of us. The family was looked up to by everyone in town, with their roots going deep into its history.

The youngest of the boys, Owen, was my age, Wyatt two years older than us, and Landon four years. All three kept catches on their arm, the cream of the crop of girls in Tallahassee. Isabel spent her youth on the futile search for a boy that could hold a candle to her brothers and father.

She was a dream girl, the most crushed-on-jealousy-inducing one the world had ever seen, as far as I was concerned. I'd often wonder if she knew the extent to which people adored her, if her bashful nature was actually genuine. By the time I met her, she was used to having teenage boys fawn over her, and girls of all ages trying to befriend her just to get a bit closer to her brothers.

When we met, she was just over 5', tan skin, athletic body, and the most heavenly face I'd ever seen. It was accentuated by a perfect, distinct widow's peak, long gorgeous eyelashes, a button nose, deep, charming dimples, and flowing Cherokee oak hair that had never been touched by dye. She spoke with a mild southern twang, and had a radiance about her that could set a room on fire.

When the time and place would come, I'd tell Matt about my vixen from a past life. I'd tell him how she was the one that got away, a relationship never fulfilled. I thought of her often, and was shocked to find her on this night, at this place.

We got home and were greeted at the door by my dog, Juice. Within seconds Isabel was sitting on the floor, hugging and kissing him as if he was her own. I had long suspected she was his favorite too.

The four of us hung out for a while longer before Isabel and I retired to my room. I felt the same familiar butterflies that I always had as we laid down next to each other. I tried to calm them, and listened carefully as she began her story.

6.

Late Spring, 1998

While my mother was in Tallahassee fighting cancer, raising me, and working a full-time job, my dad and Frankie were creating their family with two new daughters, Hannah and Sahar. I always wanted siblings and was excited when they were born. I would want to visit them often, either in Mobile, or an hour west, in my stepmom's hometown of Lucedale.

Some of my fondest memories growing up were at my aunt's house in that Mississippi town. They had a large estate in the middle of the woods, with a big family, and three older cousins that I looked up to. Jason, Jeremy, and Jeanna were their names, and they treated me like their own. As a young child, my family referred to me by my middle name, Kaleb. It wasn't until I met my cousins that I wanted to be called Josh because it sounded more like their names. They helped culture and shape me, introduced me to movies I loved like Forrest Gump and Good Will Hunting.

Their family life was a stark contrast to the upbringing that I was used to. I was attracted to the idea of having a large clan, with sons and daughters to make grandchildren and a lofty family tree.

HK

I wished my parents had stuck together, like my cousins' parents had, and became enamored with the concept of romantic love, the idea of there being one person out there for all of us.

I came home from many of these trips, unable to hide my excitement at how much fun I'd had, how grand the house was, with their huge yard and swimming pool. I'm sure my mom was happy I got to experience those things, but looking back I see how it could've upset her. I'm sure sometimes she wished she could have given me those things that I enjoyed so much.

While she couldn't provide me with a big family, she made up for it by trying to instill values in other ways. She would force me to volunteer (how's that for an oxymoron?) wherever it was she was working, stressing the importance of giving back. I didn't appreciate it at the time, but I look at it now with pride and admiration at what she was trying to teach.

She had a special way of doing that, conveying things to me. One day, around the age my mom was starting Chemotherapy, our cable went out. I thought the TV was broken and that it would come back on shortly. My mom said differently.

"I had to shut it off, sweetheart," she said. "It costs money, and it's a luxury we can't afford."

At the time, I got a weekly allowance for helping with chores around the house. I asked her if I could use that to help pay the cable bill.

"You could. Or maybe we can figure a way for you to make your own money while keeping your allowance."

My mind wandered, trying to ponder clever ways I could earn money for us. I remember there being an after school store that sold candy and popsicles to students after class was out. I couldn't carry around popsicles in my backpack all day, but I could damn sure fit some candy in there. I asked my mom if I could buy a big bag of it at the grocery store with my allowance. She said yes, and I took it to school the next day to sell for cheaper than the school was offering.

It didn't take long for me to get caught by my 4th grade teacher, who was awfully concerned by it. It was highly frowned upon, my teacher explained to my mom, for a student to be selling candy, or anything for that matter, at school at such a young age. My mom didn't understand what the big deal was. I sold chocolate for school fundraisers door to door every semester for the school in efforts to outsell classmates. The teacher advised I devote my efforts elsewhere, and suggested a local speech contest. I was interested.

I asked my mom what I should write about.

"What do you want to write about?" she asked back.

"Well, what do you write about?"

"Nowadays it's only things for work."

"What if I write about your work?"

I didn't know what exactly she did at her job. I just knew it was something helping people. Folks were always thanking her for her help when we were at her work functions. It had an impact on me, her status in the community.

She suggested a heavy topic. She'd seen several cases of domestic abuse recently at her job, and thought it should be something I should learn about. I didn't know where to start.

"Well, you tell people the facts, then you tell them how you feel about it, then finally what you think we should do about it." She helped with much along the way. It was weighty content for a 4th grader, but there I was, taking my speech around the county, winning local and regional contests, doing my best to champion a cause. The seed of putting pen to paper had been planted. She was proud, and decided it was time for the next step in manhood.

I turned 10 years old, and my gift that year was a lawn mower. Looking back now, it was another amazing attempt at instilling character traits that would pay dividends later in life. At the time, I was not thrilled.

"Mom! What the heck am I gonna do with this?"

"Well, for one you're gonna mow our lawn with it. And two, you can start making some money for yourself. You're old enough."

More work didn't sound like fun, but she insisted. It wasn't as much about the money as it was about teaching me, not just about independence, but interdependence, pulling weight and helping those around you.

HK

I could help with cable, maybe even some movie channels, I thought. In the midst of trying to get myself excited to push a lawn mower around in the hot Florida sun, I came across a magazine for a department store, selling an above ground pool for $899.99. That became my goal. I was either very ambitious or delusional. Realistic thinking was the most often traveled path to mediocrity, I'd learn later.

I started around door to door, asking each neighbor if I could mow their lawn for them weekly. I printed out flyers and stapled them to light posts around the neighborhood. I managed to get a good amount of work, and saved up a few hundred dollars. I never got the pool I wanted, but valuable lessons were learned. I knew then that if there was anything I wanted, it was best to just go out and get it.

I continued selling candy to kids around my neighborhood, away from the supervision of nosey teachers. It wasn't as much money as mowing lawns, but not as much work either.

Hell, I didn't even like candy.

7.

"Sometimes junkies fall asleep," she told me, "and I happened to fall asleep in the middle of using." We hadn't gotten to the extent of what she meant by "using," but I didn't want to interrupt.

There I was, in bed with a girl I wasn't even sure I'd ever see again. Like most around her, I'd given up hope of the person I once knew. She'd turned into someone else entirely. I had a hard time taking in the things she was telling me.

"And that's how they found me, overdosed, asleep in the car."

They were the police, and the incident she was describing was an acute OD she'd suffered just weeks ago. After being rushed to the hospital, she was taken to Leon County Jail, on several drug charges, and a count of paraphernalia.

We'd all used together in high school, to varying degrees. I had dealt with substance abuse myself and seen dozens of cases in friends. I knew she'd had problems, but wasn't sure how far down the rabbit hole she'd traveled.

Her drug of choice was opiates, which she'd already visited three rehabs for, before finally being taken to jail. There she sat, for what she hoped would be the final time, suffering opiate withdrawals with no methadone.

Hell on Earth was how she described it, waking up on a concrete floor and realizing what had happened. She explained the terror, anxiety, and physical pain in such detail that it sent shivers down my spine. She was only 21.

Look how the mighty have fallen.

"I tried to quit every day," she said, "and every night I gave up. I don't even know how it got to this point."

"What about the rehabs?"

"They didn't help. All I did at those places was learn how to do drugs better."

"What does that mean?"

"When I first got admitted, I had a problem. I'd discovered roxys and oxys, and got carried away eating them. When I went to rehab, I was surrounded by actual junkies, who explained how great drugs could really be, if only I used them right. After the first time I got out, I relapsed in days. Of all the times I'd done roxys, I had never snorted or smoked one. And I was curious." I didn't like where the story was going.

"I was still living with my parents, and I got caught using again," she said. "And they sent me to a longer program, at Shands in Gainesville." Shands was one of the best hospitals in the nation, and very expensive.

"I spent a few months there, and got out and moved in with Landon." Landon was her oldest brother and was living in Gainesville at the time, finishing Veterinary school like their dad. "That didn't last long either before I relapsed again, and got taken out of state." Out of state was to Georgia, at a program called "Bridges of Hope."

HK

"After finishing Bridges, I came back to Tallahassee and moved back in with my dad."

"So the paraphernalia they found, that was a pipe you freebased with?" The word freebase was such a nasty word, I shuddered as it rolled off my tongue.

"No."

She got quiet for the first time in the night, looking to wish away the question.

"What was it?" All signs should've pointed to me not having to ask. I wasn't thinking clearly.

"I was shooting up when I fell asleep, Josh." She sounded so shameful and embarrassed. I struggled to contain my shock.

"They found you with a fucking needle in your arm?"

"In my hand. I used to shoot into my hand." She gently rubbed at the scar tissue on the small vein opposite her palm.

My heart sank. I was dumbfounded. We both laid in silence for a few moments. I had so many more questions. Feeling the moment getting too heavy, I asked an insignificant one.

"Well, where were you?"

"In the parking lot."

"What parking lot?"

"Pockets."

"You had a fucking overdose in the parking lot that we *just* left?"

"Well, the movie theater lot next to it." I sat, speechless.

"I have to go back," she said after a few moments of silence.

"Back where?"

"Back to court. I still haven't gotten my sentence. My parents refused to bail me out when I got arrested, and the judge finally let me out after my last court date."

"Well, what do you think is gonna happen?"

"My public defender says they will offer me a few years of probation or a few months of jail."

"You know your probation is going to have drug tests."

"I'm not going to choose probation."

"What do you mean?"

"I want this behind me."

"You're going to go to jail? You think that's a good idea?" I had been in Leon County Jail, and the thought of her stuck there for three months didn't sit well.

"I've been in institutions before, one more is not going to kill me." She had a point.

"Okay, Thug Life." I joked, trying to make light of the situation. There was a difference between a luxurious rehab and bologna sandwiches for 90 days. She'd soon find out.

8.

Spring, 1999

I must have displayed signs of Godlessness early, because I was often asked by my stepmom's family if I'd found Jesus. I began seeing a counselor when my mom became ill and confided in him about phrases I heard that confused me. He told me that God was something that many people looked to, to cope with life's events. While he said He wasn't real, I spent years of my life waiting for everyone to finally tell me the jig was up, that deep down no one really believed the stuff they were saying. Like Santa Claus and the Tooth Fairy, I assumed this too would pass.

I tried to ask questions and understand what made them believe, but my skepticism was met not with answers, but instead with more church, more youth services, more drilling it into my head that I needed God. In their doctrine, curiosity was the opposite of faith, and the two seeming mutually exclusive made me resent it.

I had moved on to reading things by people I knew were real. I enjoyed being perplexed by Agatha Christie mysteries, having my imagination run wild in Michael Crichton science fictions and gripping suspense of John Grisham novels. If I didn't know the word in a book I was reading, I would keep a dictionary in my desk to look it up. I liked being called on in class to read, to show others my proficiency. I liked standardized testing, quantifying a pecking order of intelligence, and being recognized for it.

HK

I enjoyed science fairs at school, and always wanted to know what it was the older kids were learning. I was class president, and if I didn't know something, I would pretend until I did. One of my teachers, a splendid lady named Mrs. Frinks, would take me around the school to perform different projects and experiments. Together we'd administer arithmetic tests to students under various stimuli, such as classical music, or rock'n'roll, or sounds of birds chirping. Sometimes I'd race her or other teachers on the same tests. She challenged the class and me to make bridges out of nothing but spaghetti and rubber cement, or see who could devise the most efficient package to drop raw eggs from atop of the school without them breaking. She once showed the class a childbirth video to help us understand the cycle of life. She peaked my curiosity from a young age, encouraged the cerebral.

I attempted to read parts of the bible, but at the same time I heard about religious stories in church, I was learning about how thousands, and even sometimes hundreds of years ago, we believed the earth was flat, and the center of our universe. I wondered how much multiple authors writing a book from 2,000 years ago could be trusted.

During my summers in Tallahassee, I attended a camp run out of a local church, called East Hill. It was actually my idea, as my first childhood friend went there, a Hawaiian kid named Kane. I told my mom I wanted to do the same, and she was delighted to be able to tell my dad I was going to a Christian camp.

I really enjoyed the place. It wasn't overly faith-based. There was chapel once a week, but the rest of the days were great, alternating between video games, swimming pools, and an indoor gymnasium. I went back every year for as long as they would let me.

My mom would want to go to church sometimes, though not often, and when we did it was to a liberal, non-denominational church, named Unity. People there didn't dress in suits. They had on sandals, and tie dye shirts, with long hair. It seemed more like a hangout for hippies and lesbian women. They met every Sunday like traditional church, had programs and sang songs, but didn't preach the same gospel as the Southern Baptist churches I had to go to in Alabama and Mississippi. They didn't try to scare folks with threats of burning in hell or eternal damnation, or try to seduce people into being good by offering eternal bliss.

She always tried to give me free reign to form opinions for myself, something I'd grow to be grateful for later in life. She never tried to shove her beliefs down my throat. Sometimes I think she was unsure of them herself. When asked about God, she once told me she liked to imagine him up there, making tally marks for all the good and bad things people had done. She told me to make sure the good outweighed the bad, that *being* good was important to *feeling* good.

I wasn't always good to people, and maybe it showed. I was 10 years old, and had many friends, but I had a sense of peerlessness. Some of it was being a narcissistic, condescending prick to kids in school, but much of it was noticing that many children simply weren't being raised the way I was.

To say I had an unconventional childhood was an understatement, and as my mother gave me more freedom to do the things I wanted, the gap between my upbringings and the lives of others my age began to broaden.

9.

"Rock bottom sometimes begins the solid foundations on which we build our lives."

-JK Rowling

Isabel was staying at Anna's house while awaiting her next court date. I'd promised we wouldn't lose touch again, albeit not without hesitation. I was still reeling myself in from the night before, wondering where this path would lead should I choose to wander down. I had experienced firsthand the destructive effects an addict could have on the lives of those around them. I had once been the one doing the destruction. She'd burned through many of her bridges, and I felt compelled, like I owed it to her. I would

HK

help her where I could, but that would be the extent of it. That's what I told myself.

She didn't have a phone at the time, so I had to call her on Anna's if I wanted to talk to her. I wanted a more reliable way to check in, and bought her a cheap flip phone.

I spoke to her almost every day, always wondering if that was the day where she would spring back into past behavior. We hung out a few times a week, often she'd want to go out for drinks. As long as she wasn't sticking needles in her arm I guess we were making progress. I gave her rides to court-ordered drug tests, which were a condition of her temporary release.

The day was getting closer, and I wondered if she was still planning on going through with jail instead of probation.

"You're sure this is what you want to do?"

"Yeah. I don't want to be in this system anymore. I don't want to listen to one more drug counselor, I don't want to have to go to one more NA meeting. I don't want a constant reminder of what a fuck up I was. My mistakes are going to follow me around everywhere if I have to be reminded of them with a probation meeting every month for the next three years."

The jail time served as a purgatory in her mind, a way to purge herself clean of her mistakes. She envisioned herself getting out and making a real life, returning to old form.

We discussed jail visitation as it got closer. She insisted I not come. She didn't want me to see her reduced to an inmate number and a gray jumpsuit. I maintained otherwise. I'd been on the wrong side of the thick glass wall, knew how much a friend could help morale.

The date finally came, as we knew it would, and I had gotten much closer to her than I intended. I'm not sure if either of our motives were pure at the time. We always had chemistry, and I still found myself with a soft spot for her. I think, though, that maybe there was more underneath, that to Isabel I represented a time in her life when she was more golden. Maybe now she was reminiscing about how good things used to be, how everyone once adored her, and maybe she wanted a reminder of that.

Maybe I latched on because I wanted to remember how far I'd come since being an 18 year-old punk kid, chasing after a girl I was never quite able to reel in.

10.

Fall, 1999

My mom and I began a series of what I now realize were bucket list items. We went to the Grand Canyon, the Smokies, and more. Experiences and memories were more important than things, she taught me. We went camping on the weekends and had gone whitewater rafting during the summer. She was sick but managed to hide it well. She wore a prosthetic breast, and her long blonde hair had been replaced by wigs. She thought her being bald embarrassed me. It didn't.

I wish I could say I made the next several years easier for her, that I continued to help around the house, and do the things she'd taught me up until middle school. The truth is that I made things as terrible as possible, though I didn't mean to. Somewhere along the way I had just taken a wrong turn.

I was under consideration for what was called the International Baccalaureate program, a set of courses for standout students that extended beyond typical Advanced Placement classes until the end of high school. The program was intense, and intrigued me, save one minor detail. The IB program, as it was known, was placed in inner-city schools, in order to raise the average overall testing scores of that particular school. In Leon County, the chosen schools were Fairview Middle and Rickards High. The crime rate at both was severe, as well as dropout rates, and all parties involved were wary of me being in that situation. I shadowed at the school for a single day before agreeing it wasn't for me.

The de facto school I was zoned for was Swift Creek, a much more suburban environment, with many of the kids I'd gone to elementary school with. While I entered the 6th grade with several of the friends that I'd grown up with, it wouldn't be

HK

these friends I was interested in for much longer. I was always in a hurry to grow up, couldn't wait to reach my teenage years.

My first day of 6th grade, I walked to the bus stop at the top of my neighborhood, nervously excited for the next chapter in my life. As all kids did in grade school, I had my favorite outfit picked out for the first day of class, and was anxious to see what new school was going to be like.

When I arrived at the bus stop, there was a large group of students near the road, waiting for the bus. A smaller group crowded behind the local Dunkin' Donuts. I walked towards them to see what they were doing.

As I got closer, I noticed a familiar smell, cigarette smoke. By this point, I'd already been walking their way too long to turn around.

"Hi. I'm Josh."

They seemed surprised at being approached so frankly. I may have been a lot of things, but an introvert I was not. I looked them over, wondering what kids this age were doing smoking cigarettes. They were a couple years older, doing their best to grow long, stringy, facial hair.

"You want one?" A kid pulled out his pack of cigarettes in my direction.

Newport Menthol, it said on the box, a brand I'd seen.

"Sure." As I said this, I caught myself, wondering what I was doing, why I was so willing to try this without any second thought. My whole life I'd attached a negative connotation to cigarettes, never once being curious about them, and now here I was, 11 years old, instantly willing to see what the hype was about.

My curiosity silenced my better judgment, and I grabbed the cigarette as if I knew what I was doing. I did my best to hold the lighter steadily as I lit it like I'd seen people in movies do.

I made sure to take a small hit at first, not wanting to cough in front of the group. I had taken a couple drags before I started to feel a lightheadedness. I hit it again, harder, and got a rush of euphoria. It was my first experience with any mind altering substance, and I liked it. I liked it a lot.

I left my phone and keys at check-in for the Leon County Jail, and made the long trek towards D-block, where non-violent women criminals were held. It would be Isabel's home for the next 90 days.

I pressed the buzzer to notify the jail guard I was there and sat opposite the thick pane of glass that separated inmate from visitor. There was a long hallway they had to walk on the way to visitation, up the stairs and straight towards us for 40 yards.

I watched her take that walk every step of the way that day. I tried to read her body language. She was running her hands through her hair, trying to make herself look as presentable as possible, considering the circumstances. She managed to crack a smile, which was a good sign, and picked up the phone opposite me.

"Well, how is it?" She had been there a couple days already.

"It's jail." She did her best to lighten the mood. "I still have great hair, right?"

"Gorgeous. The best." I let her set the tone for conversation, and was glad to see her in good spirits. I knew this wasn't how she wanted to be seen, but better than not being seen at all.

We began with small talk, a couple awkward moments, and some silence before both of us settled and became comfortable with the situation.

I wasn't her therapist, but I knew she had things she was wrestling with. More than anything I was just trying to make the road a bit easier for someone I cared for. I could relate to her more than she realized. I too had been in and out of institutions, had hurt my family before, and had caused my parents more than their fair share of grief. I knew what it was like to be addicted to something, to many things.

If she wanted small talk for 30 minutes, I gave her small talk. If she wanted more serious, I was there for that too. Visitation after visitation we hammered away at details of how she'd gotten

HK

there. Much of our conversations were mistakes that she made, regrets she had.

Her whole life as I knew her, the most important thing to her was the approval and love of her family. She loved talking about them. There were parents and brothers and aunts and uncles and cousins galore, many of them on their way or already doctors and professors. They loved her, although she was unsure of it. They'd become unable to hide their disappointment, and tough love was the motto most had adopted.

She didn't have many other visitors, and after getting a grasp on what had transpired in years past, I didn't blame them. It occurred to me what a nightmare it must have been, left with nothing but concrete walls and bars. She had done it to herself, and expressed the torment eloquently.

"What's the worst part about being in here for you?"

"There's nothing to get lost in, nothing to lose myself in the moment with. I've got a few books, my thoughts, and regrets." Finding things to escape in, that's what life was about for people like us. Sex, or drugs, or travel, or music, or religion, we all needed something.

"I think it's helping me change, though. I feel different this time."

She told stories of troublesome folks she would use with, a whole variety of people. Nurses that stole from their doctors, women who looted from dealer boyfriends. Isabel had stolen from her parents on occasion, when faced with unwanted withdrawal. She explained, always with disgust in her voice at what she'd done.

One instance that was difficult for her to get passed was a time she had stolen a gun from her dad's safe. It was a shotgun, and happened to be the very first her brother Landon ever owned. She looked at that as the moment the trust was severed, the turning point she felt they gave up on her. It was a family keepsake, sold and shot up into her veins.

"I just don't know what the hell I was doing. I don't know what I was thinking. When I look back now it feels like that was another person. I remember one time my dad walked into my room while I was trying to smoke the last bit of drugs I had. He caught me and took it from me, and I chased him down the hall crying, begging him to give it back. I can't imagine what that was like for him." To be an addict is to not just taste desperation, but to become intimate with it, a fact that she knew well.

The more we talked, the more I saw her heal, and the more she began to show an emotional maturity like she hadn't before. She accepted responsibility and acknowledged that she'd hurt many people in the process.

All of our 30-minute sessions ended the same, with me leaving money in the jail canteen, an account for inmates to purchase snacks or make phone calls. It was an unforgiving place. It had a particular way of reminding me that things could always get worse. Leaving there always put me in a peculiar mood, greeted by the sunlight, freedom to come and go as I pleased.

12.

Early Winter, 1999

Classes at middle school were not at all what I thought they'd be. Teachers there saw a couple hundred kids a day, and I didn't build rapport with many. I didn't have Mrs. Frinks to engage me in things I was used to. I lost interest, and my energy diverted in other directions.

Although I already thought I was an adult, my new school was a level of freedom and responsibility that I wasn't ready for. I had a locker to stash stuff in, and a schedule that offered time in between classes to talk to girls. It was a first for school dances, and for more trips to the bus stop. There were periods of unsupervised activity throughout the day, and I chose to use those times to take up my new found hobby of smoking cigarettes. I wanted to do it all the time. Often it wasn't just social. I'd smoked enough to need a whole one to feel the same buzz I first did.

I liked smoking and knew there was more beyond cigarettes. We'd learned about drug education the year prior, but I hadn't taken much interest in them until I'd felt what nicotine

HK

did to me. I became infatuated with the concept of altered perceptions. Every day I walked to the bus stop, I hoped it would be the day that the kids were smoking pot instead of cigarettes. They talked about it often, but I'd never seen it.

Finally, the day came. I was still 11 years old when I got high for the first time. I loved it immediately. I was so profoundly changed by marijuana. It helped me bring my personality from an 11 to a 7 or 8, made my feelings less intense. I wondered why anyone in the world wouldn't want to feel it. I had stumbled upon a pot of gold and never wanted to let it go. I wanted to get high all the time.

I had one of the bus stop kid's older brother to thank for it, and I asked him to bring it every day from then on. I still had money from doing yard work around the neighborhood, and getting high made me want to work harder so I could buy more weed. The problem was I had no concept of moderation. I skipped classes to smoke with my friends, and snuck out at night to try my first drinks.

I didn't like the taste of beer, or the effect as much as I did marijuana, but we made ourselves chug a few warm ones that kids would steal from their dads. My mom didn't have a clue because a mom just doesn't expect her 11-year old to be drinking and smoking pot.

Every now and then I'd see other drugs. I wasn't shy. I wanted to try more. I wanted to try *everything*. It seemed like an endless list of opportunities to make me change the ways I felt and viewed things, a new world of possibilities.

The thing I saw most, was older kids eating pills. Many times they were getting high off Coricidin, a cough medicine that had psychedelic effects in large amounts. Sometimes they ate prescription pills, of all shapes and colors. I don't think even they knew what they were eating. They were young, too. We were all headed in disastrous directions.

I can't recall what I tried first, or second, or third. I remember my mom dropping me off at the local skating rink on a Friday night, and not much else. I woke up the next morning in the hospital.

On December 3rd, 1999, just four months after trying my first cigarette, I was admitted to Tallahassee Memorial Hospital, for a prescription and over the counter mixed drug overdose.

13.

Believe in yourself. Believe in your own potential for greatness. Believe that you can change the world. It is something that is within each of us. Believe in the power of one.

-Evan Tanner

"So you're dating someone in jail now?" Matt teased.

"Shut up, it's not like that." The topic wasn't a sensitive one, but not one I felt like joking about.

"You know shit is gonna get serious when she gets home."

"Nothing's gonna get serious. I'm not trying to get involved like that."

Isabel and I had been intimate many times in our life, and had regained a feeling of closeness, but we weren't together in any sense of the word. I entertained the idea a handful of times but scoffed away at the practicality of it. She didn't yet know how to manage her own life, let alone one with someone else.

"What about the girl you met the other night?" he asked.

That girl was Veronica, a bartender with lots of mutual friends at a local nightclub that I'd worked at. She was from Miami, a tall, slender, fiery, Cuban, with a pretty face and attitude to match.

Isabel had been in jail for a month at this point. I wasn't sure how to tell her about it, although I wanted to. She knew we weren't in a position in which I was going to just stay home, awaiting her release. She brought it up before I had the chance to.

"So who have you been dating now? I know you always have someone in the works." She prodded.

"I've met someone, decent." I don't know how much it could have been considered dating. We spent most of our time partying and having sex.

HK

"She'd better be cute," she said.

"Her hair isn't as good as yours."

"Oh, shut up. So you gonna stop coming to see me now?"

"That's what you think?"

"I don't know. Maybe."

"That's silly."

"Does she know about me?"

"Yes."

"What do you tell her?"

"I tell her I have a friend in jail that I visit. What else am I supposed to tell her?" Veronica didn't think much of Isabel. She didn't consider her a threat, only because she'd never laid eyes on her.

Not many of my friends cared much for Veronica. Most didn't expect it to last long. They'd seen me go through countless flings with Hispanic girls from Miami and thought the same about each one. The Cuban girls I'd dated always celebrated being domestic. Veronica had a face like it pained her any time she tried to cook or clean.

I never stopped going to see Isabel, although she called less after that day. I would feel awful if I missed a call from her, not wanting her to think I was ignoring her in lieu of being with another. As I continued to visit, the topic of conversation eventually moved from her and the things she'd done, to me and what I was doing in my life. Isabel was always supportive of my ambitions, forever asking what was on the horizon.

A friend and I had recently opened an LLC and began promoting Mixed Martial Arts events, which consumed much of my time. Combat Night was the name of our promotion, and my partner's name was Mitchell, a former student who, like Matt, had grown to be much more than that. Mitchell was an intelligent guy who reminded me of my dad, short in stature, big in personality. He had good ideas, and enough money in the bank to buy a cage and get us started. I had made lots of connections in the sport, and we'd decided it was time to capitalize on them.

There was so much more to event promotion than we'd ever realized, once we got started. We had to pay sanctioning bodies and referees, matchmake fighters with one another, solicit sponsors, purchase insurance, secure hotels for athletes and coaches, then still have to worry about filling the building.

The first few events we held were in Tallahassee, at a local venue called The Moon. Isabel had made it to one of the very first, just days before she left for her vacation behind bars. I paid extra attention to her that night as I worked the event, trying my best to make her the guest of honor.

She loved the whole idea of it, something I'd created from the ground up, to give others the opportunities that I had when I was younger. Years prior she'd watched me fight inside the same cage we used for our event, inside the same venue. She liked that things had come full circle.

She enjoyed the idea of me being the guy outside the cage instead of in it, but she knew my passion was my own competition. The world's premiere MMA organization was the Ultimate Fighting Championship, and *The Ultimate Fighter* was the UFC's trojan horse to inject MMA into the mainstream the best way that they knew how; through reality television. Fighting in the UFC was the pinnacle of what MMA fighters strived for; to compete with the best in the world, and *The Ultimate Fighter* was the most readily accessible route.

The series featured a number of fighters living in the same house, competing in a tournament where the winner, and often others from the season, were awarded a contract, along with the notoriety that being in front of an audience of millions for 13 weeks provided.

I'd recently gotten a casting call for the show. I had a history with the series, having tried out three times before. I was more interested in winning the tournament than I was with being on TV, but for one reason or another, it had always escaped me. Isabel knew I'd been chasing the opportunity for years, only to have it elude me, time and time again.

During our jail visits, I was healing up from a meniscal surgery repair that I had undergone after a fight. I told Isabel about the casting tryouts, and my hesitance to go back for the fourth time.

HK

"I'm not sure if that's the route for me anymore."

"What do you mean that's not the route for you? Of course it is. You've wanted this forever now." I didn't know if it was the fear of reinjury that was deterring me, or fear of disappointment, coming up short again. Sometimes people got signed to the UFC outside of TUF, and I was hopeful.

"The Josh I used to know would be going in a heartbeat," she said. She raised her hand up. "Believe, baby." She had the word tattooed on her left wrist. *Believe.*

Heedfulness be damned, she was right. She had always succeeded wonderfully at planting seeds in me, knowing just what to say to motivate me in a way no one else could, and this day was no different. Many of my friends had suggested it was silly for me not to go, but it wasn't until I was looking through the glass at her, that my mind was changed.

"You *have* to go," she insisted.

It occurred to me for a moment that I was taking life advice from a recovering addict who was sitting in jail, but it also occurred to me that she *was* right, I *had* to go. And I did. I went home that night and bought a plane ticket for Vegas, just days before tryouts.

For the fourth time, I would fly west in hopes of punching and kicking my way into the UFC on national television. I knew what to expect. I'd been there before. This time, it would be different.

14.

Late Winter, 1999

I was first institutionalized at Tallahassee Memorial Hospital. After the overdose, I was taken to the behavioral wing of the clinic, to make sure that what I'd done wasn't intentional. I could hear the doctor talking to my mom. She was crying. This had gotten out of hand fast.

I was embarrassed and angry at myself. My mom and I were asked a series of questions following the incident. Yes, I'd been acting differently over the past few months. Yes, she'd noticed some of her alcohol may have been missing from the fridge. Yes, she was at work often and wasn't always aware of my activities.

My mom explained how I'd begun hanging with a new group of friends. She was reluctant to point towards counterculture as a source of problems because she was the counterculture herself. She always wanted to give everyone a chance.

The other kids that were in the behavioral center had been through way worse than I had. The majority were anti-social. Many had been abused, and had intentionally tried to hurt themself. It was my first brush with real dysfunction.

She couldn't keep it from my dad, although I think she may have if she could've. That phone call had to have been awful for both of them. My cousin, Jeremy, from Mississippi came and visited me in the hospital. He was in his early twenties and told me about similar life experiences he'd had. I looked up to him, and he talked sense into me.

Give it a rest, he said. *Smoke weed on the weekends, maybe. Don't eat pills. Don't steal booze. Find other things to do if you don't like school anymore.* He handed me his old skateboard, and I was given an outlet.

Mrs. Frinks came by and told me I could still go to the magnet lab for experiments if I wanted. She reminded me of all the things I'd been curious about at the end of the last school year and gave me books to read. Others came and left. I wanted to leave too. It was just a big accident. I didn't belong there. I wanted the doctors to agree.

I was released from the hospital after a few days, but I wouldn't be home long. Once kids start down this path, it's important to reset course early, the doctors told my mom. While she had little idea of what I'd been doing, my dad had even less. He was livid when finding out the news. My mom told me he wanted me to live with him. She didn't know what to do.

I'd never been a kid who was at odds with authority. I didn't get into fights. I did excellent in class. I played soccer. I'd

HK

never displayed real problematic behavior until I got into middle school. I'm not sure why I looked up to kids who were doing bad things. I thought everyone drank when they got older. I thought all teenagers smoked weed, the exciting ones anyway.

Looking back now, as a kid, I had fascinations with public figures that suffered drug overdoses. It was a step shy of glorification; more of a curiosity at what it was like to take things that far.

I fought against living with my father. Every time I would go there he would cut my hair, and send me home with a lecture on how image is important, how I can't be running around looking like a hooligan. He was more judgemental about everything, hated if I wore long shorts or hooded sweatshirts. It was an environment shift that I knew I didn't want.

Eventually, they agreed that my mom couldn't supervise me how I needed to be. She thought it would be good for me to have a male influence in my life, if only for a few years. It hurt her to do, but it was time for a change.

15.

The tryouts in Vegas were the same process they had been before. By then the producers of the show and the UFC had seen me several times and knew who I was. I realized the tryout was more of a formality at this point. Along with 40 of the 200 other fighters that showed up that day, I was asked to stay in Vegas for the week, for further evaluation. From there, 32 would be called back to fight for a chance to get on the show.

As the producer called out those asked to stay, I hurried to pull out my phone and jot down all the names I heard, spelling them phonetically best I could. I would use them later to exercise my inner nerd and scout potential opponents, looking up records, and watching film.

Some guys I knew, some I recognized from previous tryouts. Next to me sat a short, stocky Hispanic fighter sitting with his girlfriend, who I sat next to as I filled out more paperwork. We exchanged small talk, and he introduced himself. He struck me as a shy guy, soft spoken, and carried himself differently than the general machismo of the other meatheads in the room. Kelvin was his name.

We were set to stay for a few days to undergo more extensive interviews, as well as a series of physicals and drug tests, all under strict supervision of the UFC. In the meantime, we were all stationed at the hotel. I met up with the only other local fighter from my area, a guy named Clint Hester, and we found a pocket of the hotel pool grounds to spar on. Older vacationers walked past us, looking at us like we were crazy. I'm sure we did look crazy, two big muscular guys punching each other in the head in public like that.

As fate had it, I would be in Vegas the day Isabel was released. After months of seeing her in a cramped visitation room, talking through a nasty payphone receiver, and looking at her through a wall of disfigured glass, I wasn't even there to hug her when she finally got out. I was across the country, trying to tackle the only other thing in my life that had escaped me for years.

I remember perfectly, the evening she was released. I had wandered down to the bottom floor of the hotel we were in, to a little spot called The Oyster Bar. There I found the same friendly Hispanic guy I'd made acquaintances with earlier in the week.

He told me more about his girlfriend and asked if I had one. Sort of, I said. It was complicated. We finished our dinner, and I invited him to join me for a couple hands of poker at the table.

"I can't play."

"Ah, it's not hard. I could help you out." I'd once lived with a gambler who'd showed me the ins and outs of Hold 'Em.

"No, I mean I'm not allowed. I'm only 20."

I looked at him for a moment after he told me that, realizing he did look young. I thought of memories of myself flying out to *The Ultimate Fighter* tryouts at 21 years old, not knowing what to expect or what I was getting into, blindly following a dream.

HK

"What are you doing here, being 20 years old?" I asked him. The minimum age to be on the show was 21, for alcohol liability.

"My birthday is the day before filming begins. They said as long as I'm 21 by the first fight, then I could try out."

More power to him, I thought. It was quite the story.

"You gotta tell me your name, one more time," I said. I was always horrible with names. Every year I had a New Year's Resolution to remember them better.

"Kelvin. Kelvin Gastelum."

"I won't forget it. Good luck, bud. See you soon." I went to gamble for a couple hours before heading back to my room, forgetting about my new friend 'til the next time I saw him again.

I remember trying to stay awake waiting for her call. It was a momentous day for both of us, and I wanted to share it with her, wanted to hear her the excitement in her voice when she was finally free.

I ended up falling asleep, waking up the next morning with a single missed call. A special day for both of us, and I didn't even get to speak to her.

When I did wake, it was to a ring from a UFC staff, to come downstairs and be transported to an official doctor. There, we would be tested for all drugs and blood transferable diseases; Hepatitis B, Hepatitis C, and HIV. It was procedure for all cast that were under consideration, and the standard to get a license to compete professionally in any state.

The 40 of us got called down from our rooms, 10 at a time, in groups of four. When we finally got downstairs into the parking lot I took a seat on the front row of the extended van.

"Yo, homie. You're in my seat." I heard a deep voice to the right of me as I sat down. A muscular black guy with a cutoff shirt, shaved head and goatee.

"I didn't hear anyone call a seat," I replied. I recognized what was going on.

"I called that seat, and you're sitting in it," he said again. It reminded me of a high school confrontation, juvenile posturing.

"I didn't hear anyone call shit, and I'm not getting up," I said affirmatively.

"Ok pussyboy. I'll remember that. You're the first one on my list." He got in the van and took the seat right behind me. He continued in my ear. "You know this is a fight show homie? I'll get you sooner or later."

I listened closely to every word. I had been taking names and Googling every one of them since the moment we got chosen, and I knew exactly who the culprit trying to affirm his alpha was. Kevin Casey was his name, a fighter with less experience than me, trying to make a statement at my expense.

I didn't hear much else from him after that day, although I had the feeling that eventually we'd get to the bottom of whose seat on the van that really belonged to.

16.

Early Spring, 2000

I had no idea what it was I was getting myself into. My dad arrived in town in his new minivan. I was still 11, and my two sisters were six and four years old.

You should be ashamed of yourself, he told me on the ride back to Mississippi.

You fucked up big, mister. We didn't even get out of town before he'd stopped at the mall and bought a whole wardrobe of khaki shorts and collared shirts for me.

You're gonna go to school, make straight A's, and that's the end of it. You hear me? He told me he'd kill me himself if I brought any drugs to his house. He made me sit in the back seat. I can still feel him burning a hole in me through the rearview mirror.

You're gonna go to church, play sports, and there's not gonna be any bullshit.

It was school, sports, and God, as he said it would be. He let me skateboard for a bit every night, but only in the driveway. Any friends I wanted to hang out with had to be from soccer or church. I was under constant supervision. Even if I wanted to

HK

smoke cigarettes or pot, I never would have had the opportunity.

My world had been turned upside down. Being uprooted from the town I grew up in was tough. Changing the home life I was accustomed to was tougher. Worst was, I missed my mom. The separation bothered me.

Frankie had done her fair share of diaper changing when I was young. I was fond of her family and had learned a lot from them, although it wasn't long before we butted heads, hard.

Every child is at odds with their stepparent, on some level. The defiance I had for Frankie was worsened by the abrupt circumstances. She didn't know what my move meant for *her* family, and her concern was reasonable. We grew apart. She took my sisters with her.

I see her in my mind now as a Nancy Grace character, mixed with Sarah Palin. And I don't think she'd mind that comparison. She was always calling everyone a heathen. She once made my dad go see a therapist before they got married because he told her he'd gone to a strip club at his bachelor party. She believed in the rapture. I didn't realize how immersed they were in it all until I lived there.

He forced it on me, which was ironic because it was his doctrine switch early in life that made me realize religion was a choice. Every Sunday and Wednesday we played dress up and went to church. I'd always been intimidated by the place, the judgment of it all. I learned to blend in, and look and talk like the others to not become scrutinized. I guess that was the point.

Being opinionated wasn't something that was encouraged unless the opinions were popular ones. The sentiment rang true for the whole community where we lived, in Jackson, Mississippi. I became passive and more introverted, a 180 from my personality growing up.

It was best not to challenge the things they said. I told them I let Jesus into my heart. I knew they wanted the best for me. I just told them whatever they wanted to hear so they'd leave me alone.

I got baptized, in a hotel pool, by the youth pastor at a church retreat. I remember eyeing the "no diving" sign before he dumped me in the chlorine-heavy water. It felt insane, this cultural ritual I was subjecting myself to, in front of all these people clapping. I struggled to take it seriously.

I tried to travel the path of least resistance, to barrel forward into a time when my mom would let me come back home. I struggled to accept where I lived as home. I wanted to get back to Tallahassee.

17.

"The best way to find out if you can trust somebody is to trust them."

-Ernest Hemingway

I returned to town after tryouts with a renewed sense of interest in my career. I'd always been on the outside of the UFC looking in, wondering if I would break the threshold, and at times, I'd lost focus. I had fought in, and was champion of various second-tier organizations, and made decent money, and local recognition. I grew tired, though, of having to answer people's questions about when I would be in the UFC, and having to correct their mislabeling of MMA as being called "UFC fighting."

"This is Josh, he's a cagefighter," folks liked to introduce me as. I detested the word, *cagefighter*. My friends were always needing to qualify me with the term, and it annoyed me to no end. I was many things, and didn't like being pigeonholed into a single title, and one so barbaric.

An event promoter, I would tell people that didn't know me, or maybe a personal trainer in years past. When I told someone I fought in a cage for a living it made them see me differently. It may've been in a positive, awe-inspiring way, if they were a fan. If that was the case, the worst that could happen was they may want to talk my ear off, telling stories of every bar fight they'd ever got in. Sometimes it was a more revolting response, gawking at the idea that I would participate in something as uncivilized as fighting in a cage. Either way, I didn't enjoy the response. I loved competing in MMA, but didn't like the stigma

HK

attached to it, and was at odds with a subculture of fans that wanted only to see people get hurt.

The UFC had come a long way since the days of headbutts and groin strikes. The inaugural event was held in 1993 and was the first of its kind in America to feature what would later be known as MMA. The promotion served primarily as propaganda for a family named the Gracies, and their signature martial art, Brazilian Jiu-Jitsu.

The story was a fascinating one. During the early 20th century, many Japanese sought refuge in Brazil. With them, they brought the art of Jiu-Jitsu, which the Gracies took and added to, making it their own. Brazilian Jiu-Jitsu combined joint locks with chokes, and the family had been using it to beat martial art styles of all kinds in Brazil. MMA there was named "Vale Tudo," Portuguese for "anything goes," and they wanted to cash in on the appeal to American fans.

The UFC held several events before struggling with sanctioning laws and the legality of it. Senator John McCain, in particular, began a campaign against the sport, calling it *Human Cockfighting*, and trying to get it outlawed nationwide.

That was years ago. It had become well regulated by this point and deserved more respect than it got. The MMA boom could be traced back and attributed to a handful of men; UFC President Dana White, and owners Lorenzo and Frank Fertitta. With the help of the Nevada State Athletic Commission, they made Las Vegas a home for more than just boxing, and it grew from a fringe sideshow act to a legitimate worldwide sport.

UFC President Dana White, as he tells it, was a boxing instructor in Boston at the time, and convinced his old friends, Frank and Lorenzo, to purchase the organization from its founders. The Fertittas were already successful in the casino business and agreed to buy the company. They dumped millions into the sport, and were ready to bail, before one last Hail Mary, bankrolling a reality show called *The Ultimate Fighter*.

Knowing the details of the storied history of the UFC and TUF made me want to be a part of it even more, and I was excited to finally have a chance to fight inside the iconic octagon. I was anxious to carve out my own piece of history on the largest stage in the world, and I was finally getting my chance.

While I was waiting for that opportunity, it brought me great joy to know that when I got home, I'd be able to see Isabel. I was still dating Veronica, and couldn't spend time with Isabel as I wanted, but I still planned to help her in the ways I'd pledged. Most importantly, I'd promised to help get her a job.

I had a ton of folks in town who owned restaurants and sponsored our events. One was opening a new sports joint, and I told him that I had a close friend who needed help getting work, as a favor to me. I promised that she would be a good addition to his staff. He agreed to bring her in for an interview and hired her on the spot.

Isabel made it clear how much she appreciated me vouching for her. I was going out on a limb, hoping it wouldn't come back to bite me in the ass. Just as I'd come back from my trip with a renewed sense of interest in my career, she was feeling the same about life. Isabel was free, no jail, no probation. She was excited about being able to work again, and becoming self-sufficient. She'd moved in with her brother Owen's girlfriend, Stephanie. Stephanie was the cheerleader type and was one of the only others that knew all of Isabel's story, and still gave her the benefit of the doubt.

Proving everyone wrong was the name of the game in her mind now, and that came in the form of her independence. Waiting tables would not be enough to get by, so she began to take up the only other profession she'd known most her life, being a housekeeper.

18.

Late Spring, 2000

I needed an outlet. Skateboarding was cool, but not very many kids skated in Mississippi. Most of them wore cowboy boots to school. My mom suggested I take up an instrument, and I loved the idea.

HK

For all the detractions I had about my dad, one thing he never did was censor pop culture for me. Music was always important, and he'd take me to the CD store frequently as I was discovering different types of genres.

My first four CD's were Green Day, No Doubt, Rage Against the Machine, and Boyz II Men. I'd gotten those years ago, and had since moved on to things my friends liked, or my parents. My mom played Bob Marley frequently, my Dad U2. Jeremy gave me a Pearl Jam album. One of my favorite bands was Nirvana, and it made me want to play the guitar like Kurt Cobain.

I remember going to the music store on my 12th birthday. I wasn't allowed to go around the neighborhood and mow lawns like I did at my mom's, so I didn't have any money for myself, but my dad said he'd buy me a guitar.

I had never thought of actually learning to play an instrument. No one I knew at that age played anything besides the xylophones at school. I spent hours at the store, trying out guitars, twisting knobs, pressing buttons on amplifiers.

He bought me what would be my most prized possession for years to come: an electric, black, six-string Ibanez. The package came with a small amplifier, and within hours I was home, plotting my foray into rock'n'roll superstardom.

I played that guitar until my fingers bled. I fell in love, with youthful curiosity. I began taking lessons twice a week and learned to play all my favorite songs.

With my guitar I was able to express myself in a way I never had. I enjoyed drawing and painting when I was younger, but it didn't make me feel like music did.

I joined the chorus at school and participated in local plays and musicals. I was the Wizard in Oz, Santa Claus in the Christmas show, and everything in between. It helped give me an identity at a time when I wasn't sure what mine was. I still missed my mom, and I still wanted to go home, but it felt better with something to throw myself into again.

"Go confidently in the direction of your dreams. Live the life you've imagined."

-Henry D. Thoreau

    I flew out to Vegas on October 28th, for what would be a series of life defining moments. There was a production member there for me at the airport, and I collected my luggage as we waited for the last remaining fighter. When he arrived, it was none other than my Mexican friend, Kelvin Gastelum. I was glad I had made a mental note of his name. We rode together to a UFC corporate office where the production crew from FOX met all the fighters to take pictures and check our weight .

    As soon as we arrived, I sat down at a table in the middle of a large room, filled with film sheets, cameras, food table for staff, and a makeup corner to pretty up fighters for photos. Sitting across from me was a charismatic fellow who introduced himself as Gerard. He was too small to be a fighter in my weight division, and I pegged him as a staff member before he explained himself. A producer of the show, he told me, with a chatty story of how he got interested in this sport that he'd since become consumed with.

    Filmmaking was his passion, and before working for *The Ultimate Fighter* he'd just completed an MMA documentary that was being released soon, dubbed *Once I Was a Champion*. It chronicled the story of Evan Tanner, a former UFC middleweight champion who wandered into the desert one day and never came back. Evan was an enigmatic figure, and there was much acclaim in the MMA world about his film.

    He had an incredibly thick Scottish accent, tickling to the ears, as he explained to me a bit about the season. The show had done less than stellar ratings over the last few seasons. The concept had grown stale. Much of the time in between fights that were recorded was the kind of debauchery one might expect from a reality show; lots of drinking and arguing amongst cast members. Sometimes fighters would play pranks, throwing each other's mattresses in the pool, or sabotaging each other's food.

HK

The production wanted to depart from the reality show feel, and focus on a documentarian approach. The cast was picked with a more serious tone in mind, and the narrative, as he explained it, was to concentrate on the level of competition; to capture the raw emotion that such an intense competition could impose on a person. The fights themselves, combined with weight cuts, isolation, and the stressors of living in a house of 14 natural alpha males, motivated and hungry, would provide plenty of drama to not have to rely on conventional reality show antics.

I shared with him about my failures in the past, how with each repeated attempt the tournament took on more of a unique personal sentiment to me. I told him I wasn't even planning on coming, but I had a good feeling this time.

After speaking with Gerard for a few minutes, I was called over to have my weight checked by another UFC employee. My weight class was 185 lbs and I was floating around 195, right on track. Following a quick step on the scale, I was directed towards make-up, where a pretty lady introduced herself. She moved quickly, powdering my face, and spraying my torso with unnecessarily cold water. Last, she strapped a pair of extra large MMA gloves on my hands.

"Ok babe, you're all set."

I sat there for a moment, staring at the gloves she'd put on me. *UFC* in big, bold, white letters. I had seen them hundreds of times before, but never worn them, or even better, had a UFC employee put them on me.

This is the real thing.

It would be a familiar feeling over the next several months, many gradual, incremental realizations that after all these years, things were all finally falling into place.

20.

Fall, 2000

My dad's family and I moved from Jackson, Mississippi, to Knoxville, Tennessee, while I was still 12. My dad was a graduate of UT and was thrilled to be back in The Rocky Top. My step mom didn't seem to appreciate the move, as she headed further from her family.

I gained trust back, and my dad eased up on the supervision. I was able to hang out with people outside of church and sports. The social dynamic in Knoxville was different. There weren't as many country bumpkins. I made friends more easily.

My closest friend was named Carlton. He enjoyed skateboarding like me and was the only other person I knew that could play guitar. He could play piano too. I was jealous of that. It felt good to be competitive about something I cared about again. I played soccer and did homework to appease my dad. Music was something I strived to improve at, for myself.

I learned to read notes, and sing off a music sheet like Carlton did. I practiced skateboarding more and was allowed to skate around the whole neighborhood now. I did things that were constructive, in the name of competition.

We sang Incubus' "Pardon Me" in the school talent show. I had a crush on a girl, and it was her favorite song. I thought impressing her would get me laid for the first time. It did, just not by her.

I was on the bus home in eighth grade. Our middle and high schools shared transportation, and the high schoolers dominated the buses every day. There was one girl, a senior, who was the bossiest. She had big boobs, and sat in the back seat and told people what to do. They listened.

She had a younger sister that was in my grade. The older one was better looking, and we were the last ones on the bus every day. My stop was the new neighborhood on the route, with construction and dust that clogged my skateboard bearings. Her's was the trailer on a field beyond that.

Every day I felt the tension grow. She'd call me back to the back of the bus and ask questions. She asked me if I'd ever had sex before. She talked a lot. She said she didn't have a car because she lived with a single mother who spent her money on alcohol. She smelled like booze too sometimes, and cigarettes. The aroma triggered things in me.

"My sister says you play the guitar."

$\mathcal{HK}$

I wondered if she'd told her I was good. It didn't seem to matter. My stop arrived mid-conversation, and I picked up my book bag. She grabbed it by the strap and pulled me back.

"Stay." It was one word only, but I knew what it meant.

My heart was racing. I was nervous, excited, scared, anxious. I'd touched a few boobs, and fooled around with my crush from school, but I knew what was coming. When we got off the bus stop, she pulled out a pack of cigarettes and handed me the first I'd had in years. She might've been 18 years old by then. I'd just turned 13.

She fucked my brains out on the trampoline in front of her trailer. She bounced up and down, switching between facing me, then away. We were in a giant field, with not another person in sight. I remember looking back to make sure one of her sisters wasn't watching. She got annoyed at my distraction and rode harder. I came, and she didn't get off me. I didn't have any experience having sex, but I knew that wasn't supposed to happen.

She rode the last bit of me that I had left, and handed me another cigarette; a reward of sorts. She told me her mom was gonna be home soon, gave me a pack of matches, and sent me on my way.

I didn't care that I had miles to walk. I didn't care if my parents asked where I'd been, or if I smelled like cigarette smoke. I didn't care about any of that. I'd just banged a high schooler, and in the realm of 13 year-olds, I was the fuckin' *man*.

21.

"Everyone sees what you appear to be, few experience what you really are."

-*Niccolò Machiavelli*

The UFC had recently inked a new television deal with FOX, increasing its exposure enormously. This season would broadcast to a much larger number of viewers than previous ones with Spike TV, and the new network was likely the driving force for the show's structural change. Isabel had always said everything happened for a reason. Maybe this was one of those times.

Better late than never.

One of the new features was a segment in the first episode, introducing cast members and families. In all 16 previous seasons, fighters would arrive in Vegas by themselves; no coaches, no friends, no family, just their cups and mouthpieces, ready to fight for a chance to compete in the UFC. This time, we'd be allowed guests, people that were meant to be woven into our story, to introduce us to the world with a context more than just face and body.

My mom was first on my list. I had a wild connection with her, and how she applied to my fighting career. At the time, I had a combined 12-3 record in my fights. All twelve fights that my mom had been there for, I'd won. The three I didn't win, she had missed. She'd never once seen me lose, and while I didn't much believe in superstitions, I told her she was my good luck charm.

Mitchell was second on my list. He and Matt both were, although Matt was not able to afford the trip. Mitchell and I had been doing our promotional thing for months, and if I ended up winning the first fight I'd be staying in Vegas for seven weeks to film, and he'd be flying solo. My third guest was a grappling instructor I'd been working with, and the fourth was Gary, my friend and manager. All these guests left one vacant spot to be given. My career interested Veronica, but something did not feel right. I decided, hesitantly, that she could be my fifth guest on the show.

The Ultimate Fighter was a reality show that placed heavy emphasis on confidentiality, to ensure that results were not revealed before airing. Because of this, they'd taken our cell phones, beginning the moment we were picked up at the airport. They were the ones communicating with our guests at this point, although in all of their pre-emptive genius, they did not take the hotel phones out of the rooms. I'd always been good at

HK

remembering numbers and didn't need my cell phone to get in touch with the people that were supposed to be coming.

As luck would have it, the day everyone was set to arrive, Hurricane Sandy would ravage the East Coast, halting all flights departing the area. Halting all flights, of course except one. Had I not remembered their numbers and called to get news of the storm, I would've been bombarded with the situation that was on the other side of that door when I finally got a knock. Four of my five guests had gotten held up, and couldn't make it to Vegas in time for the first day of filming.

There I found myself, sitting on my hotel room bed, alone, next to Veronica. I wasn't even sure about bringing her in the first place, and there she was, a girl I'd known no longer than a couple months, being the one and only person that represented me to the whole world. The cameras rolled, and I knew with utmost certainty that the wrong girl was sitting on the bed.

22.

Early Summer, 2002

My stepmom may have been the only one that wanted me to leave as badly as I did. She and my father argued daily, and weeks went by when she and I didn't talk. When my stepmother was angry with my dad, she would take it out on the stepson. When my father was angry with her, he'd confide in me about it. It made for a very *us vs. them* scenario. Sometimes I thought she genuinely hated him. She had a sharp tongue, and I could feel the conflict coming to a head. My presence was disruptive to her.

Summer break was approaching, and I'd be returning to Tallahassee for a couple months. I planned on not coming back, and I got what I wanted.

I expected my dad to keep the reins of my future in his hands well into high school, but he'd had enough. I was a source of problems between him and his wife, and I'd adjusted well enough to try things again at my mom's. As much as I'd always wanted to be part of a big family, I wanted nothing more than to just go home.

My mom had beaten cancer by this point, and gone back to dating men. I told her things would be different when I got back. I did my best to not be rebellious, to be respectful. I returned to mowing lawns, and still played music every day. I was productive and worked hard. The curiosity in me from years ago was never satisfied, though. I saw my life take a detour to my father's only because of a single mistake. I thought I wouldn't let it happen again.

I didn't plan on fucking it all up. There was just no one to stop me. I was home by myself every day that summer. Free time and disposable income were the enemies. Like years earlier, my mom was none the wiser as to what I was doing. She wasn't expecting me to come home and pick up where I left off, but that's what I did. I went right back into the fire.

The bus stop kids and their siblings had grown older. Their indulgence had evolved. I knew after living with my dad that not all kids acted the way they did. I knew many of them struggled to determine what was right and wrong and that I knew the difference. Sometimes, wrong just felt good.

"Get in!" I heard my devious bastard of a friend Baxter yell from the back of a pickup truck, as I walked outside to see who was honking. Most of the kids my age had siblings that could drive now, a whole new level of freedom and danger.

I hopped in, not thinking twice about it. I hated the idea of missing out.

"Where are we going?" I asked. He had a mischievous look on his face.

"We're going picking."

I didn't know what that meant. It was hard to hear over the wind in the back of the truck, so I just sat along for the ride. A ride is what I got.

HK

"The meaning of life is to find your gifts. The purpose of life is to give them away."

- Pablo Picasso

The film crew wrapped up the first scene as I said goodbye to Veronica and got ready to head downstairs to the sauna to lose the last few lbs before the official weigh-ins. Once there, we would pile into a hallway upstairs, all anxious to step on the scale at 185 lbs. Combat sports employ weight classes to separate different sized athletes, and our weight class was middleweight. Being the bigger man in the cage was a competition in itself. After weighing in, we'd then be able to eat and rehydrate back to our natural weight, which for me was between 205-210 lbs. The cut was grueling, but I'd done it fifteen times before and had become adept.

The feeling in the air was unreal. There we were, 28 prizefighters, all hungry and thirsty, literally, figuratively. They'd found the perfect group of athletes, an all-star cast to compete, including nine undefeated fighters, and over 200 cumulative wins between us. I had a name in the regional MMA circuit and was one of the youngest cast members on the season at 24 years. I'd taken my first fight at 18, and had my fair share of time in the cage.

Some fighters knew who I was. Some tried to make small talk. I was there to win, but I also wanted to do my best to represent where I came from. I was friendly with those that were friendly with me, keeping in mind that all of us were chasing the same goal, and would possibly have to fight each other soon. We sat in the hallway and did our own feeling out process of each other. Only half of us would make it into the house. The losers on the following day would be sent home immediately, and none of us yet knew who we'd be fighting.

I waited for my chance to weigh in, a quick hop on and off the scale before going to a banquet room reserved for our own personal buffet. I packed back on the weight with carbs and liquids, just as I'd done many times before, and returned to my room, patiently awaiting further instruction.

Within a couple of hours, we were called downstairs to load up in the van and be taken to the UFC training center, which would be the location for all fights, future weigh-ins, and training sessions during our tenure with *The Ultimate Fighter.* I went down and loaded in the van with seven other fighters, taking a seat next to my friend Clint Hester. My Scottish lad, Gerard was in the front driving.

"What the hell are you doing driving a van? Don't they have errand-boys for that?"

"Part of the gig man," he said. Being a producer included being around the fighters 24/7, making sure not to miss out on emerging storylines in the weeks to come.

"Do you know who we're fighting?" I asked, always looking to become privy.

"Of course I do," he laughed. "You'll be finding out soon." Soon was never soon enough.

We left the hotel and headed to the training center. As the van doors opened and I entered the facility, I could not contain the smile on my face. No one wanted this as bad as I wanted it, and no one had any idea of what I'd gone through to get there. I absolutely couldn't believe that I'd considered not coming.

As we strolled through the main entrance, we were greeted by some of the sport's most iconic images, plastered on a wall. There stood a collage of every successful fighter since season one, in a series of before-and-after pictures walking into and out of their fights. I took a moment to take it in; the stories told, in hundreds of photos. Georges St-Pierre, Matt Hughes, Ken Shamrock, BJ Penn, the pictures seemed endless. It was crazy to see the heroes who had built this thing from the ground up, all displayed in one place, in a gut-wrenching, eye-opening display of all the emotion that went into the sport. Glory and defeat were both powerful, moving things to be captured in a picture, and it was the perfect introduction of things to come.

The double doors across from the collage were unusually flimsy, begging someone to punch a hole through them at any

HK

given moment. I was one of 28, and walked in front as I made my way through the hallway into the UFC training center. I'd watched 16 seasons prior filmed in the same building. I was familiar with what I was seeing, but it was all so surreal in person.

Immediately to our right was a large cage, much larger than the one Mitchell and I used for Combat Night. Corporate sponsors lined the floors and posts. Harley Davidson, Miller Lite, FOX. Huge names were funding what we were doing.

Ahead of us was a large wrestling mat area, with three of the most recognizable personalities in the MMA world; UFC President Dana White, accompanied by opposing coaches for the season, UFC light heavyweight champion, Jon Jones, and perennial contender, Chael Sonnen.

The show's strength relied heavily on the draw of the coaches, and the two there were sure to turn heads. Jon was a master of creative violence, an unstoppable force in the cage. Chael was the best mouth in sports, a genius of fight promotion, a testament to articulation and charisma. Never before had two such high profile fighters been cast as coaches for *The Ultimate Fighter*, and it made a statement from the UFC to let the public know that the stakes on MMA reality television had just been raised.

Once all of us had made our way towards the mats, Dana began his speech. He told us we had the opportunity to become the future of the UFC, and to make the most out of it. We were there that day not only to meet our coaches, but to find out who we'd be facing the following afternoon. Everyone was still eyeing and sizing each other up, and Dana began to read the list of names. One by one, I saw potential teammates and opponents face off with their opposition until finally my name was called.

Josh Samman. I walked forward, fists clenched. The intensity in the room was through the roof, and I was giddy as a school boy.

Leo Bercier. It was one of the few names I didn't know, and I watched for who would be the first to move forward. A Native American fellow with the most giant head I'd ever seen stepped forward. I put my hands up, stared into his eyes, and attempted to soul gaze for a moment, making a mental note of his name to research when I got back to the hotel.

They announced the rest of the matchups, and we headed back to our rooms. I immediately called Mitchell to get info on Bercier. He found his record and some fight footage easily, realizing quickly that he was a one-dimensional fighter, relying strictly on striking to finish opponents. He'd amassed an impressive record of 7-1, with seven first round knockouts. A one-dimensional opponent, but a dangerous one.

I made a couple more calls to friends and family with the numbers I remembered. I cursed myself for not writing down Isabel's new number before I left. If I were to win my fight, I'd be taken immediately to the house where filming took place, without saying goodbye to anyone other than those with me.

I dozed to sleep that night as I performed my ritualistic pre-fight thoughts. I imagined every possible scenario, walking myself through the fight hundreds of times before it actually happened. For my whole career, I'd had at least a month to visualize and prepare for an opponent. This was a much different dynamic, discovering the identity of my adversary less than 24 hours before competition.

I didn't mind, at all. I was ready.

24.

Late Summer, 2002

They grew like wildfire in North Florida. They were everywhere. I'd been prompted on what to look for when we got there. Search low to the ground, make sure it bruises purple, and under no circumstances pick one if it doesn't have a complete ring around the stem. I was in the middle of a cow field on the outskirts of Tallahassee, skewering around for mushrooms; *Psilocybe cyanescens*, and *Psilocybe azurescens*, to be exact.

I hadn't tried a new drug in years. The whole experience started before I even felt the effects of it. The way my friends explained it, mushrooms were a wonder drug that allowed you

$\mathcal{HK}$

into parallel universes, where you could hear smells and taste colors. I couldn't have been more excited. Every kid had different views of what they thought was cool, and this is what I was attracted to. It started at the bus stop and never stopped.

The thing about mushrooms was that we had to trespass onto someone else's land to get them. They grew the way most fungi grows, via spores, in any animal's feces with a two or more cylinder stomach. For now, it was just cow shit.

We hopped the fence, empty bags in hand. We agreed to meet in an hour back at the car where we'd parked down the road, then all ran in our separate directions. It was the middle of broad daylight, and I realized we hadn't discussed what happens if we got caught. I tried to find a tree line and stay out of sight.

We reconvened at the car in an hour, as planned. We'd filled our grocery bags full, and I remember wondering whether it was enough or not. I didn't know how much a person needed to get high.

We went back to a friend's, who lived outside our neighborhood, and began sifting through all the mushrooms one by one. Some they threw away, some they placed upside down on a cardboard box to dry, and many got thrown into a large strainer, to rinse before putting in a boiling cauldron. It was unlike anything I'd ever seen. I made mental notes as I watched.

The magic had yet to come. It would be hours before the concoction finished cooking. Halfway through the process, they'd added tea bags to the mixture, and a little bit of grape Kool-Aid. When it was ready, I wasted no time. I liked the taste. I had to be told not to drink so fast, that it was my first trip and to be easy with it. At least they'd adopted some concept of moderation.

We waited and waited. I was convinced it wasn't going to work, that I needed more. I stood up to go back to the pot of Kool-Aid, and it hit me all at once. A tingling sensation radiated from my legs outwards. My ears began resonating in a slow hum.

I felt a sense of euphoria, calm at first, then intense. My friends told me to relax and enjoy it. I was enjoying it. Everything was pleasant. The walls melted and rebuilt themselves before my eyes. It was like a dream, but I was awake and had full control of my faculties.

I didn't yet know about synapses. I didn't know what synesthesia was. I knew only that there was a wonderland behind my eyelids, and that I'd reached a corner of my mind that hadn't yet been explored.

25.

"You were put on this Earth to achieve your greatest self, to live out your purpose, and to do it fearlessly."

-Steve Maraboli

My chance had finally come. After years of waiting and dreaming, dedicating my life and neglecting relationships, multiple injuries, and downfalls, I had finally captured the opportunity that had eluded me for so long. Across from me stood the only thing in my way. Only a couple hundred people in the world had gotten the opportunity to chisel their legacy into UFC history, and I wanted so badly to be one of them. My mom and the rest of the crew had finally made it into Vegas, just in time to see the fight.

The bell rang, and I darted across the cage, throwing a few stiff jabs before shooting underneath Leo's guard to take the fight to the mat. Considering his striking ability and my reluctance to have any uncertainty of victory, taking the fight where I could exploit a difference in grappling skill was the most sound plan of attack.

As soon as we hit the mat, it became apparent how inept he was at moving correctly to escape. I realized then that I'd finally done it. I had trapped the untrappable, my white rabbit, in the form of a sweaty, heavily-breathing 31 year-old Native American. I realized there was no way he was going to return to his feet, and I yelled loudly as I moved into the mount position on top of him.

"You ready?"

HK

I'm not sure who I was talking to. Maybe Leo himself. Maybe Dana and the coaches. Maybe my family and friends; not just the few that made it there that day, but the dozens who'd watched, helped, and stood by my side in pursuit of my dream. I didn't plan on yelling, it was spur of the moment. It was my way of saying "I'm here. I finally made it. This motherfucker isn't slipping away this time."

I rained down punches with both fists, a signature finishing move of mine throughout my career. The technique was not a gimmick, or something I did for flash or show. I did it in my fights because it was brutal and violent. Steve Mazzagatti pulled me off, and I was overcome with elation. Winning four fights in six weeks was a daunting task, but I was one step closer.

I told my mom I loved her, and sat to watch the rest of my future opponents perform. After the fights finished, we said our final goodbyes to our loved ones as the cameras caught the drama and gravity of the situation. Veronica let out some crocodile tears that made me cringe, and I tried my best to feign an authentic goodbye.

We were hurried back to the locker rooms to await the coaches decisions for team picks. Chael had been awarded the first selection of fighters while Jon was given the right to choose the first fight. The tournament format would largely depend on who won which fights, as the winning team kept control of fight order. We gathered back at the same mats that we'd met on the day prior, now with 14 instead of 28. The names began to rattle off.

"Luke Barnatt." Chael chose first and went with the tallest guy in the room.

"Clint Hester." Jon selected his first pick. The two had hit it off earlier in the day, and it came as no surprise to anyone.

"Uriah Hall," third chosen, and he was handed a black jersey by Chael and his coaches. I was wondering when my name would be called. I thought I would've been one of the first.

"Josh Samman." Jones' second pick.

Not bad.

Not being picked first took some pressure off my back. One by one, the rest of the teams were chosen, all the way down to the very last fighter.

"Kelvin Gastelum." The little fucker had made it, the youngest kid to ever be on *The Ultimate Fighter*, at 21 years and a day. He didn't seem to mind being the last picked. He exuded an attitude as if we all had another thing coming, and no one knew it but him.

26.

Fall, 2002

I tripped on mushrooms for months. It became my drug of choice, partly by circumstance. Shortly after moving back, my mom randomly drug tested me to see if I'd been smoking pot. Somehow, I passed. I was convinced it was a mistake. It made me hesitant to smoke anymore, and mushrooms didn't show up on a piss test. I'd wait til my mom went to sleep at night, then sneak out and get picked up. I'd roam around cow fields, then the city.

I started 9th grade at Lincoln High School, following the most exciting summer of my short life. Things were so much different at mom's than they were at my dad's. I had independence, whether it was good for me or not. I was always walking a fine line, wanting to take things as far as I could, without betraying my mom's trust. I pushed the limits.

I had girlfriends early into high school. More accurately, I came sprinting out the gate, trying to date several at once. They all lived within a couple miles of each other, and at night, if I couldn't find a ride from the older kids, I'd skateboard down the road for hours until I got to one of their houses, and risk my life by going inside. Many had dads that would've castrated me had I been caught. It was the kind of thrill-seeking I thrived on.

I wanted cash for the upcoming spring break, but it became winter and the grass had stopped growing, so I had to find other ways to earn. I'd go to the local grocery store, and purchase items that were on sale for buy one get one free, then wait for them

HK

to go off sale and return them both for double what I'd paid. They'd only do returns in gift cards if I didn't have the receipt, so I'd stand outside the same grocery store afterwards, and sell the cards for cash.

I'd go to the movie theaters, and collect ticket stubs people threw on the ground, then halfway through the movie run out and tell customer service there'd been an emergency and my friends had to leave. I'd say they asked me to refund their tickets for them. They never argued.

Spring Break came, and with it left the virginity of half the girls in our class. Everyone our age was having sex. It was the most debauchery filled, unsupervised week any of us had ever seen, a bunch of teenagers stumbling around St. George Island, horny and wasted. Everyone lied to their parents about who was chaperoning. Like the theater ticket trick, I look back now and can't believe the stuff that flew under the radar.

When there was no booze to drink, or mushrooms to eat, or girl's houses to skate to, my friends and I would skate up to the grocery store, and videotape ourselves doing dumb shit. The stunt show *Jackass* was popular on MTV at the time, and we tried to replicate various segments, and make originals of our own. We'd push each other around in shopping carts, or get the local Hungry Howies to give us leftover dough to make dodgeballs with. Our risk aversion was horrendous, our regard for safety non-existent. I'd soon paid the price.

27.

"What would you do if you weren't afraid?"

-Sheryl Sandberg

Tor was a mystery.

The next time I found myself inside the cage, we were halfway through filming the season. The pecking order of the teams had been decided. I liked where I stood in the talent pool, although I didn't like the fact that I had to wait so long to fight again. Filming only lasted seven weeks, and I had three more wins to get through in order to participate in the finals.

The team dynamics had already been carefully laid out by social situations and activities we'd been put in, each member falling into their respective roles through long days of wrestling and sparring, then returning to the fighter house. It was a mansion in Vegas, giant, but shrinking by the day.

My team consisted of six other fighters, all with their own unique personalities and peculiarities that began to come out after living together. It was seven grown men, sleeping in one bedroom.

My closest friend in the house was Clint, our team's first pick. He was a good fighter, athletic to no end, and had the capacity to learn quickly. What stood out most about Clint was his innate ability to get along with everyone. Never once did any of us see him get angry or upset at a single thing. He was the consummate portrayal of composure.

There was Bubba McDaniel, the most experienced in the house. He'd been around the block of nearly every MMA promotion in the world besides the UFC, and had the wear and tear to prove it. He was a good-hearted southerner that probably never went to school long enough to do anything other than labor, which for him, was prizefighting. He reminded me of Matt, and while he rubbed many the wrong way, he and I hit it off. Bubba had lost his first fight a few days prior, to Kelvin, who'd been a huge underdog.

Another likable teammate was Dylan Andrews, hailing from New Zealand. Like Bubba, Dylan had a good amount of experience against tough competition and was an amazing training partner. He was a leader of the team, well liked by everyone, and had wisdom beyond his years.

There was Collin Hart, the quietest of the bunch, although he gave the impression that there were gears turning in there. He was a talented grappler, hailing from the lineage of one of the most elite BJJ coaches in the world, Cesar Gracie. There he lived in Northern California, getting high with the rest of the Californians, while training for a show that none of us were too sure how he got on in the first place. He didn't say much in the

$\mathcal{HK}$

house, instead spending his free time making elaborate slingshots, and contraptions out of sticks and rubber bands. I liked him because he was intelligent, and enjoyed playing chess, helping me pass the time between training sessions.

Also on the team was Adam Cella. With a quick wit and a sharp tongue, Adam could make even the most somber person laugh. He often commanded the room's attention, everyone wanting to see what he would say next. Although he'd competed in several dozen kickboxing matches, he was the least experienced of the group in MMA. He'd been on the receiving end of a devastating knockout the week prior, courtesy of Chael's second pick, Uriah Hall.

Adam wasn't the only one on our team who'd been knocked out, as seventh Team Jones member Gilbert Smith had gotten the consciousness kneed out of him, in a fight that he'd picked himself. We tried to tell him calling out the tallest guy on the other team wasn't a good idea when he was a whole foot shorter, but he was adamant.

Gilbert's knockout came courtesy of 6'6" Luke Barnatt, the tallest middleweight in UFC history. He'd flown over from England, having just picked up MMA a few years prior after owning a fashion shop in the UK. He was an intellectual, and a pleasure to live with, though I thought we may end up fighting in a later bracket.

Also on the opposing team was Zak Cummings, a friend who I'd ran into at several previous tryouts. We had a comical connection, as he was the only one that had tried out as many times as I had, knew what it was like to be chasing this damn thing for years.

There was Jimmy Quinlan, a cop from Boston. He talked with every bit of Bostonian accent that he could muster, and described everything as "wicked." He had an inability, or unwillingness, to pronounce his "r"s correctly, and we rubbed each other the wrong way from day one.

Kevin Casey was also on the opposing team, the guy I'd gotten in the altercation with in the van. His tough character facade faded quickly, although he kept it up as long as cameras were rolling. His nickname was "King" he explained, because every man has a right to be a king, with a queen, and a kingdom. He was a king he said, not the king. It was poetic, at least.

Kelvin Gastelum, the youngest of us all, the last pick, the chubby little Mexican, was fresh off his upset win against Bubba. Kelvin was young, inexperienced, had a shitty diet, and from what his team members said, never won a single round in practice. He did have one intangible that managed to carry him to success, an intensity that he could flick on when it came fight time, that let his opponent know that he was going to be a handful.

The 6th member of Team Sonnen was Uriah Hall, the Jamaican ninja with spinning attacks. He'd given us the spectacular knockout against Adam Cella, and looked to be a front runner for the show.

The final member of team Sonnen was Tor. He'd flown under the radar while I'd researched potential opponents. Tor was quiet, with an aura of intelligence. He doubled as an engineer in his native land of Sweden. Besides his nationality and unique day job, we didn't know much about him. Whatever else I was to learn about Tor would take place inside the cage, as his team had picked the two of us to compete next.

The fight started evenly, both of us vying for dominant position and inside control. He fought safely, as I expected him to, doing his best to thwart my attacks in the opening minutes of the bout. It was not particularly exciting, until the end anyway.

It finished the way most the fights in my career had, referee pulling me off of an unconscious heap of bone and muscle below me. With a second first round TKO stoppage, I was one step closer to becoming *The Ultimate Fighter*.

28.

Late Winter, 2002

I was with one of the bus stop kids, skateboarding at the same Dunkin' Donuts from 6th grade. We were daring one another to do tricks, trying to one-up each other. The kid I was

HK

with was good at skateboarding, and I was doing my best to keep up.

He did one, I did one, he did one, I did one. Finally, he did one, I tried to do one, and seconds later I was on the concrete, clutching a broken leg, feet and all dangling from right above my ankle. I'd suffered a break of the tibia and fibula, and was on the ground, yelling in pain.

I'd never broke anything before. It was loud, then shocking, then painful. My friend ran and threw his weed in the bushes, then tried to wave someone down from the side of the road.

The man he waved down was a neighbor, and he rushed over to help. He gave me his cell phone so I could call my mom. I gave it to my friend and told him the number. He looked terrified.

"Hey.. Uh.. Ms. Cheryl?" He stumbled and stuttered. "Yeah. Josh is here. He says his leg is broke. What do I think? I.. Um... It looks pretty broken." I cussed at him and told him to give me the phone back. I told my mom I was calling an ambulance and to meet us at the hospital. She said she was close, and to wait there.

She got there the same time the ambulance, and rode with me to the hospital. The first thing they did was stick a needle in my arm.

Hey there. Haven't felt that one before.

Everything went dark, and blurry. My leg stopped hurting, and I forgot where I was. I would come to every so often, and open my eyes to see my mom beside me.

I don't remember how long we spent in the hospital. The break was so bad that they had to put a full leg cast on. A cast below the knee could not bear the break, so one had to be made which carried the weight on my kneecap. It was horrifyingly painful, trying to get up the first few nights to use the bathroom. I finally resorted to pissing in bottles, my mom sleeping on the couch next to me to empty them when needed.

I'd never been injured before, never had to rely on anyone else. I was just 14, and wheeling around high school in a handicapped chair. The cast went all the way up to my crotch, and I couldn't use crutches.

There were perks to being handicapped, if only temporarily. I was the first one allowed out of class and the last one in. Girls would all volunteer to wheel me around, and help me with my stuff. The doctor prescribed lots of medicine.

The first time I ate a painkiller it wasn't like I'd found the holy grail like marijuana was. I never loved it. It was just there. I didn't have to go anywhere to get high, didn't need to worry about drug tests, or sifting through cow dung. We went to the store and picked it up. Shit, my mom even paid for it.

29.

The Tor fight was short, but I left the cage more battered than I'd have liked. I limped down the cage stairs with my left thigh in a knot, and a rib popping out with every breath. I'd managed to get a few good weeks of training in with the team, but the rest of the time filming I'd be rehabbing injuries, with continuous cryotherapy between ice bath and sauna. In the meantime, I had some of the brightest minds in martial arts to learn from.

Jon Jones was lead. He was more of a team captain than a coach, as he didn't do much technical teaching. MMA was something that came naturally to him, which can transfer into a difficulty explaining theory. He was an inspiring person to be around, with the charisma and attitude of a champion, but not too egotistical to prevent his team members from drifting in whatever direction we were most comfortable in. Most of the team were older than he was, and several of us had more professional fights. Jon enjoyed success by the boatload and brought with him people to help us achieve the same.

Frank Mir was an assistant coach. Anyone who'd ever watched a Mir interview knew he was well spoken, with confidence that didn't hesitate to delve into the realm of pompousness. I had an ex that told me I reminded her of Frank, or maybe the other way around. When I met him, I saw what she saw.

HK

One of the first conversations I had with him was about his tattoo above his stomach. *Two bodies, many minds, one spirit* was the transcription, a clever allegory for his love with his wife. She had the same inscription on her lower back so that the two tattoos were uniform with each other when sleeping belly to back. Corny, but I liked it.

With Frank came Ricky Lundell. Ricky was a genius; a physical phenom in his own right, and the mental acuity to match. Ricky was better at analyzing details of a fight than anyone I'd ever met. He taught applicable techniques and emphasized tiny nuances within the game. I looked forward to every bit of instruction he could afford to spare.

To complement Ricky and Frank's grappling expertise was Bubba Jenkins (yes, another Bubba). Bubba J was a 5x national wrestling champ and had defeated a who's who in the sport. Like Jon, he was an athlete who things came naturally to, while still having a respect for work ethic. "Are you out-working or just working out?" he would yell all practice. "You gotta be *comfortable being uncomfortable*." He had all sorts of quips and motivational slogans that he'd picked up through years of world class coaching and wrestling camps.

In addition to those was John Wood, MMA coach to the stars. Of all the coaches, he had the most actual experience training MMA fighters, and successful ones. He owned Syndicate MMA, one of the largest gyms in Vegas, and a hot spot for UFC fighters of all sorts to come and visit. He had competed on a much earlier season of the show, before having to retire from injury.

Last was Stonehorse. First name Stone, other part of first name Horse, no last name. Not that we knew of anyway. He was Jon's first ever striking coach and was one of the most hilarious people I'd ever met. He was an old Native American, like the guy I'd beat to get on the show, that grew up on a reservation. Some days he would be full of energy, hollering around the room about 720 spinning back elbows and triple flying knee strikes. Other days he would be calm and cool as ice, waxing poetic about what it meant to go into battle, and embracing true warrior spirit.

It was a dynamic group of individuals, our coaches and fighters, all from their respective ends of the Earth. We were all there to work towards a common goal; a tournament win for Team Jones, while still keeping our selfish interests in mind. The coaches, for their part, realized who they favored early, and all of us got to build our own little relationships with one another.

The whole time filming was going on, there was this special feeling between the cast, the coaches, and production that this was going to be a good one, this was going to be a turning point in our lives. All the fights were exciting. People were getting finished left and right. The payoff wouldn't come for months, but the suspense of delayed gratification in filming was a thrilling experience.

The production team allowed no contact with the outside world. No phone, no internet, no television, no email, not even any radio or music. They gave reason for confidentiality concerns for contact with loved ones, and cited copyright laws on the music, although I was convinced it was a scheme to make us go crazy, and do it on camera. There wasn't any instance where anyone lost their shit. No super confrontational scenes like the producers may have been accustomed to.

I thought of Isabel often. I wondered how she was doing. I wondered if she'd relapsed. I wondered if she'd done good on her promise to do well at her job. I wished that I could've called her.

30.
Early Spring, 2003

"In 2012, 259 million prescriptions were written for opioids, more than enough to give every American adult their own bottle of pills. Four in five heroin users begin by misusing prescription painkillers."
-American Society of Addiction Medicine

First, the doctor gave me too much. He gave me a ton. But then my tolerance grew, and the pills slowed. It wasn't that my mom was vacant. It was just easy to keep things from her. She'd

HK

never been a mischievous child and didn't have the capacity to understand the mindset of one who was.

I kept eating painkillers. I didn't eat handfuls like I had that one night years ago. I kept myself on a steady diet. A few throughout the day, and more at night when she'd go to sleep.

I didn't have my prescription anymore, so I had to buy them elsewhere. They weren't hard to find. The only problem was I was running out of money. My leg wasn't ready for lawn care, and my get-rich-quick schemes weren't sustainable. There were only so many grocery stores and movie theaters in town, and some had caught onto my tricks. My morals changed with my drug use, and petty strategies for fast cash morphed into full-fledged theft.

The manager of the Hungry Howies in the grocery store shopping center was a nefarious character, and had made an offer to all the bus stop kids; that he'd pay cash for anything we stole from neighboring stores, at half price value. We all did it. Sometimes we dared each other to take things as outlandish as bags of dog food, just to see if we could. It became a challenge.

Some of my friends began to steal other things. Some of them stole things from people we knew. *What's the difference?* They'd ask, on occasions when I didn't join them. Many times they'd go around at night "car shopping," taking things out of unlocked vehicles. Many of those cars were the same customers that had paid me to mow their lawn. I never stole from those ones and tried to make my friends skip their cars.

There was one neighbor that I could not resist. He was in his 40's and sold weed. I could always smell it coming from his house, and people constantly stopped by for minutes at a time. I'd asked him once if I could buy some, and he acted like he didn't know what I was talking about.

I knew that he knew what I was talking about, and I wanted to find out. He left his side door open all the time, even when he left, to let in and out his tiny yappy dog that guarded the house. One day Baxter the bastard and I were feeling ballsy and wanted a gander at whatever he was selling.

We tossed the yappy dog a treat and tiptoed over and in. The hairs on my neck stood. The house reeked of weed, although we couldn't find any. That's all I'd gone there for. I didn't want to plunder further, and I was ready to leave when Baxter found something else entirely. Sitting right on top of his dresser was a giant wad of cash. We sat there for what seemed like forever, adrenaline pumping.

I wanted to leave it. Baxter wanted to take it. People didn't call the police when drugs went missing, cash was a different story. Baxter said that if I didn't, then he was going to anyway. We compromised, and left some of it there, hoping maybe he wouldn't notice.

When we got back to my house and counted it, it was a little over $800. We split it up, and Baxter went back to his house. I called my drug dealer, bought a half ounce of weed, a bottle of painkillers, and hid the rest.

It was the first time I'd felt sorry for stealing something. The thrill wasn't worth the way it made me feel afterwards. There would be much worse consequences than a guilty conscience.

My mom came home the next day and asked me where it was.

"Where's what?"

"The rest of the money, you little shit." She was furious. She already knew; otherwise she wouldn't have been cursing at me. I kept playing dumb. She was giving me a chance to own up, and I failed. She'd come home at lunch and looked through my stuff once the neighbor called her, asking if she'd seen anyone at his house the previous day. I wasn't even cognizant enough to realize she'd already found it.

She went into the kitchen and called the police. I bolted out the side door and ran as fast as I could. My leg hurt, and my heart was beating out of my chest.

I didn't know where I was running. I tried to cut across to the next neighborhood and ran directly into a squad car. I turned to run the other way, and he got out and chased me. I'd been sprinting for minutes, and he caught up quickly.

He tackled me to the ground. I didn't resist once he reached me. I laid there, face in the grass, and let him cuff me. I wondered how I'd fucked up so badly.

HK

31

"That word, tournament, I want you to keep using that word." I listened carefully as Chael spoke. I was explaining my journey to him about the show, and what it meant to me. I was surprised to have him express interest in my story.

He had come in and set the tone for the season. Jon was not sure what to expect of the typically brash and confrontational Sonnen, but Chael had made it clear to the cast that he and the coaching staff of both teams were there to cater to us. This was our opportunity he said, and he wanted to help make the most of it.

Chael visited the house often and was cordial to our team. He was excited to be a part of the whole thing and took a different approach to the coaching gig than many of those before him. The norm was to keep fight picks private, shrouded in mystery to thwart the other team from knowing who would be fighting next, who would have to make weight in the coming days. Chael would be forthright, and tell us who he thought had a good chance to win, and sometimes even what order he wanted to pick the fights. The show, to him, was less about silly games of deception, but rather determining who was the best fighter swimming in the deep talent pool of our season.

"I want to win the tournament. And I want to fight Jimmy next," I told him. Jimmy and I were still butting heads, and I thought he was an easy scrap to advance to the following round. I explained to Chael that I was there to win, and take the least amount of damage doing so. I was already injured from the Tor fight and wanted someone I knew I could put on a dominating performance against. I set my sights on Jimmy, and I was going to talk it into existence. Chael seemed to be pleased with my approach.

Usually, when fighters were asked who they wanted to fight, the tough guy response was *whoever you put in front of me.* When I was asked, I always had a response prepared. We had the same conversation, moments later in Dana's office, with him and Jon both present.

"I think Uriah wants to fight you," Chael said. Fight picks in the opening frame of the tournament were determined by which team had won last. When given the option, Uriah had chosen Adam, the least experienced fighter, to take out. It didn't bother me that he wanted to fight me.

"Why should I care who Uriah wants to fight? If he continues winning, then we'll get the chance sooner or later anyway." I knew that Uriah and I were the strongest two seeds in the house, and so did they. Dana saw the same thing I did; that the most climactic possible finale was between Uriah and I. Everyone expected us to keep winning. Grandiose visions filled my head of toppling the favorite, on a live stage in front of thousands. The climax would be much more dramatic after a whole season of build-up.

Chael pulled me aside again, after our meeting. "I like what you did in there Josh. That was impressive. Remember, the squeaky wheel always gets the oil. Use whatever you can to your advantage, whenever you can."

I left the room knowing I'd made an impression on him. I was taken aback that he was going out of his way to instill any success in my future while I was preparing to punch a hole in the head of one of his team members.

The remaining eight contestants convened on the mat, where 14 had stood just weeks earlier, and 28 only days before that. The picks had been made, and I'd gotten what I wanted. I was matched with Jimmy while Uriah drew Bubba, who was brought back for a second chance. Dylan would be fighting Luke, and Kelvin would face Colin. We were down to the final couple fights, and the suspense was building.

32.

Spring, 2003

I was arrested at 14 years old and booked for burglary, grand theft, and resisting arrest. I spent the night in juvenile detention center.

HK

While detained, my mind shifted back and forth between being remorseful for what I'd done and wanting to get home to my bottle of painkillers. I was drug tested while I was there, and my mom discovered I'd been smoking weed again, and eating opiates I hadn't been prescribed to in six months.

She asked if I'd been doing it the whole time. She couldn't accept that drugs were the cause of all this, that it had all happened under her nose. I lied, told her I hadn't. I'd hid the pills and weed in a different place from the money. I knew she hadn't found them because the police didn't mention them. They were more concerned where the rest of the money had gone. Baxter had the other half. I didn't rat the bastard out.

They released me the following evening. When I got home, the dope was still where I'd left it. I ate a few, and went to sleep in my own bed, happy. I swore to never go back to that place, to stop being a troublemaker.

It wasn't just about not wanting to be in a cell again. I cared about hurting my mom. I'd never seen her so angry. My dad and I had grown apart since I moved out, and it was just her and me, as it had been much of my life. I didn't want her to give up on me. As soon as this pill bottle was done, I told myself.

Last one.

I didn't get a chance to finish them. I showed up to school the following day, and a girl I'd been dating said Baxter had been calling non-stop. He said he had to talk to me, but wouldn't tell her what about. I called him back at lunch. He said the police had been at my house all day. I knew what they were there for.

My mom had waited til I went to school that morning, and continued her search. She had a feeling the things I'd failed my drug test for were still in her house. She found them and called the police.

My next class was AP science, with Coach Mike Crowder. They called him Coach because he led the high school wrestling team at Lincoln. He talked to me once about joining. I wish I would've listened.

I went to my next class, not knowing what else to do. It was out of my hands. I watched the seconds tick by on the clock, the longest hour of my life. When the deputy finally entered, I didn't run. I grabbed my book bag and walked calmly towards my fate.

33.

"Strive to be a man of value, rather than success."
- Albert Einstein

We had a couple days until I'd fight Jimmy. The matchups were determined, the remaining players left with nothing to do besides train, wait, cut some extra pounds, and talk, which really was the only thing to ever do.

I walked into the kitchen the afternoon after the picks were made, and found the whole house engaged in a conversation over the dining room table. Rarely did a topic have the whole group involved, and I was curious what they could be talking about.

Familiar voices bantered back and forth. One was getting louder as the conversation progressed. I recognized them as Jimmy and Kevin Casey. They were on the same team but argued often. Last time they'd gotten into it, it was about the legitimacy of Casey's Brazilian Jiu-Jitsu black belt, and his accomplishments on the international grappling circuit. Jimmy had won multiple world titles at his skill level, and Casey was claiming the same. Jimmy called bullshit. He'd earned points for being a skeptic, gained a few more for calling Casey out on it, and hit the jackpot by admitting he was the only other nerd that had actually scouted the other fighters extensively.

The argument this afternoon was different, and struck my interest as I began to listen. They were having an ideological discussion, rare in a house of fistfighters. They were speculating specifically on the origin of the universe, and creationism. The conversation intrigued me, but I preferred only to spectate for the moment.

"C'mon man. You supposed to be smart. You tellin' me that we're here just by chance, that someone didn't make all of this?" Casey put his arms out as he spoke, motioning to all of us, the giant

HK

house we were in, the spectacle we were all a part of. He was animated and convincing.

I had heard the same words from Isabel and several others many times. I'd been a part of this back and forth; one infinitely firm believer, one equally doubtful non-believer, neither of which understanding how the other didn't see their point of view.

The astonishing thing to me was the specifics of Jimmy's rebuttal. Almost verbatim, he said to Casey the same things I'd tried to express to others. It was music to my ears, and had it not been for his awful accent, I'm not sure I could have said it better myself.

"Yes. I think it's all a giant coincidence. I think that if we were to somehow lose all the information collected here on Earth, and forced to start over, that the religions of the world would be different than the scripture written today. The scientific information would represent itself identically." Tor was the only one sitting on the side of the table with Jimmy, nodding in agreement. I realized I'd be fighting the only two people in the house with the same belief structure as me.

The rest of the group seemed incredulous to the idea of someone blaspheming, so confident in the absence of a higher being. Whether or not Jimmy convinced them otherwise was not important, because the interaction had served its purpose; with those couple of short sentences of conversation that I'd caught, Jimmy had successfully changed my whole perspective of him.

I cooked dinner as they argued for a few more minutes, before they finally agreed to disagree. Once they finished, Casey went to the living room to play pool, one of the only recreations afforded to us, while Jimmy went to help Kelvin cut weight for his fight against Collin.

Cutting weight was an acquired skill, with all sorts of different techniques used to get down to the required weight one competes in. A method in particular that Kelvin was using involved covering himself with layers of blankets and hot towels, in order to break a sweat and lose some of the water weight the body carries. He was struggling, and Jimmy came to the rescue, in one of the most amusing ways possible. He was sitting next to Kelvin as he sweat.

"A long time ago, in a galaxy far far away...."

It wasn't more than an hour after discovering Jimmy's cosmic views on the world that I was hearing him comfort Kelvin by telling him, from start to finish, the entire story of Star Wars.

No way.

It was a strange and confusing thing, Jimmy going from the person I disliked the most, to becoming one of my favorites, just two days before our fight. There was no avoiding it now, and I didn't mind fighting friends, but it made me less excited about it. We had a conversation that night, after my revelation.

"How are you feeling?" I asked him, genuinely curious. It was such a unique situation, living amongst those that we were competing against.

"I feel good. Almost on weight. You?"

"Another 10 lbs or so." We small talked for a few minutes before I brought up his earlier debate with Casey.

"I heard you talking earlier. You sound enlightened." He laughed, unsure of whether I was being sarcastic or not. I assured him I wasn't. We discussed our beliefs a bit, getting cordial, before he seemed to not be able to contain the question much longer.

"So, what is it about me that you don't like?"

"I'm not sure," I confessed. "Something about you just rubbed me the wrong way." Had to have been the accent.

"Why is it you don't like me?" I asked back, assuming he didn't.

"You have a confidence about you that makes people uncomfortable. It's abrasive. You think you're smarter than everyone. I can tell you're bright, and you might even be brighter than all of us, but I don't think you're as smart as you think you are." His answer was clear and concise, as if he'd spent time thinking about it before I asked.

I knew already that I had this problem, the character flaws he described. It was something I didn't like and was always trying to rid myself of.

HK

He gained a ton of respect with his answer. I told him I appreciated the honesty, and that he had changed my opinion about him within the course of the last few hours. It didn't matter much how much I liked him. One of us had to lose, and sympathy for my opponents wasn't something I could allow.

34.

Summer, 2003

After my latest run-in with the police, I was institutionalized for the second time in my life. The juvenile jail was no different than adult jail. Four-inch thick metal doors with electronic locks kept us in. There was barbed wire around the fences, and the food was the worst I'd ever had.

The jail that summer was overcrowded and understaffed, and spent many days on 23-hour lockdown because of it. When we did get out for an hour, violent criminals mixed with non-violent offenders. Many were in gangs and got in fights while inside. Each time they were handed another assault charge and put on lockdown.

I had internal struggles of whether I belonged there for what I'd done, or if it was all just a case of bad luck. I talked to a therapist for the first time in years and tried to convince her I wasn't like the other teenagers there. It was the second time I was surrounded with dysfunction, and began to wonder if this pattern would continue.

The therapist believed I wasn't like the others, but it wasn't up to her. I had to stay until my court date, where it would be up to the judge. The court relied on a shirt system for the jail employees to communicate with the judge in the simplest way possible; colors.

Blue was reserved for the worst behaved. Any day that an inmate would violate a rule would result in a demotion back to blue shirt status. After three days of uninterrupted good behavior, an inmate was promoted to green shirt. After a week, they earned a red shirt.

I touted my red shirt with pride. I wasn't a hooligan, as my dad had called me for years. I thought the red shirt would save me. It might have, had I went to court with it.

I was there for almost three months. Just before my day in court, the jail did a cell inspection and found a JS I'd etched into the concrete bed when I'd arrived at the beginning of the summer. They took my red shirt and threatened charges of vandalism. There were initials and profanities etched all over the cell from people over the years. I tried to say it wasn't me. They checked the cell logs and found no one else with the same initials.

It sounded trivial, but what happened to kids when they went to court was heavily determined by shirt color. It told the judge who adapted quickly, who felt bad for their mistakes, and who continued to cause problems.

I went that day with a blue shirt on, like the rest of the thugs that had been punching each other in the head for months. The judge looked at me like he looked at them, and sentenced me in the same way. I was forced to yet another institution. It was a six to twelve month military camp in the middle of the woods, named West Florida Wilderness Institute.

This is not happening. This can't be happening.

I cried. I wouldn't be seeing Tallahassee for a long time.

35.

"Victory belongs to the most persevering."

-Napoleon Bonaparte

I knew, he knew, the whole room knew who wanted it more. The fight itself was more of a formality, an afterthought. It went how most of us thought it would go. A takedown, even a good slam by Jimmy, some scrambling, me showing him I wasn't one to go quietly, and him conceding that I indeed wanted it more. The fight ended the way the previous two fights on the show had ended, with the referee pulling me off my opponent. He wasn't

HK

asleep this time, instead submitting to strikes before losing consciousness.

I did a slow victory lap after the fight, trying not to celebrate flagrantly after I'd beaten my new friend. I jogged around the perimeter of the cage and something on the outside caught my eye. A particular tattoo. A face tattoo.

Mike fucking Tyson.

Iron Mike was a well-known MMA fan that went to UFC events frequently, but his presence that day was a huge surprise. My favorite fighter of all time wasn't even an MMA fighter. He was a boxer, and there he stood right in front of me clapping with a satisfied grin.

He came and congratulated me after the fight. "You's a real violent fighta Mr. Josh. I liked that vewy much." He spoke through his thick upstate New York lisp. I couldn't believe the master of violence, a guy I'd watched and wished to embody in the ring, was congratulating me, complimenting me on my violence. It was an incredible moment on the whole adventure, and one of my fondest memories.

I talked to Jimmy a bit after the fight and sat down to watch the other three bouts that day. Dylan beat Luke in what would be the fight of the season, Kelvin knocked out Collin in perhaps the quickest fight yet, and Uriah knocked out Bubba, breaking his orbital bone with one punch. Both Uriah and my performances would help to grow the rivalry between us. Everything continued to be nothing short of fireworks.

We were told that we would be rewarded the next day for our performances, in the form of a field trip. It sounded silly, a group of men excited to pile up in a van and get out of the house, but it was something to look forward to. For over a month the only time we'd left was to the gym twice a day.

Our coaches decided on the trip, a local state park in Nevada called Red Rock Canyon. It was a stretch of land nestled in the mountains, named after the color, blood red, with a large peak right in the middle, overlooking the city of Las Vegas.

When we got there, it was beautiful. It reminded me of trips to the Grand Canyon early in life with my mom; nostalgic memories of magical views, overlooking landscapes that made me understand the ideas of God and heavenly bodies.

Dylan and I were the most excited to be there. The terrain reminded him of his home in New Zealand, and he couldn't hide the glee on his face. The two of us hurried to the summit, with the coaches and rest of the team trailing behind, and camera crew doing their best to keep up with 30 lbs of gear.

We made it halfway up the mountain before one of the producers entered babysitter mode, and told us to stop climbing. Coincidentally, or maybe not coincidentally, Dylan and I, the two so anxious to get to the top, were the only ones on our team to have a fight remaining. Metaphorically indicative of who wanted the most out of this thing, maybe. Either way, they couldn't afford the disaster of one of us getting hurt.

We obliged, reluctantly, but not without hopping up another 20 feet to take one last mental photograph, as we still didn't have phones or cameras. It was a refreshing moment, a helpful reminder of the world outside. We stayed until the rest of the team caught up, and made a promise to each other that we'd come back one day and get to the top, unbounded by limits to the heights of which we could climb.

36.

Fall, 2003

West Florida Wilderness Institute was an eye opener. It was isolation like I'd never known. We weren't under lockdown like at the detention center, but instead 30 miles from the nearest town. Swamps and neighbors with shotguns surrounded the perimeter. Escape was not an option.

Sometimes I didn't want to escape. I missed home, and my mom, a theme in my life by now, but there were times where I enjoyed the solitude, being in the woods, away from everything.

Many of the employees were ex-military or military wannabes. Everything was strict. Each morning we woke up to a bullhorn, had five minutes to make our bed, brush our teeth, and stand at attention. We had even less time to use the bathroom and shower.

There was marching, cadences, and uniforms. Several times a month they would make us run laps in combat boots around the track. Other times they'd pick us out of the group at random and make us clean the kitchen or bathrooms the whole day. I thought my dad's was a lifestyle change. This was night and day.

We spent hours on end in the hot sun. The food was better there. They had sweet southern ladies in the back, cooking grits, mashed potatoes, pork chops, and anything else we wanted. It was the best thing about the place.

They kept us fed because they kept us working. We dug holes and trenches, and laid concrete. We built fences and gardened plants. There were lakes, horses, and cattle. I learned to kayak, climb, and more. There were even some mushrooms growing in the field. I didn't think of touching them.

There was a single kid I identified with, out of all 40, the only other from my hometown. His name was Justin, "Juice" for short. He was a few years older and was there for drug charges. Like me, he read books and played chess to pass the time. He gave me my first copy of *Gorgias*, and said he wanted to grow up to be a philosophy professor. I didn't know if they let criminals become college professors, but it sounded nice. He preached what my mom preached, that we had to be good people in order to feel good. He enlightened me, and I looked up to him.

There was an employee, named Mr. Shannon, who was the alpha of the camp. He had no neck and lifted weights every chance he got. He was an intellectual too, and would pull Juice and I out of activities that he knew we didn't like. He'd talk to us about everything, from girls, to boozing, to things he'd done that were illegal when he was a kid. He found a way to connect like other counselors couldn't. He was a male influence in ways I never had before, and helped me through the process.

The camp was performance based. Like the detention center, we were assessed on our behavior day to day, except now we were judged by an intricate point system that required a set number in order to graduate from the program. Numbers appealed to me, so the system came naturally. The same was true for Juice, and we worked the program the way it was meant to be worked.

Both Mr. Shannon and Juice were martial arts enthusiasts. Mr. Shannon had been a hand-to-hand combat instructor in the military, and Juice took Kung Fu at a Shaolin studio in Tallahassee.

They talked about it often, and I could only sit and listen. I liked watching boxing, but didn't know enough to contribute. It was the only topic I couldn't keep up with in discussion, and I so desperately wanted to.

37.

"..Because the warrior path, like true love, leaves us open to the greatest joy and the greatest sorrow, the greatest freedom and the greatest uncertainty."

-Pedro Olavarria

Dylan and I were up on a sleepless night, the eve of our final bout of filming. Somehow, we'd gotten on the topic of what would be worse; losing a spouse or losing a child.

"I couldn't fathom being able to say goodbye to someone I'd built a life around if given the option." All my life I'd had two deep-rooted fears; not fulfilling potential, and growing to be old and alone. Gerascophobia was the clinical name for it. I suggested that maybe if one lost a child, at least they'd have their spouse to grieve with.

Dylan scoffed at my answer. "That's because you're a fuckin' kid, with no kids of your own. A kid is like... It's like you." He lacked the words to explain what it was he felt for his children, but his eyes lit up when he talked about them as if magic tricks were going on in his mind. He showed us pictures of his son and daughter every day the whole time we were there, both around seven years old.

HK

"I don't know what I'd do without them. And my wife would never forgive me if I let something happen to them. She'd kill me."

He tried to explain how a child was an extension of himself, with a love that couldn't be described. I didn't have kids, and had never lost anyone close to me, so I was speaking in ignorant hypotheticals. I took Dylan's words as I took many of his words, for that of wisdom, and hoped that I would never have to deal with either situation.

The next day arrived, and I'd gotten the fight I asked for. I stood across the cage from Kelvin, the dark horse of the whole tournament. There I was, one punch, kick, knee, or submission away from my destiny; the culmination of years of struggle and strife. I was moments away, less than five minutes surely, from what I expected to be my finest moment. It was to be the moment when I could finally relax for a minute, and look back on all that I'd done, at everything that had become of my career.

This game of Mixed Martial Arts had many ways to look at it. I knew the sport contrived of chaos, doused in differences of ounces and milliseconds. I knew that anything could happen and that everyone had a chance to win on any given day. This fight though, I had convinced myself that I had a 100% percent chance of winning. Maybe 98% or 99%, because everyone can get lucky now and then.

Too much confidence and not enough respect, that was my undoing. I'd watched Kelvin win upset after upset, seen his intensity in the cage, his versatility in both knockouts and submissions. In my mind, I just failed to see any way he was going to beat me.

The bell rang. From the first second, until the moment it was all over, I kept waiting for him to make a mistake. Such was the name of my game often, waiting to capitalize on the mistakes of opponents, and most the time it worked. This time, there were none.

We fought back and forth for the majority of the round, as I realized I was not going to walk through him as I'd anticipated. I was still confident until the end, the last minute of the first round, when almost unexplainably, he'd made his way to my back. His forearm was pressing against my Adam's apple, doing his best to choke me unconscious. Exactly how he got there would be a question for later. For now, all I could do was tap his leg frantically, ending the fight, and saving my trachea.

The ref split us up, and Kelvin ran around the cage, screaming, almost in disbelief at himself that he'd actually done it. I was in disbelief too, and laid there on the cage floor, listening to his cries of celebration. It was one of the worst feelings of my life. I made a mental note of how it felt. Such was a tool I'd done many times over the years, making notes of unenjoyable moments to try to ensure they never happened again. I wanted to learn from my mistakes, but this was one that was going to be hard to swallow. I sat there until the referee told me to stand up, so he could read the official result. I went to the locker room to chock up my tears and try to figure out what the hell went wrong.

I had been in fights before. I had lost before. I knew that seconds were of magnified importance. I didn't think about all those things before the fight. I went into it with just as much hubris as I'd come across as having to others. It was a disastrous combination, mixed with someone who was determined to defy the odds.

In my sport, one's dreams coming true sometimes relied solely on the development of other's nightmares, and that's what Kelvin had done to me. To come so far and lose at the very end was heartbreaking. After the long, arduous road that was *The Ultimate Fighter*, my journey had come to an end. Although the final four was nothing to scoff at, never would I be able to claim the title of TUF winner.

After a loss, every minute of every day was dedicated to hypothesizing where it all fell apart. What could I have done differently? Where did I stray from the path? If I had a time machine, what's the very moment I would go back to? The hamster wheel of analyzing loss was something I'd have to get used to if I was going to survive the things to come.

HK

38

I graduated from WFWI in six months and was back at home getting into trouble almost immediately. I returned to Lincoln High School, and barely finished the year. My experimentation was not done. It wasn't just easy to repeat the same patterns of behavior; it was nearly impossible not to.

I had a new image when I came back. Nobody knew someone who'd been to jail before. I didn't know how people would look at me. Some girls thought it was cool. Some kids were scared. It was amusing at first but tired quickly. I didn't adapt well.

It was a time in my life that was filled with intense substance abuse. I tried harder drugs, synthetics I'd never done before. I did LSD, and ecstasy. I snorted cocaine for the first time, and liked it. I found kids that did it heavily. I sought them out, and attached.

I never stole again, though many people I used with did. I thought it put me on some moral high ground, being a junkie but not a thief. I was 15, and met a group of kids who had just finished high school. We were at a party on their graduation night, and they saw me doing a line in the bathroom. They'd done coke before, but didn't know where to get any. I told them I could help.

I never sold cocaine. I facilitated its use, between a group of rich kids, and a drug dealer named Fatso. They weren't comfortable going to that side of town, let alone Fatso's apartment. He kept pit bulls and guns everywhere, and made a point to intimidate people. He liked me, though. I made him lots of money.

The crew of guys I'd met did just that; crew, at the rival high school, Leon. Each of them had a scholarship to different Ivy League Universities, all for rowing a damn boat. Harvard, Princeton, Brown, Columbia, they were all going in different directions, to the best schools in the world, and they wanted one last summer of fun.

They'd give me piles of their parent's cash to get them bags of blow. I'd tell them it cost double what it did, then spent the rest on my own habit. They knew what I was doing, that I needed them for my own addiction. We were friends, but there was a function of us all using each other.

We would binge until the early hours of the morning, playing Tetris of all things. They were avid enthusiasts of the game and were surprised when I kept up, or beat their scores.

"You're a smart kid huh?" There was one I was closest with, that I engaged with the most.

"I used to play puzzles a lot."

"So why are you all caught up with this shit?" He'd seen me on benders, always wanting one more. It was different than the painkillers, more than just a physical dependency. I really liked the stuff. It was the kind of desperation I'd told myself I wouldn't taste again. The land of cocaine addiction was an ugly place, changed people's personalities, including my own. The nights were thrilling, the days empty.

"You guys are the ones with bright futures, what are you doing with the stuff?"

"Well, that's kind of the point. We've got our futures secured. What's your plan?"

I didn't like the interrogation. "I'll cross that bridge when I get to it." The birds were chirping, and the sun was up. If I had a problem, I wasn't going to admit it.

39.

"How does it feel to be on the losing end of the biggest upset in TUF history?" The producer asking the questions didn't pull any punches.

Felt like shit. I walked out.

I'd seen more than half the cast members cry under the pain and pressure of the last two months. I'd promised myself I wouldn't be one of them, but there I was, in tears from dashed dreams of hours earlier.

I stepped into the backyard of the mansion. The first person I called was my mom. After all this time of isolation, we

HK

finally got our phone back, and the first call I made went straight to voicemail. I called my step dad, Jeff, who answered after a few rings.

"Josh! What the heck man, how are you? How was it?" He was excited to hear from me. I couldn't even muster the politeness to sound remotely enthused. I felt bad about it afterwards.

"Let me talk to mom, please."

"Well hey to you too!" He joked, before handing her the phone.

"Hey honey.." She waited for my response, knowing it would be one of two extremes.

"I lost today, just now." I fought back emotion in my voice.

"Oh honey, I'm so sorry... I know how bad you wanted it." She paused a moment before continuing. "Well, you got far if you fought all the way til today, right?"

"Yeah. Just not as far as I wanted."

"I know. You'll get 'em next time sweetheart." There wouldn't be a next time, not for this accolade anyway. I didn't say that.

"Yeah, next time."

"When are you coming home?"

"I'll be back tomorrow."

"Do you have a ride from the airport?"

"I'll call Matt."

"Okay, call me later. I love you."

"You too."

We hung up, and Gerard walked outside to join me on the lawn.

"You know that was your fight, we all knew it." He echoed my mom's sentiment, emptily. "Next time."

He gave me his number and told me to stay in touch. He wasn't allowed to show favoritism on the show, but had been rooting for me, he said, and wanted us to keep in touch. He challenged me to a game of chess to get my mind off the fight. I obliged, and a friendship began.

Finally I called Veronica. I wasn't thrilled to talk to her, or anyone, considering the turn of events. She made matters worse when she answered. Right away, she began talking about herself, complaining about a pop quiz her professor had sprung on the class that day.

After two months of not speaking to anyone in the outside world, I sat there, puzzled that this was the first thing I was listening to. I wanted to tell her it was over, right then and there. I decided to save that conversation for later. I told her I'd be home in a day or two, and that I had other people to call.

I didn't call anyone else. I went upstairs, packed my stuff, and got ready to leave. Everyone was engrossed in their phones, catching up with friends and family. We'd all talked about who we were going to call first, and all the things we'd do when we got home. Most of them had already lost weeks ago and had gotten over the sting of it. I wasn't afforded that pleasure, and was condemned to make the flight home with an inescapable displeasure in myself.

I finally got back to Tallahassee and tried to find the joy of returning to real life. The first thing I did was pet Juice for an hour, and roll the biggest joint I'd ever smoked. I enjoyed being high once again, as I reflected on my experience.

Outside of the five folks I'd chosen to be brought in at the beginning of filming, I contractually couldn't divulge the results of the tournament to anyone else. It was a huge deal, one FOX emphasized in great detail. Anyone who broke their non-disclosure agreement was subject to a penalty of up to five million dollars, which they reminded us of several times. They'd scared us enough to make me not want to tell a soul.

When I finally met all my friends for a big dinner the next night, I had to hide my disappointment. I tried to live in the moment and enjoy the company I was with, attempted to pretend like my mind wasn't elsewhere. I was happy to be home but still distracted, trying to digest the events of days prior. It would be months before I was able to see the tape.

I got a text from a random number, another distraction, this time a welcome one.

"Hey. It's Isabel. I heard you're back."

"Yeah, I am. I want to see you."

HK

"I want to see you too. I'm sure you're busy... Tomorrow, maybe? Sake?"

"Tomorrow sounds good, and sake sounds great."

"Love you. I'm happy you're home."

"I love you too."

After that text, I too was happy to be home.

40.

Late Summer, 2004

"If I assess my life realistically, no one but me knows how much I like to get high, and how boring life feels without it all."
-Personal journal, 15 years old

My first foray back into society was a failed one. After discovering the extent of my drug use, my mom filed a motion for a Marchman Act, and I was institutionalized for a third time at age 15.

Because I fought it at every turn, it made it difficult for her to get me admitted. While my drugs of choice were against the law, I technically hadn't been arrested and had to be assessed at an intake clinic. I was first taken there, then to a longer term program called Disc Village.

Juice from WFWI had been to Disc and talked about it often. It was after his trip there that he'd failed a probation drug test and was sent to WFWI. That's the order it should've been. Mine was backwards. Disc was lax. It was similar, but with far less structure. It was performance based, but nothing militarily styled. We didn't have uniforms. We got to call our friends. It was a cakewalk.

Easy or not, I still wanted to go home. It was at the discretion of my mom whether I could, although it was recommended that I finish the program once admitted. That's what she wanted me to do.

I got back to my books. I read *The Electric Kool-Aid Acid Test* and *One Flew Over the Cuckoo's Nest*. I was influenced by Ken

Kesey, Bukowski, and others. I realized there were loads of intelligent people that glorified drug use, that it wasn't just a character trait of degenerates.

Like WFWI, there were things that I enjoyed about the place. I learned about addiction and the substances I'd been using. I discovered why I'd been feeling the way I was, so depressed after long nights. I learned the difference between immediate and delayed gratification, about dopamine and serotonin receptors, and how different drugs damaged those pathways.

I was introduced to Narcotics Anonymous, and found utility in sharing my stories. I realized I had a problem. I admitted it. That was the first step, they said.

Unlike WFWI, there were plenty kids there that I could relate with. Most grew up in Tallahassee. I identified with the ones that had been arrested. I felt sorry for the ones that had been caught only for weed and had over reactive parents. Like usual, I lost my patience with the whole thing.

There had been escape attempts before. If the patient was court ordered, it was common for them to go to a higher security program after being caught. If they were voluntary, they'd get terminated, and forced back on their parents. While my situation was unique and my consequences uncertain, I was getting antsy and began plotting. My house was only 20 minutes away.

Disc had lots of flaws to exploit. It wasn't meant to hold people that were escape-threats. One of their sillier policies was to take us to a local barber shop for haircuts, as opposed to cutting hair on-site. The haircuts were weekly, and the employees that took us each chose different ones. I'd ask around, to see where all of them liked to go. I found the one that went nearest to my house and asked him to go just a bit further.

Mile by mile, he drove closer. He didn't know where I lived, of course. He was just going to the place I told him I liked to get my hair cut; the Hungry Howies shopping center. By the time we pulled up, I couldn't believe that I'd just gotten him to drive all the way there.

I sat in that barber's chair, anxiety and anticipation coursing through my veins as I grappled with whether or not to

HK

execute it, and how so if I was going to. I hadn't thought that far ahead. My mind raced as I tried to work out the kinks.

Finally, the haircut was over, and I had to make a choice.

"Can I go to the bathroom?" The restrooms were in the rear of the barber shop, which led to the back parking lot. It was the same one I'd been skateboarding in for years.

"Sure."

Fuck it.

I calmly walked to the back of the barber shop, opened the bathroom door, and locked it from the outside, trying to be tactful. As quietly as I could, I closed the door, went out the exit, and broke into a sprint. There was no turning back.

41.

Her skin had regained color. Isabel no longer smelled like cigarettes, and her hair was in curls, which she knew I liked. She looked good, but I always thought she looked good. More importantly, she had her old energy back, the glow and aura that only she could radiate.

She was making progress, and in the short time I'd been gone, she'd been promoted at the restaurant. Her boss texted me, thanking me for the recommendation, and singing her praises. She wanted to regain the trust of the people around her, and she was succeeding wonderfully.

We liked to pretend that sushi dates were something that were exclusive to us. They were a special nostalgia driven tradition, something we used to always do. She poured the sake into the small shot glasses, perfectly without spills.

"Cheers," she said, "to fresh starts. I want to know all about it. Are you happy?"

"I should be happy, yeah. I can't tell you much, but I think a lot of things are about to change for me." If there was one person I wanted to spill my guts to, it was her. I didn't have five million dollars to spare, should she let any details slip, and I promised I'd explain in due time.

HK
86

I was more interested in what was going on with her life. I was still dating Veronica, so I wanted to keep the date friendly and platonic, but I struggled.

"Have you met anyone?" I asked, hoping she couldn't see the question eating at me.

"Of course I have. I meet people all the time," she deflected.

"Have you been with anyone?" The question wasn't beyond our personal boundaries.

"What do you think?" I didn't know in which direction she was insinuating. She didn't give me time to answer.

"You still with that girl?" She wasted as little time as I did.

"I am," I said with disdainful emphasis, defiantly, as if it wasn't Isabel that had been on my mind the last two months. "I was with her when I left. I've only been back two days."

She cocked her head to the side with a tight-lipped smile, hesitating before nodding, and letting out a single chuckle. *Come on motherfucker, you know what we're doing here. You know how this ends.* Sometimes I think my whole relationship with Veronica was predicated on trying to rebel against Isabel.

I was the first person to bring up relationship status. Maybe it was then that she knew she had me again. Little by little I could see that sneaky confidence coming back behind her eyes.

"Congrats," she said instead. "Good for you guys."

She brushed it off and kept the conversation moving, telling me more about work and what she'd been doing since getting back on her feet. Her dad had helped her get a car, and she was on the way to making her own payments, along with car insurance. She sounded so proud, and I was proud for her.

She told me more about her new house, and how happy she was to finally have her own room again, with a big comfortable bed, not made of concrete. Her roommate Stephanie and I weren't the best of friends, but I was grateful for her giving Isabel a chance when not many others would. Isabel was still cleaning houses, doing everything she could to support herself for the first time in her life. Validation was always at the forefront of her mind.

"Which of your jobs do you like more?" I asked.

HK

"Keeping house, of course. I get my privacy. I'm not at the mercy of customers. I get to make my own schedule, and I'm good at it. It's therapeutic for me." I hated cleaning, and wasn't sure how it could ever be considered therapy, but I was glad she had something like that in her life.

"So, how long before we see it?" She asked, back to the TV show.

"A few weeks. Not long."

"On what days?"

"Wednesdays."

"I work Wednesdays."

"Well, you'll have to take off for that one."

"I'll see what I can do." Non-committal was nothing new from her, but it was good enough for me. I had commitments of my own to think about, and I drove home from dinner that night, alone, with those decisions heavy on my mind.

42.

Fall, 2004

After escaping from Disc, I headed not home, but to my school, Lincoln. It was almost lunch break, and all my friends who had cars would soon be leaving.

Several trails led from the back of the shopping center into Tom Brown Park, then to our school. I didn't take a single one of them. I ran in a straight line, faster than I ever had, through bushes, trees, and shrubs. By the time I stopped, my ankles and feet were covered in blood from all the cuts on my legs. It was one of the most intense moments of my life.

I got near the school and heard the bell ring from the road. I tried to catch my breath, and worked myself into another sprint. My feet pounded the concrete as I picked up speed.

I got on campus, and ran, literally, into the school Student Resource Officer. I *couldn't fucking* believe it. I'd been gone for not even an hour before I'd delivered myself to the police.

He took me into his office and asked me what I was doing there. He knew I wasn't a student anymore, and being on campus was against the law. It was then that I realized...

He doesn't know what's going on.

I told him I was there to meet my girlfriend for lunch, and that it wouldn't happen again. He wrote me a trespassing warrant and told me I'd be arrested next time, then sent me on my way. Much like the Disc employee who'd driven me to my house, I imagine it was not a good day for him when he realized what had happened.

I posted up outside campus, halfway in a bush, wondering when he was going to come zooming back around the corner. I saw one of my friends first and waved him down. We went back to his house, smoked a blunt, then went to a mutual friend's.

Nero was older and had a house of his own. He sold weed, and hung out with questionable folks. I knew it would be a safe place to go for the moment. He had a family member in law enforcement, and he'd get a warning call before any police came kicking in doors.

As fate had it, the cops didn't kick in any doors before I ran into them again. I was in the back seat of a car, coming home from a party. Nero was driving, drunk, with the owner of the car in the passenger seat.

I don't remember how he lost control, or hitting the tree. I remember waking up and seeing both bodies slumped in the front seat. The airbags were deployed, and there was broken glass everywhere. We were a mile from the house. I used one of their cellphones to call the police, then tried to wake them both up.

Nero woke. The passenger didn't, not at first anyway. I was terrified. An ambulance came, then the police. He asked me for my information. I gave him Baxter's information, the only other complete name and DOB I knew that was my age.

Nero's officer-family-member showed up on the scene and let us walk the rest of the way home. Nero left without a DUI, and for the second time in a month since escaping from rehab, I'd been face to face with the law.

HK

The accident was the talk of everyone, and word traveled fast. The next morning, there were eight or nine of us, sitting in the living room. All at once, everyone's phones began to ring. The first person to answer looked startled.

"Shit. Turn it to channel 13." That was the local broadcast station. I did not have a good feeling.

There I was, on TV for the first time in my life, under giant letters. "MISSING PERSON." The picture they'd chosen was one from elementary school, for extra effect.

Nero's phone rang too, and I knew who it was that was calling. They had to have known where I was now. I didn't mind. The whole situation had been sapping. I wanted it to be over.

I went with the police when they came, and they took me back to Disc Village. They called my mom, who was on the other end of a phone when I woke the next morning.

"Why didn't you call!?" She was crying, hard. It's the single thing I feel worst about doing to her. I had called, only once. It went to voicemail. I should've left one.

There are many times in my life that I look back and wonder what I was thinking. While the escape itself was one of those things, I still understand the feelings that were behind it. In my final days at Disc, I had an overwhelming sense of *I don't need to be here anymore*. While addiction is something that comes and goes for those who suffer from it, I'd learned all I was going to learn there. I knew that drugs had been the catalyst for most my behavior since I was 11, and I had no desire to be that person again. I told my mom that, and my drug test upon arriving back at the program reinforced what I'd said. I loved marijuana and was never going to stop, and while I'd drink socially, for several years I'd never take a drug again, including while I was an escapee.

The incident, while alarming, made her want to bring me back home. The details of what had happened made her lose confidence in the program. She and the director butted heads. The director terminated me from the program and recommended to the judge that I be admitted to a higher level facility. Such recommendations were usually heeded, and the day after being taken home from Disc, a Sheriff was back at my house.

I didn't know where I was going, and neither did my mom. By dumb luck, the officer misread the court order and took me back to Disc Village. When the director got there the following day, she was furious. She called my mom to come pick me up for a final time, and officially gave up. I had won.

43.

"He tried not to look long at her, like staring at the sun. Yet, like the sun, he saw her even without looking."

-Leo Tolstoy

It was the moment we'd all been waiting for, the season premiere of *The Ultimate Fighter*. We were at The Hobbit, a local restaurant sponsor, where we'd set up viewing parties for the whole season. Everyone was ready to see how the kid from Tallahassee did in his big broadcast debut. Besides FSU athletics, there wasn't a lot for the town to rally behind nationally, and the city was beaming with support.

The season would be a success, I was sure. I knew I'd done well, and although it would be a long time before I'd shake off from the loss to Kelvin, I realized that no one would know I'd been defeated until the last episode.

I waited anxiously as the show introduced us, one by one. Finally my face popped on the screen, and the restaurant burst into applause. It felt amazing, to be the thing that everyone was so excited about. I was on cloud nine, and hoped for more moments like it.

My phone was going nuts, ringing non-stop, hundreds of texts from people I hadn't seen or talked to in years. I was fine with that. I was never bitter at those I'd lost touch with that decided to drop a line only when things were going great. That's how things work. That's how people work. Most had still been part of the journey and contributed somehow along the way.

My mom was to my left, and she was to my right. It was not the right she. Veronica exuded a sense of entitlement, in a room

HK

full of people that had been with me much longer. I couldn't shake the feeling that she was out of place, and I knew I wasn't the only one to feel it. I should have ended it sooner, but I'd procrastinated. It would be addressed soon, I had a feeling.

After the brief scene of Veronica and me in the hotel room, it cut to my fight. Short and sweet, and broadcasted to millions of viewers at home. It ended just how I'd remembered, with the referee pulling me off. The restaurant graduated from applause to a certified uproar. People were standing on chairs, high-fiving each other, taking pictures and videos, capturing the moment.

I looked next to me at Veronica. She was face deep in her phone, sending her friends a shot of the few brief seconds that she was on TV. She hammered the nail in her own coffin, and triggered a chain reaction that would go hand in hand with the catapult my career had just been launched from.

Everyone wanted to party. There was no way I wasn't going to join them. Veronica had to work in the morning and said she wanted to celebrate on a different night.

"Can we just go home? I have to be up early." I couldn't believe she was even asking.

"I'm not going home right now, I'll meet you at your place later if you want."

"Are you serious?" She seemed shocked that I wanted to enjoy my moment.

"Are *you*?" I was angry by this point, and trying not to make a scene.

"Fine. See you later then." She walked out without saying bye to anyone.

Matt excitedly rounded up the crowd for the next destination.

"Where we goin' dude?"

"Tell everyone to meet us at The Strip. I gotta go do something first."

"Do what? Where?"

"A quick stop. I'll be there soon." He grinned and said okay.

I walked into Isabel's restaurant and found my friend, the owner. He congratulated me, and I thanked him. I asked him for one more favor.

"Can we get her off work?"

"Sure, tell a manager."

She had on her work uniform, the one I teased her about that she hated, short shorts and high socks. She looked stunned when she saw me.

"What are you doing here? You're supposed to be out celebrating, Mr. TV star!"

"I came to see you. You're off work now, you have to come with us."

"What do you mean I'm off work?"

"I mean I just got you off work. Clock out and come on."

"Your phone hasn't stopped ringing since you've gotten here, you've got all those people waiting on you, and you came here for me?" She smiled.

I never went to Veronica's that night, or any other night ever again. I was ready for the next stage of my life, and it was full steam ahead.

44.

Winter, 2004

I calmed down after rehab. I'd tried what I needed to try. I wanted to return to regular life, whatever that meant. Because of the run-in with the officer at Lincoln, the administration would not allow me to go back to school there. My mom asked me which of the others I wanted to attend, confident in my ability to convince them I wanted to be there.

I did want to be there. Despite all that happened over the years, it was a huge goal of mine to defy the odds and complete high school the same year as my class. My friends were all over the county now. I chose the school with the most of them, Leon High, where my boat rowing friends had gone.

HK

I adapted much better this time around. It was easier when I didn't go looking for trouble right away. I found a girlfriend instead. It sounds silly, talking about girlfriends while so young, but anyone who remembers teenage years knows that dating was serious business.

Beth was her name, and she was a large part of helping me transition back into a semblance of regular life. She wore a bright smile and was always so well put together; the student body vice president, and homecoming queen. I'd always found a way to date outside my league.

While the school admin did not like me with her, her parents were always supportive. That made me feel good. They let me stay at her house on weekends, and trusted us together. It was one thing I was adamant about not ruining.

My relationship with my mom improved, although she kept getting angry with me for smoking weed at the house. She'd caught me several times since being home, and would take it and give it to her friends who smoked.

One time she came home and found it, and told me to get out. It was the last straw. I didn't blame her. She'd had enough, done all she could do to raise me, and I agreed. I was ready to leave too. When I moved out, it was on good terms. She had an enormous sense of relief it seemed, to be in the next stage of her parenting relationship, one in which she would watch and love from a bit more distance, with faith that I'd make it work.

I stayed at Beth's for a few days, then to another friend's, named Jacob. He had a similar childhood to mine, with a single mother, named Theresa. She was a young mom, flirtatious and permissive. She was the first person my mom openly disliked. I loved her. She cooked Italian food every night, and cleaned up after us.

She took me to school while I was still trying to attend. It only lasted a few weeks. None of my credits from classes I'd taken at WFWI counted towards a diploma, and I had several attendance failures from being in and out of school for so many years. I'd fallen too far behind. I couldn't catch up, and dropped out.

I thought I was done with subcultures and atypical lifestyles. When I moved out, I realized I was wrong about all of it. The transitions were just starting.

I got my GED, which gave my mom some much-needed faith in me. I got a job and started Tallahassee Community College, and she gave me her old vehicle so I could get there. Beth and I got a Golden Retriever puppy and named him Juice.

My mom decided to take a final leap and bought a house to rent to me. My independence was important to both of us. I got a couple of the bus stop kids to rent the other two rooms. One had gone on to manage the old Hungry Howies, and the other worked construction with his dad.

I was 16 years old, and despite self-inflicted hardships, was leading a fortunate life. I had a good girlfriend, an awesome pet, and a new house full of old friends. I was still ambitious, and community college wasn't challenging. I needed something to throw myself into.

I was driving home from school one day, when I took a wrong turn and stumbled upon an old busted down warehouse that would change my life forever.

I knew what it was when I found it. I'd heard of it before. The busted up letters barely hung on the brick exterior.

Shaolin Kung-Fu.

45.

"A love not expressed is a love not experienced."
                                        -Pastor Fran Bueller

Isabel and I jumped in, head first. It moved fast, but I didn't mind. Making up for lost time, I thought. There was no feeling out process, no physical exploration to be done, no games, as there usually were with typical relationship beginnings. We had been saying our *I love you's* for years now, only now they were more intimate. I was swept off my feet again in no time. She'd not so much walked back into my life as she had stuck her head down and crashed right in. It was a tactic I could appreciate.

Veronica had no idea why I never came over that night. I didn't feel obliged to explain it to her. She was a fling, a temporary diversion from the things that mattered. I got a salty text from her days later.

"You think you're some kind of celebrity now? You're never gonna love anything more than that stupid sport." I didn't answer, and it was the last thing I heard from her for a long time. In all fairness, I'd heard it before, complaints of being too absorbed in the sport. There weren't many things I'd ever loved as much as MMA, although I didn't think I was any kind of celebrity. I just had a clear path ahead of me, with someone I had an impossible time saying no to.

As for TV stardom, I was far from it. Instead of notoriety for my hard work and success, the series painted me as a villainous character, something I wasn't exactly grief-stricken about, but it did teach me a lot about the depths to which people became emotionally involved with folks on TV that they'd never met.

In the day and age of social media, it was easy for the public to access on-air personalities to tell them exactly what they thought of them. The response to my personality was less than stellar, which is probably the understatement of the year. I had people who didn't even have Twitter accounts, creating them for the sole purpose of telling me what an asshole they thought I was.

Watching the show, I did look like a prick. I thought back to the conversation I had with Jimmy, him telling me I had a confidence that made people uncomfortable. In the professional MMA realm, I had a nice streak of finishing opponents in the first round, I'd been a coach, a gym owner, a promoter, and matchmaker. I felt those experiences put me ahead of the other fighters in the house. I thought I was better, and it showed. A certain amount of brass was to be expected of prizefighters, but in the context it was shown, people simply did not like it.

I began writing contributions for a website called BloodyElbow.com, doing episode breakdowns with a behind the scenes look at things that weren't shown on air. I wasn't divulging results, or spilling details of future fights, instead just trying to tell my side of the story. Production felt it was enough to tamper with their planned narratives, and I got a stern warning call from a tyrannical executive producer, telling me to shut the fuck up. That was the end of my blogging for *The Ultimate Fighter*.

Tallahassee had no love lost. They didn't give a shit what the rest of the world thought. I had great support, hugs and handshakes everywhere I went. Isabel was around to witness most of it, and she beamed with pride as I did. It was mutual, immense feelings of being proud of one another. She had made such a turnaround, returning to her old form more with each passing day.

As for the rest of the episodes, we still watched at Hobbit. The same crowd showed up every week to cheer me on, even on episodes I wasn't fighting. Instead of Veronica, it was Isabel watching by my side. No one really asked where Veronica went. There were no awkward feelings bringing Isabel around my friends. They all loved her. Everyone always did, and with her by my side it felt like natural order in the world had finally been restored.

46.

Late Spring, 2004

When I walked into the Kung Fu gym, two older men were wrestling on the mat. What they were doing didn't look like Kung Fu. They stopped rolling around, and the larger one walked over and introduced himself. His name was Brian Orkin. He reminded me of Mr. Shannon from WFWI; a nerdy meathead with thick muscles and thicker glasses.

For two hours a day, he and a friend rented out the Kung Fu building, and I happened to show up during those hours. I joined them that day, then came back and tried to Kung Fu the following afternoon. I decided quickly which one I liked more.

They split their classes into two categories: striking and grappling. Striking referred to various forms of boxing and

HK

kickboxing. Grappling was what they were doing when I got there, combining traditional wrestling with the Brazilian Jiu-Jitsu submission techniques the Gracies had been teaching for years.

I didn't yet know what they were doing was "UFC fighting." The first time I'd watched a whole UFC fight was at Beth's house. It intrigued me, but it wasn't something I meant to pursue. It wasn't until I heard some of the guys at the gym talking about their upcoming fights that I put the pieces together.

I was still a kid, and martial arts became an avenue through which I could continue learning after traditional education. Fighting satisfied my mental appetite as well as physical, at a time where I was getting neither. I now had another channel to direct my love of excess into.

Every day I went to the gym, grappling, hitting, and getting punched by grown men. We hurled medicine balls around, and kicked bags, and all suffered together in that musty, shitty gym. Most days I worked out so hard I threw up. I felt like a caveman, and I loved it.

I had a case of asthma I'd been fighting since I was a kid, and it took me a while to get it under control. Once I did, I began to see results, and people noticed. I liked that they noticed. I'd always been the skinny kid, and it was a good experience finally gaining muscle. Because people knew about my past drug use, they assumed me getting bigger was more of the same. At first, I was flattered, folks insinuating that I could've only had the results I did because of steroids or artificial means. It got old fast though, the notion that I'd taken shortcuts. Even my own friends and family asked me about it. It made me want to work even harder, made me want to do things the natural way to spite them.

MMA became popular at a pivotal time in my life. I'd carried a sense of failure after dropping out of high school that I was looking to cure. Throwing myself into competition was a way to combat that. I didn't plan on making a career out of it. I just wanted something to work towards, some of that delayed gratification I'd learned about at Disc Village. I told them to sign me up, and they did.

They didn't realize I was only 16. I didn't realize I had to be 18 to fight. When the two intersected, it was a bit of a funny moment. Patience, they told me, my time would come.

47.

"If you were all alone in the universe with no one to talk to, no one with which to share the beauty of the stars, to laugh with, to touch, what would be your purpose in life? It is other life; it is love, which gives your life meaning. This is harmony. We must discover the joy of each other, the joy of challenge, the joy of growth."

-Mitsugi Saotome

Besides fitting in by my side at The Hobbit, Isabel grew into her own as a part of our new business, Combat Night. Mitchell's girlfriend, Brandi, had taken a class with Isabel at Tallahassee Community College, one of the only Isabel had ever went to. Isabel shared a special social intelligence with her brothers, an ability to shapeshift with her surroundings while still keeping an identity all her own. She was my intellectual superior in this sense, by far. She knew how to fit in and make friends with anyone, anywhere, and when she found someone she liked, she knew how to make a good impression. Brandi was someone she really liked. The feelings were reciprocated all around.

"I'm guessing you guys dated in high school?" Mitchell asked me after our first interactions.

"Something like that," I said. I wish it would've been that cut and dry.

"I like her a lot," he said.

"Yeah?" Everyone adored her. I just wanted to hear the reasons out of his mouth.

"Yeah. She reminds me a lot of Brandi."

I could see the similarities, but wanted him to elaborate. "How so?"

"I dunno. She's country, but still kind of hood." I laughed at his description. He didn't know anything about Isabel being in

99

HK

jail, although I still called her Thug Life from time to time. As for being "country," she preferred the term "southern," but she was certainly both.

Isabel was always looking up to people to learn new things, adapting in social situations. We were at a time in our business' growth where we were expanding from Tallahassee and Jacksonville to Orlando and Miami, and our projects began to need more hands on deck. Brandi helped, and Isabel followed suit.

Brandi worked the front desk as guests and fans came in while Isabel and I set up VIP around the clubs. She would take hours to personalize the invitations and reservation cards, writing each letter perfectly in decorative fashion, starting over immediately at the slightest mistake. Meticulous attention to detail was something so attractive to me, someone I didn't have to micro-manage. Isabel took great pride in the things she did, and became my right-hand lady, doing all the things I wanted in a partner for both love and business. She carried the same enthusiasm for Combat Night as we did, and fit like a glove in our small knit group.

After an event once, I wanted to show appreciation for her help. I bought a dozen roses and showed up at her house; a typical gesture, but one with which I fought back feelings of puppy love. My butterflies flew in figure eights when I saw her reaction. I'd never seen a girl get so excited over flowers. She was blushing and started waving her fingers in front of her face in elation. "Eeeeeeee," the expression she let out when excited.

"You know they're just flowers, right?"

"Do you know the last time a boy bought me flowers?"

I didn't, and thought for a moment about it. "High school," she said. Three years was a long time, in the realm of pretty girls not getting flowers.

After that day, I made sure her vase stayed full. Every week, every other week, however often was necessary. I don't know who it brought more joy to, me or her, but it was something so fulfilling. I knew that anything I could to light up those brown eyes and dimples was something I wanted to do over and over.

It was all so fanciful, but another crossroads loomed ahead. Getting out of Tallahassee was part of growing Combat Night, and my own MMA career. I had already made plans to move out of town with my other roommate Brian, and Matt. Brian was an easy-going animal lover, and had played baseball with Isabel's brother, Owen. Brian wanted in on the adventure out of town.

I'd sold everything in my gym and began to look for homes in South Florida. Neither Isabel nor I liked to talk about it. I was excited, and I knew she was excited for me, but Miami was a seven-hour drive, and we weren't sure what effect the distance would have on our relationship. We were riding the train as long as it lasted, feeling maybe that the honeymoon would be coming to an end soon.

I remember us watching the Grammy's that year. One performance that stuck out to Isabel was Rihanna's song "Stay." Isabel was a sucker for attaching movie and music themes to her life, to our lives, and it rubbed off on me. The particular song struck a chord in her, and she sent me a link to it a few days after, except for instead of Rihanna, it was a version of Vin Diesel singing the song to his wife on Valentine's day.

The link came with a short text: "Be my Vin Diesel?" It was funny, and sweet, and had all the poetic humor that she was great at capturing.

For several years, I'd let my guitar sit idly as a decoration, not playing it much, and certainly never to impress anyone. Not once in my life had I ever played for Isabel. I always had such a complex about it, her being surrounded by musicians growing up.

I finally got the balls to pick up my guitar and learn the chords to that song that night, and played it for her when she came over. I did my best Vin Diesel baritone voice impression, half joking, half trying to sound good. She joined in soulfully, and there we were, drunk in a golden moment. To have been a fly on the wall, we looked silly I'm sure, but it was another step towards exposed vulnerability.

That's what I felt being in love was, a series of events of putting yourself out there for the other person to accept or reject.

HK

And silly was good. Silly was comfortable, and complete comfort was a thing I couldn't find with just anyone.

48.

Spring, 2006

Fighting became all I thought about. I loved it more than I'd loved skateboarding, more than music, more than anything. It consumed me. I spent most of that year inside the gym, and I was finally getting a chance to show everyone what I'd learned.

I was in the back, one month after turning 18, getting my hands wrapped. I'd never been to a live MMA event, let alone competed in one. I'd never even been in a real fistfight. Behind the scenes was crazy. Next to us one coach was slapping his fighter in the face to ready him. Outside, people were sprinting up and down the hall. Orkin told me not to worry about them, to stay calm. He said it was okay to be nervous. Fear was okay, as long as I didn't let it paralyze me.

Violence had become an escape from the mundane, a chaos to lose myself in. Before fights, athletes went through training camps; 8-10 weeks of intense diet and exercise, several workouts a day, and lots of bumps and bruises along the way. I'd done mine diligently. I hadn't smoked or drank in months.

We were in the Valdosta County Convention Center in Georgia, and on the other side of that locker room door was an arena full of screaming fans. I'd brought 50 or so from Tallahassee, and the anticipation was palpitating. If I won, jubilation. If I lost, embarrassment and shame.

People are rarely put in situations where there's so much to be gained or lost over the course of minutes, or seconds. That's where I'd put myself, inside that ring. I was 18 years old, standing across from a solid brawler. Orkin was behind me, giving instructions before the fight.

Relax. Breath. Relax.

I was relaxed, until the bell rang. It was all a blur after that. Punching, kicking, heaving, kneeing. I could hear my mom screaming in the background. The first round ended, and I dragged myself back to my corner.

I had to puke. I held it in. I'd been trying to listen to my coach the whole fight, but there was so much going on. The 60 seconds in between rounds flew by, and I stood back up, wobbly legged. It hurt to breath.

The second round began, and we staggered back towards each other. More punches, more knees, and an uproar from the crowd. It surged the last bit of adrenaline I had left in my body, as I pushed him into the corner and unleashed a flurry of sloppy, looping punches. It was enough to win the fight. He covered up, didn't respond, and the referee pulled me off. I'd done it. At 1:37 of round two, I'd won my first MMA fight by TKO.

I dizzily returned to the locker room to take it all in. Orkin cut my handwraps off and handed them to me.

"Keep these, kid. You'll thank me later."

I threw up, and sat in the back until I'd gathered myself. When I returned to the arena, the first person I saw was my mom. It was a mission to get her there, but I was glad she'd come. She hugged me tighter than she ever had before. My grandma stood behind her, grinning widely. Beth and my friends were further back, and broke into celebration when they saw me. For a split second, I was the coolest guy on Earth.

It gave me great pride to be able to compete and succeed at this thing that few dared to attempt. I didn't care if it was a fringe sport that people thought was going to get me hurt. I didn't care about the stereotypes I had to deal with. I didn't care about the knuckle dragging mouth breathers I had to train with, or the stigmas that came with fighting in a cage. I dealt with it all, because I'd finally fallen in love with something.

49.

My mom had left me first; that was the way that I justified it. I'm not sure I needed justification anyway, me finally moving away from home, but I was never sure that I could've left her, had

HK

she not left first. Luckily for all of us, she'd found someone to go with.

Her health was declining, showing signs of Fibromyalgia, and possible Multiple Sclerosis. It wasn't something I often saw, because I was never around her late at night, but Jeff would tell me more than she was willing to admit.

It was her health struggles that were the reason for them leaving in the first place. They had a grand scheme, both of them leaving their comfortable jobs to sell their house to buy an RV and travel the nation. They had dozens of national parks planned for their voyage across the US, to set up shop at and enjoy the wilderness.

It was a lovely plan, one that I was excited for them for, until it all began to unhinge. When they left their jobs, it cancelled their health insurance, and not even a week later, days before they were set to embark, Jeff fell ill. He'd been a habitual smoker for 40 years, and his body had waited until the final hour to punish him for it. He developed a severe cough one morning, and decided to have it checked out before they departed. Within days, he was diagnosed with a rare respiratory infection, Mycobacterium Abscessus. There was little-known cure.

In an instant their plans were thwarted, reducing Jeff to a hospital bed at Shands in Gainesville. He was released shortly after, but relegated to outpatient care, with intravenous antibiotics for several months.

There were multiple factors at play, none of them good. Besides him being sick, neither of them had jobs, neither of them had health care, and they had no home except the RV they'd bought. Worst of all, Jeff did not quit smoking. He tried several times, but failed. It made me angry. What he decided to do with his lungs was his own decision, but I was relying on him to take care of my mom.

Their plans were impeded, but I refused to bail on mine. Miami bound I was, whether or not Isabel or my mother were happy about it. Isabel was not, I knew. Isabel wasn't without a temper when she didn't get things she wanted sometimes, and when she cancelled on a lunch date one day, I chalked it up to her

HK   104

throwing a fit. We were supposed to go to Hopkins, our favorite sandwich spot. She texted me minutes before we were to meet.

"Can we do this later?" she texted.

"Do what later?"

"Lunch. Or hanging out. Or whatever it is we're doing."

Whatever it is we're doing stung.

"Okay..?"

"I'll come by later."

She did come by later. The first thing I noticed was a band-aid with a cotton ball on the inside of her forearm.

"What is all that about?" I said, pointing at her arm.

"I don't want to talk about it right now." She'd left it on for a reason, but bailed at the last minute when it came to telling me why.

"Anything I need to know?"

"Yeah, but just not now please."

"Yes there's something I need to know, but you're not going to tell me?"

"Can we just.. Later. Please." I was usually one to badger. Something in her voice told me to stand down.

"Why do you love me?" She asked, suddenly. She didn't sound like she was fishing for compliments, she sounded desperate for answers.

"What? Where is this coming from?"

"I wanted to know if you knew why you love me."

I pondered for a moment to give her a thoughtful answer. A good explanation escaped me, and I made a mental note to work on it.

"I've always loved you. Why do you love me?"

"I've always loved you, too." She said that because it was the kind thing to say. I didn't know how true it was.

"Well, why now?"

"Because you saw value in me when I didn't feel valuable." She'd thought about her answer. She and I had an understanding of what was going on. We both knew that me sticking with her through her bullshit was a personal investment, and it was present on her mind. She didn't want the whole thing to be in vain, for her

HK

to turn out to be fool's gold. It was as if I was only one that had remembered the old Isabel. That was my best asset, it seemed.

The conversation was out of left field, and I wasn't sure what she was getting at. I was leaving in a week for Miami and figured she was just unsure of everything.

"I'm sorry. I just worry about things," she said when I pressed further. She was worried, and couldn't hide it. "None of that matters, because you're leaving soon anyway."

"Well that's being short sighted isn't it? I'll still see you for my birthday, right?" I was moving the first week of March, and we'd planned to meet in Orlando on the 14th to go skydiving. My mom and I shared a birthday, and Isabel was joining us.

"Of course I still want to come," she said. "I'm sorry for being negative."

It wasn't the send-off I expected, but I let it be. I tried to put the thought out of my mind, although intuition told me something was wrong.

50.

Winter, 2006

"It is a frightening thought, that in one fraction of a moment you can fall in the kind of love that takes a lifetime to get over."
-Beau Taplin

After my first fight, I came back and celebrated for weeks. I'm not sure if it was the culture of a college town bleeding into younger ages in Tallahassee, or if every place in America was like that, but everyone my age partied, a lot.

By this point, I'd moved out of the first house with the two bus stop kids, and had a falling out with both. I'd deemed it better to put them in the past. Between training and partying, I'd lost Beth as well. I wasn't good to her, and she moved on.

I moved into a better home, on a road called Lakeshore. The place was huge, and beautiful; 2,700 sq ft, on seven acres, with no neighbors in sight. I lived with a nerdy kid named Chris, and a revolving door of other roommates, one of whom's uncle owned the house, and agreed to rent it to us temporarily until they demolished it for a commercial building. The kid moved out early, and I took over. The uncle charged me $500 a month, for the *entire* house.

It was an incredible thing to have at 18 years old. I'd paid rent in the last house with child support that my dad had been sending my mom. She didn't want to tell him I'd moved out, and felt bad keeping it, so she gave it to me to help pay bills. Between that and financial aid, it wasn't hard to support myself.

At Lakeshore, I charged my roommates a fair $300 a month, collected the bit off the top, and paid for anything else I needed with my new hustle; throwing house parties. I'd always coordinated our spring break trips, collecting money and making reservations for hotels. I had a knack for getting people together in one place. I enjoyed entertaining, and being the reason everyone was having fun.

My graduating class was still in high school. We used to have to wait for a friend's parents to go out of town to throw parties, and we now had a spot all our own. It was more than just mine, it was something all of us in town shared. I was just the one to collect the money from it.

I invested in keg shells and taps. I bought ice luges, speakers, and outlandish party accessories. I bought a hot tub, a throwback to the above ground pool I'd wanted all those years ago.

I charged $5 a head to get in, and it became a thing. Because of the size of the land, and room for parking, it allowed us to have parties on a bigger scale than anyone had ever had. Halloween, New Years, any and every special occasion was brought in at Lakeshore.

Fighting, throwing parties, and hooking up with girls, that's what I thought life was about at 18. We all did. Being the house where everyone went to hang out helped that. It was always the same cycle. I'd take a girl out for dates, lose interest in her, but continue sleeping with her.

I'd fought again and won. When I trained, **I split my time between the MMA gym, Tallahassee Fight Club, and the local**

HK

Gold's Gym. I was sitting at the Gold's smoothie bar with my friend Chris, when one day when two girls walked up. Chris was friends with both. I knew only one. The other girl I'd never seen, but couldn't take my eyes off. I'd never had someone catch my attention so strongly. I got choked up trying to introduce myself.

"Hey, uh. I'm Josh." I stuck my hand out and squeezed too tightly.

Smooth, dufus.

"I know who you are. My friends come to your parties, and my brother goes to your fights." She fluttered her eyelashes a bit, breaking me down. I was nervous and did the first thing I could think of, inviting her over.

"Yeah? We were thinking of having people over tonight if you wanna come." I hadn't even asked her name yet.

"I'm not sure I can tonight. Maybe this weekend?"

I pulled out my cellphone and handed it to her. She cocked her head to the side, then finally shrugged her shoulders and began to type. She put her number in my phone, saved her contact, and handed it back to me. I looked down to see her name.

Izzi Monroe <3. The heart was a cute touch. I wondered who was putting the moves on who.

51.

I could smell the ocean as we got closer. I loved it. When we got off the interstate, white sand lined the sides of the roads, and I knew we were close. It had been a rollercoaster of a 24 hours, packing our whole house into the U-Haul, taking turns driving it in one fell swoop, all the way to South Florida.

I had emptied my bank account to get us somewhere to live. The whole $10,000 I had earned on *The Ultimate Fighter* was what I gave the real estate agent, to find us a house and pay for several months of rent in advance. It was the only way anyone would rent to three young kids from North Florida with no credit.

Our home was in Hollywood, Florida, a small beach town a few minutes from the coast, nestled between the more urban communities of Miami and Ft. Lauderdale. When we got there with the truck, it was the first time we'd actually been inside. We'd packed all of our stuff into the U-Haul quickly and unorganized, and things poured out the back when we opened the door.

Isabel had been calling the whole day, asking if I was there yet, and making me promise to send her pictures. I opened the front door with my phone out, camera rolling, documenting the first look at my new home.

Juice wagged his tail as he led the way. Brian and his dog, Athena, followed close behind. There was tile floor everywhere, all the way through the living room, into the kitchen, and eventually to a fenced-in backyard with a humble pool. I backtracked towards the bedrooms and found the master with an office leading into it. We'd decided before moving that I'd pay more for the bigger room and private bathroom.

The whole day was exciting. All three of us had lived in Tallahassee forever, and we were charged up about our unknown futures. I signed the paperwork with the landlord and began to get settled in. Part of my new life, as well as Matt's, was training at a new gym, MMA Masters. Fighting in the UFC meant a rise in the level of competition, and a need to improve my skills if I wanted to remain successful. I had done well on the show, but I could not be having any more slip-ups like I did against Kelvin.

The new gym was a big adjustment from the roles Matt and I had been used to. For the last several years I'd been the coach, the leader, the one instructing others on techniques and training methods. In our new gym, I had equals and higher ups. I didn't mind the change in dynamic. It was nice to have coaches teaching me new things, and training partners that challenged me.

After a long day of unpacking, rearranging, and sending pictures, I finally sat down to call Isabel.

"Do you like it?" she asked.

"I love it. It's perfect."

"I can't wait to see it. When can I come?"

She knew she could come anytime she wanted, although I wouldn't end up seeing her again until Orlando. It would be a life

HK

changing event, as many of my junctions with her were. Until then, ignorance was bliss.

52.

Late Winter, 2006

"You alright dude?"

"I think I'm in love."

"You know that's Wyatt and Owen's sister, right?"

Fuck.

"How would I know that?"

"She just told you her brother goes to your fights. And they have the same last name, dummy."

"There's a million Monroes in this town."

"Yeah, and they're all related."

The family had a strong presence in Tallahassee, a captivating thing that people wanted to be a part of. Of all the positive traits, they were defined most by thick moral fiber, and strength of character. They were the kind of folks that never said a bad thing about anyone, wouldn't join in if someone was getting trashed on. They'd stick up for people, and give everyone the benefit of the doubt.

Owen and I had hung out a few times while young, although I never realized he had a little sister. We'd since went to high school together before I'd dropped out. I hung out more with their middle brother Wyatt, and while I wasn't particularly close to either, I looked up to them, and their oldest brother Landon. Everyone that knew them did.

She was the girliest girl to have ever had three brothers. I was enamored by her beauty but hated the fact that she was their sister. She wasn't someone I wanted to lust over. I didn't call. She waltzed into the house a few days later with her friends.

"Dick move, getting a girl's number and not calling," she said. She'd later tell me that it got under her skin, the first in a long game of push and pull.

Izzi was flawless, the dreamiest girl I'd ever met. She

radiated warmth and depth with her presence, and southern charm that could work a room with grace like I'd never seen. There might as well not have been anyone else there. Anybody that grew up in Tallahassee could attest to it. I was smitten.

She came around often. She helped us throw parties, stopping by beforehand to clean the house, and drink with us before everyone else got there. She called herself my sidekick. Izzi was amazing at cleaning, even then. Her first stepmom used to drag her around and force Izzi do the brunt of her housekeeping duties, and her experience showed.

She'd invite all the kids from her class, I'd invite mine, and between the two of us, we knew everyone in town. I took her on dates when we weren't partying. Our first was to a sushi restaurant. Early in our relationship, I would never try to hook up with her. I'd finally found somebody that I wanted to treat right. I knew that she was different than other girls.

She'd heard my reputation before I met her. Like not calling, she'd later tell me not trying to be sexual with her made her wonder what was wrong, as if the others I'd been with were more adequate. It's hard now to look back and comprehend what a disconnect we had on how we felt about each other.

There were other prominent families in town. There were the Antonellies, up to their Italian noses with money and privilege. There were the Braffords, a tribe of folks who'd had nothing but daughters. There were the Hosfords and Hunts, who the Monroes were closest with, and spent all their weekends at the beach.

The youngest of all the family's siblings were around Izzi's age. She wasn't just the youngest of the siblings, she was the youngest of cousins too. She did what we'd all done our whole lives; take after the habits of the kids we looked up to. We were all trying to act older than we really were, and she was the best at it.

Wyatt had once told me he was nine years old when he first smoked weed, and Izzi hadn't been much older. She partied, hard, in a way that made Izzi her mother's daughter. She had a lifetime of keeping up with the boys. Substance consumption became her biggest conflict early in life.

HK

Just one more. It was what we had in common most.

53.

"Isn't that what being young is about? Being the one person in history who lives forever?"

-Vanilla Sky

We were in the hotel room, minutes before my 25th birthday. We'd both gotten to Orlando late in the evening. She sat there, fiddling with a hair tie, not making eye contact. A tear ran down one side of her face as she stared at the floor, not sure where to begin.

I had no idea what was going on. I had so many other things happening that I'd forgotten about her odd behavior that day weeks before. Her single tear grew to a steady stream, and she stumbled...

"I'm not sure how to tell you this."

I had never gotten a girl pregnant before. This was kind of how I'd imagined it going. I wish that would've been the news.

"I have Hepatitis." She uttered, no longer able to contain it. I sat in silence, stunned. My jaw felt like it dropped to the floor. She filled the silence. "Hepatitis C." I was frozen in disbelief. I blew up.

"What the *fuck* Isabel?! How long have you known?"

"Only a few weeks. That day. I didn't know how to tell you."

The emotions were creating a crescendo as I thought about what I was hearing. Not only was Hepatitis a life-threatening illness, it was also a career suicide for me. Some of the only requirements for me to fight professionally were clean piss and clean blood, meaning no communicable illnesses.

"You know I could never fight again if you got me sick? You know that don't you?"

I had worked my whole career towards one goal: fighting in the UFC, trying to build a legacy in the sport to be proud of. I had other ways of making a living, but competing was my passion, and one I'd invested an awful lot of my life towards. I thought of the countless hours of sacrifice I'd put into it, and it made me upset that she'd been careless with that, even if she didn't know.

She cried harder. She explained to me the best she could between drying her cheeks and catching her breath. No, she didn't know, she pleaded. She didn't want to hurt anyone else, she said. She asked if I wanted her to leave. Her bags were still packed.

Before that day, it had crossed my mind before, the chance that she'd been infected sharing needles. I knew that when she began to prefer her drugs intravenously, the risk for diseases skyrocketed. I knew she'd been through these things, and I'd tried to hush them in my mind for months, only to have them finally bubble to the surface.

She sat there bawling, her face in her hands. I didn't know what to do. I realized it was the first time I'd ever seen Isabel cry without restraint. Seven years, and through everything, I couldn't remember her ever shedding more than a tear. There she was, sobbing on a hotel bed.

I was dismayed, concerned, scared for her, scared for myself, but more than anything it hurt to see her cry like that. Everything that she'd been working towards putting in the past had come back to blow up in her face, with a fierceness. How do you put your mistakes behind you when you have a constant reminder of them pumping through your blood?

I looked at my watch, 12:02 in the morning.

What a birthday present.

I moved next to her, feeling weak. It was a colossal pill to swallow.

"Please promise this won't change anything for us." She pleaded, trying to keep herself together.

This changes everything. I wanted to tell her. I held my tongue.

"I don't know what to say." My words felt cold as they came out of my mouth. I tried to compensate by holding her close. I let her cry as a million thoughts rushed through my head.

HK

I don't know how one person can attach themselves to so many junctures in another's life, but she had a knack of doing so, in the most dramatic fashions. Had a gun been pointed at my head, forcing me to choose between Isabel and my career, my choice would have been my career. I thought about the possibility that this would be our last weekend together romantically. It hurt me to the core. I didn't know how I'd even begin to explain myself to my friends, coaches, everyone who'd supported me through my whole journey, if I was so reckless as to choose a mate that could spell the end for it all.

Make it through the weekend, I told myself, still trying to take it all in. I didn't know what else to do.

"Do you want me to go home?" She asked again, unable to hide the desperation in her voice.

"Of course not. Please stop talking like that."

"Promise me this won't change anything," she said again.

"There's no way this doesn't change things, Isabel."

"I don't want you to stop loving me. Or stop looking at me like you do."

"I can't just stop out of nowhere, and what does that mean? How do I look at you?"

She sniffled again, wiping big, wet, brown eyes. "I don't know. Like you think I'm the prettiest girl in the world." Her voice cracked.

My heart sank through the floor. Christ, what a line. Of course she'd say something out of some princess fairy tale, and I ate it, hook, line, and sinker. She nailed it, with the most simple elementary words, the way I felt when I looked at her, but she wasn't supposed to know that.

"I'm not going to look at you different," I said, trying to gather myself from being stripped raw at her answer. I was struggling to contain my own emotion at this point. I'm not sure I'd ever been good at giving anyone comfort, and I certainly wasn't doing a good job of it now. I was too busy reeling myself in from the news, seeing her cry, hearing her plead.

If we'd hit a ceiling of vulnerability before, we were now through the roof. It was the deepest I'd ever seen into her soul. It was her laid bare, saying *take me or leave me* like she'd never done before. I wondered if I'd even be able to leave. I wondered how I could say no, because could I really *ever?*

The computer on the bed cycled through the Pandora station that had been on since she arrived. Stateless' "Bloodstream" began to play. If God was up there, he had a cruel sense of humor.

She cried harder, and slammed it shut.

54.

Early Spring, 2007

"A dream is just a dream, that ends in nothing, and leaves the sleeper where he lay, but I wish you to know that you inspired it."
-Charles Dickens

There was something about Izzi and her family being on the opposite end of the belief spectrum, at a time in my life where I was still forming my own conclusions on the supernatural. Izzi hated that word for it, supernatural.

She engaged in my inquisition, helped me get to the bottom of what people with faith thought, better than most in the church had. It was her conviction that was romantic, and I tried to coax it out of her any chance I got. I was curious at how people were captivated by faith, and she satisfied my curiosity. Whether or not we agreed was irrelevant. It was the trait of being opinionated that was appealing to me, to both of us.

I wasn't rejecting the notion of something greater completely, just challenging modern Christianity. There weren't many people that she'd heard do that. My roommate Chris was one of them. He introduced me to Dawkins and other pretentious atheists that were public figures. I wanted to question people without sounding condescending, but wasn't sure how good I was at it. She'd tell me to stop blaspheming, that He could hear me. Sometimes it would be her questioning me.

HK

"I don't understand how you can say that you don't know where we came from. What do you think happens when we die?"

"What happened to us before we were born? If your parents didn't take you to church, you wouldn't believe what you do now."

"Well I'm glad they did!" *The Monroes go to church more than the pastor*, a joke around town. Church and FSU Football, those were the things they hung their names on. "Did yours not?"

"They did. A lot. How you can have certainty in something you've never seen? I don't consider capacity for illusion to be a virtue."

"Don't use big words to try to make me feel stupid." She wasn't dumb. "I *have* seen him, everywhere. He speaks to me, in so many ways." She elaborated, citing things she'd seen throughout her life that weren't explainable otherwise.

"I understand it may seem like some coincidences are too much to describe, but they're still just coincidences. Neither of us knows where we came from, the difference is I don't make up an answer." I didn't pretend to be able to wrap my brain around String Theory, or multiple universes, or any of the other ideas that Chris and I watched on the Science Channel. I just knew I didn't believe the bible.

"So you're seriously telling me you don't pray before fights?"

"I don't pray before fights."

"Oh Lord. Well, I'm gonna start praying for you."

Religious differences aside, we grew closer. As incredible as she was, it was also what she represented that I was attracted to early. She was the forbidden fruit, the thing I was beginning to think I'd never fully have. I was the same to her, something that she wanted but no one would ever allow.

We hung out for months, more than she told anyone about. The secretiveness of it made it exciting, but gave me a complex of our relationship. If her brothers were around, she'd act differently. I don't know if she ever let anyone kiss her around them. They were non-confrontational, but they weren't soft. They'd grown up in the woods, and went to Fairview, the urban school I'd almost attended for the IB program. Izzi talked about Wyatt getting in fights from time to time.

She was so keen on judgment from them, and it trickled down to me in a powerful way. I wanted to tell them about her and me, at least give them some sort of hint before they found out elsewhere. She refused.

Because of the nature of our relationship, I never knew which Izzi to expect. When she was affectionate, it was mind numbing. When she was cold, it was painful. It was as if Izzi held a mechanism that with the press of a button, she could make my heart flutter.

She made me a CD that I kept for years. "Wild Horses" was the first track. The rest was filled with Fleetwood Mac, Led Zeppelin, and Bill Withers. Things like that made Izzi her father's daughter. Her favorite movie character was Penny Lane from "Almost Famous," and she'd often say she was born in the wrong decade.

I made her plenty of CD's. She enjoyed contemporary music too. She liked Ben Harper, and wrote an essay on Gnarles Barkley's song "Crazy." Music was something we always shared. I was too scared to play for her. That part of my life was something only people from years past knew about me.

This part of my life, people only knew fight Josh. She didn't care much about fight Josh, and I couldn't figure out why. Fighting was becoming the aspect of me people cared about most.

She'd never watched it, and I made her one day.

"So are you gonna get a bunch of tattoos like them?"

"No. I don't like tattoos."

"I bet you'll change your mind. When am I gonna go watch one of your UFC fights?"

"I didn't think you'd want to. And it's not UFC fighting yet." I had to explain to her the difference between local MMA and what we were watching on TV. I had to explain to her I wasn't even a professional yet.

"Wait, wait, wait.. You're not even pro?" She nudged me in the ribs with her elbow, teasing.

"Shut up. I could be."

HK

"Yeah, yeah. Sure you could." She stole the remote and changed the channel. I felt deflated. I texted Orkin that night and told him to get me a professional fight.

55.

Isabel still had dried tears on her face when we woke the next morning.

"Today is gonna be great," I told her. We were parachuting in a few hours, and I woke up intent on not letting the previous evening ruin the day. I tried to not think about it, pretending like I didn't want to run to the clinic right then and there to get myself tested.

We drove from Orlando where we were staying, to Titusville, a rural town closeby where they'd throw us out of the plane. It was my mom, Isabel, and a few friends. We'd coincided the weekend around our first Orlando Combat Night, happening the day after my birthday.

We got to the airstrip, and my adrenaline rose. Feeling nervous about something was a nice distraction from the night before. My mom and I had been skydiving once. Everyone else was going for their first time.

We all strapped onto our tandem partners and asked in which order we wanted to jump. I'd go first, followed by Isabel, then mom, then the rest. As we began to ascend, I looked at her for a sign of how she was feeling.

She was the calmest body on the plane, staring stoically out the window. I'm not sure she'd ever been on a plane in her life, and there she sat, with the resolve of a jet fighter pilot.

"You scared?" I yelled over the sound of wind as they opened the doors, revealing the ground more than 15,000 feet below. She smiled at me sweetly and shook her head, showing not a morsel of fear. I believed her.

I jumped out head first, feeling the blast of cold air rush against the bare skin on my face. Below me, I could see the Florida coastline, towns and cities, fields and farms. For 90 seconds I had no worries in the world, not a thing in life to do but feel the endorphins. That's what we're all here for anyway, endorphins.

The freefall was quick but powerful. I hit the ground with my heart beating out of my jumpsuit, still in invincible bliss. Isabel landed 20 yards away, unhooking from her instructor and running towards me. My mom and friends followed one by one until we were all on the ground. Maybe it was the prospect of near death that was intoxicating, or perhaps the people I was with. Either way, there wasn't a thing in the world that could have troubled me in that moment.

We took pictures next to the plane and began the ride back to Orlando, to get ready for the rest of the weekend. On the way home we didn't say a word about what she'd told me the night before. There was nothing more to say. She couldn't do a thing, but let me decide for myself, and that's what she did.

I had decisions to make, but first, research to do. I didn't know a lot about Hepatitis, or the differences between the types. When I got home, I spent the whole night in front of the computer, reading what had to have been every article on the internet ever written about the disease.

Isabel had done the same, and we talked back and forth as I read. Contraction percentages through sex, we learned, were not particularly high; 3-5% from women to men over the course of a year. The risk, it seemed, was in careless interactions that inevitably happened between couples. A scrape, or cut maybe, left without a band-aid. Sharing a toothbrush, and having a bit of blood from exposed gum. Spotting during menstrual cycles. All those things were much more common as methods of contraction.

I researched what it does if left untreated, and what the treatment process was. It was only in recent years that a possible cure had become available. Isabel explained that she'd have to make a decision whether to undergo treatment, or ride it out for 20 or 30 years until her expiration date. It was an unfathomable decision for a 22 year-old to be posed with.

The possible cure was a combination of drugs, called alpha interferon and ribavirin, that patients took for 48 weeks. The alpha interferon could only be introduced into the body through

HK

a small self-injecting needle, and the ribavirin was to be taken twice a day, three pills in the morning and four in the evening. I cringed at the thought of her ever injecting herself with anything again.

There were several downsides, besides the abundance of medicine and needles. It wasn't anywhere near a sure fix. It was around 50% successful, and less so in females. Worst were the side effects. Over the course of one's treatment, the percentage of patients who reported one or more of the side effects was alarming:

Fatigue 70%
Headache 66%
Muscle soreness 64%
Fever 41%
Joint pain 33%
Nausea 46%
Loss of appetite 25%
Diarrhea 22%
Depression 36%
Irritability 32%
Insomnia 39%
Skin reaction 28%
Hair loss 32%

She had watched one of her friends undergo the treatment while in rehab. Whenever she talked about what it was like, she always had a disdainful look on her face. She would squint her eyes and shake her head a lot, exuding a mix of fear, confusion, and disgust.

"It was terrible," she said, "watching her go through that. She turned into a different person. She slept all day, and when she was awake, she was awful to be around. And she started to lose her hair." Isabel was petrified, beside herself at the fact that she'd have to go through a year long hell just for a *chance* to kick a disease that she didn't even know she had until weeks ago.

"That insomnia rate seems pretty drastic," I said to her as I read.

"Insomnia? *Fuck* Insomnia! My fucking hair is going to fall out Josh!" She protested, struggling to find a more emphatic word than "fuck." She got her point across.

My mind thought back to her sitting across the glass in Leon County Jail, joking that at least she still had great hair. It was a trademark of hers, and would soon be slipping through her fingers, should she choose to undergo treatment.

"I thought all of this was behind me," she said. "I don't know why it has to keep following me." It really was tragic. I wondered what she thought the reason for this was, in the mind of someone who was convinced everything happened for a reason.

I must have had told this girl that I loved her at least a million times in our lives, and now I felt like it was time to put up or shut up. Prove it or move on. It was all or nothing at this point.

I thought long and hard before starting the conversation about our options. I wanted to help her get through this, but I wasn't sure if I was the person for the job. I thought back over the years and the struggle that I'd had to be a good man, to fight my selfish side. She'd had a remarkable impact on my life. She made me a better person. I thought this may be my chance at finally repaying her. I told her there was no way I could stay with her if she didn't start treatment.

"And then what?" She asked.

"And then it's all over, for good." No more reminders of the past.

"Why do you want this? Why do you want me?"

"I know I want you in my life. If we're going to be together, then I need you to get better. And you should want to for yourself."

"I do want to for myself, but you can't make me start this, then up and leave me halfway through it when I'm sick and bald," she said prudently.

"I'm not gonna do that. And hush, you're not gonna be bald."

"You're sure that I'm what you want?"

"I'm sure."

HK

"Okay. I'll go back to the doctor this week."

The whole thing made me feel valiant. I hoped the decision would not come back to haunt me.

56.

Summer, 2007

"When you're in love, you want to tell the world."

-Carl Sagan

"He thinks he's gonna be some UFC star, married to lil' baby princess." Chris and a friend were giving me a hard time about Izzi. They weren't lying. That is what I thought was going to happen. I'd just won my first pro fight, and was on top of the world. I felt in love for the first time in my life, not just with fighting, but with another person.

I was in love, but we all were. I felt like a character in "There's Something About Mary," and Izzi was Cameron Diaz. She was a soul bandit. She put it on me like no one ever had; curled my toes, dizzied me, made me never want a different girl. I didn't have any problem telling anyone. I told my friends, her friends, anyone that would listen. She thought I said that about every girl.

I'd held the cards only briefly. She was in control now. I was always available for her, dropped whatever it was I was doing when she called. She had me by the balls, and dragged me through hell and back with them in hand.

My shallow 18 year-old self had signed up for a pro fight to impress a girl, and once I'd won, there was no turning back. I quit college to pursue an MMA career. That meant no more financial aid, and because I was no longer a minor, no child support. I sold weed to supplement income.

I'd hustled sacks here and there, but had never bought it in bulk. I had a friend from Miami that I'd known for years. He gave me a scale and started me with small bags. My credit with him grew, and with it, the amount he gave me. When I ended up getting the paycheck from my first fight, I signed it all over to him, because that's how much I'd owed, $1,200.

I sold pipes too, and different paraphernalia. I still threw parties for money. My spending habits exceeded my income, and I had no help from my parents to pad my ignorance. Within months, I was broke again. I called my Orkin and asked him to sign me up for another fight.

"How 'bout next week?" He said. I hadn't anticipated that response. My last three fights had months of preparation beforehand. It wasn't just Izzi that I was eager to impress, but Orkin too. I told him I'd accept the fight.

The fight was in Atlanta, Georgia, against a sub .500 Franz Mendez. I was 1-0 as a pro and thought I was invincible. Any dominance I'd shown in previous fights was absent, as he took me down and smashed my nose with his elbow in the first minute. I remember being on bottom and hearing it shatter. I reached up instinctively to set it straight, and he immediately rearranged it sideways again. I couldn't breathe. Blood was filling my mouth from the back of my throat, as well as from the outside. I'd fought grown men before, but this was not what I'd signed up for. He took my back and forced a submission before the end of the first round, and in an instant, my facade of indestructibility vanished.

I'd brought friends to this one too, although neither my mom nor Izzi were there. I remember that being the only thing I was relieved about. I went back to the locker room and hung my head. Theresa, my friend's mom, barged in, furious. She wanted Orkin's number so she could call him to give him a piece of her mind, signing a kid up for a fight like that. The whole thing left a bad taste in my mouth, blood included.

I looked at my phone. Several missed calls from my mom, and a text from Izzi.

"How did it go? I prayed for you."

HK

57

"That's the shit I remember: wonderful stuff you know? Little things like that. Those are the things I miss the most. The little idiosyncrasies that only I know about.. Oh she had the goods on me too, she knew all my little peccadilloes. People call these things imperfections, but they're not. Ah, that's the good stuff."

-Good Will Hunting

"Lots of blood tests for the next few weeks, then if everything looks good we start in May." She was back in Tallahassee and had gone to see her doctor.

"May? That's the earliest you can start?"

"Yes, and I need you to be sensitive about this stuff. It doesn't make me feel good to have to be doing it. Don't be hurtful please." There was a maturity in her request.

"Ok. Well when do I see you again?" I asked.

"When do you want to see me again?"

"Whenever you want to come down."

"I could come this weekend maybe," she offered.

"Yeah? I'd like that."

I was excited for her to see my new home, and I wanted to make a good impression. I was never much for scrubbing and polishing, but I did my best to clean the house. I went to the store and bought ingredients to cook; steak and shrimp with her favorite bottle of Pinot Noir, a dozen roses, and a dozen candles.

I got wax everywhere, and felt silly trying to clean it up as she walked in. I had the same familiar boyish love feelings I always did on her arrival. The hours of preparation was worth it when I saw her face. The lights were dimmed, candles lit, flowers in a vase, wine poured, dinner perfectly timed and on the table.

"You did all this for me?" she said, leveling me with a smile. She stood on her tippy toes and gave me a longer than usual kiss. It felt good, succeeding at being romantic.

When we woke the next morning, we began a practice that became a fixture of our day. Each wake was spent in one of two ways. If I was facing to my right, I was woken by Juice, tail wagging, goofy dog smile from ear to ear, hot panting in my face. I didn't mind the dog breath, because if Juice woke me, it meant Isabel was still asleep. I'd turn and see her looking peaceful, lost in dreams. Most times she'd have a bit of drool just under the side of her mouth, and conditioned herself to wipe her cheek when she woke up, just incase.

If she got up first, it was different but equally lovely. She'd tiptoe to the kitchen and get us both a large glass of room temperature water, because that's what the doctor told her to do in the morning. She'd then crawl back to bed and cuddle, and wake me with kisses. They weren't aggressive, just light and gentle. She was the only girl I'd ever dated that didn't complain if I hadn't shaved in days.

"Open your eyes," she'd finally whisper if I took too long. Many days I was already awake, pretending I was still asleep, feeling her lips on my face.

We laid in bed that first morning until we'd made up for lost time, and I got up to go to the gym. "Can I go with you?" She asked. I liked the idea of her being excited about being active. I bought her a membership her first day there.

As we walked out the door, she asked me to look at something on her car. "It started flashing a funny light last night," she said. I turned the car on and looked in the dash. It was an exclamation mark blinking inside a wheel, indicating faulty tire pressure.

I checked the PSI on her tires. The recommended pressure was 35 lbs/PSI on her Honda Civic. Two of her tires were 30, one was 45, the other was 15.

"Babe, what the fuck? Who did these tires?"

"I did! They looked low so I put air in them on the way down."

"Do you know how to measure air pressure in your tires?"

"How do I do that?"

"You're 22 years old and no one's showed you how to do this yet?"

"I'm sure they tried and I wasn't paying attention or something. Stop being mean about it." She felt like she was being

$\mathcal{HK}$

scolded. I tried to explain but she became defensive, and I dropped the subject.

When we got to the gym I went to sit in the sauna, a routine I'd done for years. Isabel asked to join there too. The location was co-ed, allowing her to come with. I opened the door for her, and she took a seat on the bench closest to the heating element. I sat on the one above her.

"Come next to me, butthead." she said.

"You come up here, it's hotter."

She rolled her eyes and climbed up.

"How long do we sit in here?"

"As long as we can."

"Well, how long is that?" She'd never been in a sauna before.

"Usually, Matt and I have a contest to see who can sit the longest. The rule is you don't leave before someone who came in before you."

She thought for a second. "I came in first."

"Right, so I can't leave until you leave."

"I can sit in here longer than you," she said competitively. I told her I'd been doing it for a long time, that we had sauna contests to see who could withstand heat the longest. The whole practice we did was to get better at cutting weight, and to condition ourselves to discomfort. I was good at it, I told her, and that there was no way she'd beat me.

"Okay." She said defiantly.

While we were there, I had something I needed to confess. *The Ultimate Fighter* was nearing the end, and in a few weeks, my fight with Kelvin would air. Until that moment, everyone still assumed it was Uriah and me in the finals. The only people that knew that Kelvin beat me were my mom and coaches. I felt like I had misled Isabel, and needed to tell her before she watched me get choked out on TV.

"I have to tell you something," I said, as both of us broke a sweat.

"Oh Lord," she said sarcastically. "What now?"

"Hush. It's nothing bad. Not too bad anyway."

"Okay, well what?"

"I get beat in the last episode, against Kelvin."

"Phhhhh. Baby.. You think you needed to tell me that for me to know?"

"What do you mean you already knew? Who told you?"

"No one needs to tell me anything about you. I can tell from how you talk to people that it didn't go how you wanted. I was wondering when you were going to tell me, brat." She'd always had a read on me, knew if something was bothering me, or if I was in thought, sometimes even exactly what it was I was thinking about. I realized it was one of the things I loved most about her.

"I don't care about any of that stuff. I'm proud of you, and I love you no matter what." Her words were endearing.

"I love you too. I really am gonna sit in this sauna longer than you though."

"We will see," she said, sweat dripping. We sat, and sweat, and sweat some more. The temperature was 180 when we got in, and nearing 200 around the 20-minute mark. Most grown men didn't last 10 minutes. I was impressed.

200 degrees became 220. 20 minutes became 30. Me being impressed became me starting to wonder if my girlfriend who had never stepped foot in a sauna was going to beat me in a sauna contest.

"Are you sure you're feeling alright?" I asked her.

"I'm feeling fine," she said, seething with moxie.

"We can get out whenever you're ready."

"Right after you." I realized this was one of those times where she was reading me, and I was hurting.

She got quiet for a bit, staring into I'm not sure what. It reminded me of the plane before we were about to jump, nonchalant and indomitable. I wondered where it was she went in her mind during those times.

After long enough in the heat, reality becomes an alternating wave of euphoria and discomfort. We were beyond that point. I wondered how the hell she was still sitting there. I was

HK

expecting her to burst out of the room at any moment because that's what I wanted to do.

Did she really not mind it? Was she just waving her masochistic feathers, taunting me? *You think this is hell?* Was she teaching me a lesson about everything in life boiling down to how bad we want it? *Was she even human?*

She was likely just showing the competitive capacity of a girl who grew up with three older brothers, but I was nearing hallucinations and decided it had gone on long enough. I told myself it was for her safety, to protect my ego.

I ran out of the sauna gasping for air after 40+ minutes. It was the longest I'd ever spent in there. I sat on the chair outside, dizzy, recovering. She had a satisfied, smug smirk at my concession of defeat, strutting out after me. It seemed like a trivial event, nothing more than a funny story. It would come into play one day though, right when I needed it to.

58.

Fall, 2007

The Mendez fight showed me an ugly side of the sport, one that I knew was there but never wanted to be on. The bout wasn't even sanctioned, and wouldn't be counted on my record, but I didn't know that at the time.

I had a badly broken nose, and my whole face was swollen. I couldn't train, wasn't in school, and drank every day for weeks. Izzi didn't like this version of Josh. I'd sometimes wake up after drunk nights with several outgoing calls to her. It made me cringe. She came around less often, and I cycled through other girls when I was lonely.

One came and didn't want to leave. She was a blonde girl, named Jacky. I didn't even like blondes. She was a close friend of Beth's, and I was never able to take her seriously, because of her not caring about her friend like that. Self-righteous, I know.

Beth had been long gone, headed to mortician's school. It shocked me when I'd heard what she wanted to do. It took a special kind of person to handle the dead, and to deal with their families on the worst days of their lives. She and I talked every now and then, but I knew she harbored resentment.

People noticed that Jacky was sticking around, even when I didn't want her to. They joked that she was going to kill Izzi and me in our sleep. Jacky heard about the jokes of derangement, and it made her complex worse. If life was still imitating art, it had turned into Vanilla Sky, with the part of Cameron Diaz being stolen by Jacky, and Izzi into Penelope Cruz.

Izzi made most girls jealous, but Jacky was the only person I'd ever met that actually didn't like her. She would say bizarre things about Izzi when she got upset. *Sorry I'm not like little Ms. Perfect.* She'd come to parties, and make things uncomfortable.

Izzi never had to compete with a girl before and had no interest in doing so. She shared her brothers' passiveness; it was the only character trait in them that frustrated me. She was intimidated of Jacky being older and had a million other boys to choose from anyway.

Whenever I wanted Izzi to come back, I'd have to go a few weeks without seeing Jacky. I did, and she agreed to come to a fight, the first one since I'd lost.

It was the most nervous I'd ever been. I got my hands wrapped, and walked outside to see Izzi and my mom while the earlier bouts were going on.

"Should I kiss them for good luck?" She said, pointing to my wraps with superstitious charm. It sounded like a lovely idea. I went back to the locker room, my nervousness subsided, as I let my mind get swept in the superstition with her.

I wanted to try using my kicks in the fight. I'd been working on them in the gym, but never used them well in the cage. A training partner was holding the pads for me as I warmed up. In the locker room, folks have a bit of an unsaid contest, to see who can kick the loudest. We were winning.

Out of nowhere, he flared his arm as I kicked, and my foot landed directly on his elbow. It stung, and when I tried to put it back on the ground, I fell under my own weight.

Shit.

HK

Within seconds, it was swelling and discolored. The fight before mine was just starting, meaning I had 10-15 minutes before I was supposed to walk out. I sat there, told everyone I was fine, and mustered mental strength I didn't know I had. I thought of Izzi outside, and everyone else I'd brought.

I didn't walk out for my fight. It was more of a hobble, trying to put any semblance of awkward bounce in my step to hide the fact that I was hurt. When the fight began, I didn't do any kicking. I dragged my opponent down, put all my weight on him for five minutes, and limped back to my corner.

When the second round began, I did more of the same. I landed on top of him and passed into a mounted position. Something in my mind screamed urgency. The last round had been boring. This wasn't what I'd brought everyone here for.

He was covering the front of his face with both forearms, leaving his temples exposed. I don't know what it was, but something told me to hit him with both hands at once. It worked, well. I felt how powerful the impact was. It was loud, with a sick, wet, packing noise. I did it again, and again. The guy fell asleep, and the referee stopped me.

I surged with adrenaline, doing a victory lap around the cage. It wasn't until they announced the winner that I even remembered my foot. I looked down, and it was the size of a softball.

"You are something else kid," Orkin said, shaking his head.

"What do you mean?"

"I mean you're a fucking maniac. One moment I'm looking for a commissioner to tell them you broke your foot and can't fight, and the next minute you're in, there smashing heads with both hands." He had a huge smile on his face as he cut my wraps off. He handed them to me, like usual. I'd overcome a hurdle, used an obstacle to show character. It felt good to have impressed him.

59

"She wasn't doing a thing that I could see, except standing there leaning on the balcony railing, holding the universe together."
                                                        -J. D. Salinger

"Why you so good to me?" There was thick twang on the other end of the phone as I answered. It was a quote from Forrest Gump.

Isabel had several voice impersonations that she did. She could replicate any of our friends' accents on a dime, and had other go-tos that she liked. She could be the Queen of England, or her friend Shaquita from jail. The one she was talking to me in today was Jenny, the female heroine from Forrest Gump.

The finale of TUF was nearing. We were the first season to have every cast member receive a UFC contract, and we'd been told to get ready to fight, though we didn't yet know who we'd be facing. Isabel didn't have money to buy a plane ticket, and I knew she wasn't going to ask me to get her one. She was still headstrong, trying to be independent.

I knew there was no way I wasn't having Isabel there, although she didn't know it yet. I didn't ask if she wanted to come, I didn't ask when she could leave, I just bought the tickets and sent them to her, including money to buy new clothes with. Her Jenny impression was the response when she'd received it.

In the package was another gift, a pair of movies; *Eternal Sunshine of the Spotless Mind* and *The Fountain*. Eternal Sunshine was one of Jim Carrey's serious films, in which a couple undergo a procedure to remove painful memories of each other. In the film the procedure is botched and all their memories are irreversibly removed. Through their loss they still manage to find themselves at the end of the movie, reunited; a "what is meant to be will be" story. Truth be told, if I were given the option to erase some of my memories of Isabel, I would have, plenty of them. But there we were, together in the end.

The Fountain was a film directed by Darren Aronofsky and composed by Clint Mansell, both of whom I was fans of. In it, three stories over separate timelines intertwine into one, all telling the same tale of a man trying to immortalize the woman he loves.

The first timeline portrays the hero, a Spanish conquistador, searching for the Fountain of Youth so that his queen can live forever. The scene opens on a piece of jewelry made from the queen's hair, before the Spaniard is sent on his mission. He goes to travel across the world to Mayan ritual grounds, where he fights tribes of men before climbing the final tower, to wage his ultimate battle. In the end, he finds the fountain he's in search of nestled right below the Tree of Life.

The second story portrays a modern age doctor searching for the cure for his wife's terminal illness. During his long nights at the lab, his wife pens a book, before finally telling him that he has to finish it, moments before she passes away. He's haunted by his inability to save her, and the incompleteness of her story.

The third is a sci-fi version, set in the future as an amalgamation of the first two timelines. The hero is in a vehicle heading towards a nebula in the sky, called Xibalba. He is accompanied by the tree he planted with the ashes of his wife. *Death is the Road to Awe* is the title of the song in the background, as their shuttle reaches the star and explodes on impact in exultation.

I never equated The Fountain with Isabel, but that was the one that struck a chord in her. "Can this be our movie?" she asked, after watching. I didn't know couples had movies. Girls were the ones to pick those things I guess. If they did, it was probably *The Notebook* 99% of the time.

After thinking about it for a moment, I understood, the story of a warrior and the queen that touched him, the story of a sick woman and a man by her side. It was unobservant to have not drawn parallels earlier.

She went to the mall that day, sending me pictures of her in the dressing room for hours, asking which ones she could get. She was the most gorgeous thing I'd ever seen, and I told her so. I don't know why I was so blinded by her, I'd been with beautiful girls my whole life. She dizzied me in a way others never could, even with just pictures.

I attached the package of gifts with a small note and inscription. "Meet me in Montauk," the phrase from Eternal Sunshine. It was an anchor that was a special place for both characters. For us, Montauk would be Las Vegas, and we'd be there in less than two weeks.

60.

Early Winter, 2007

I was 19, and realizing that life had a way of being seasonal. Things were up, down, up again. Izzi and I weren't a couple, but she gave me enough to keep me around.

When I was training and competing, I was happy. When I got home from the last fight, I had a broken foot, and couldn't do a thing. The doctor had given me a bottle of Percocet. I sold the whole bottle to a friend, and Izzi had been there while I'd done it.

She and I never talked about taking drugs like that. She'd never once asked me about Disc Village, though I knew she knew. I tried to separate that part of my life from her. I was embarrassed by it, avoided the conversation like a recovering alcoholic avoids a bar.

I hadn't eaten a pill since rehab. The extent of Izzi and I partying together had only been drinking, and smoking occasionally. There was once that she and a friend had stolen some Xanax from her parents, but I didn't join them.

"Why'd you get rid of all those?" She asked after my friend left with the Percocet.

"I'd rather have the money."

"What if I wanted one?"

That's how we started. I wasn't hard to convince. An outsider may have thought it was her taking drugs because I was, but it was the other way around. For all I know, it could've been both of us doing it because we thought it was what the other wanted. I wanted to party however she wanted to party, and she knew I'd be an easy target. At her worst, she was just as cunning and manipulative as any of us.

HK

While I didn't set a good example for her drug use, I damn sure hadn't started it. She'd tried plenty of things by the time she met me. She had a friend whose boyfriend fed them all sorts of things, gave them all their "firsts." Even when I remind myself of that, looking back at it now is horrifying, thinking what it turned into, how far she took it. She had far more factors at play than just me. Some thought it was in her DNA. Some of the very people that would tell me that were her family members. The males in her life stuck with things from the earth, she and her mother took to things made in a lab. At one point or another, we all became casualties of it.

We never did hard drugs together. We ate valium here and there. I still had no interest in opiates, nor would I ever again, not that that was of any significance. What narcotic we indulged in didn't matter to her, or the people that knew what we'd been doing. I was the weed dealing, cagefighting, atheist, high school dropout, and now I looked like a pill pusher too. All the folks that had questioned my intentions with Izzi finally had something to throw rocks at.

Drugs had a way of making things more turbulent. My relationship with Izzi took a turn for the volatile, and other areas of my life began to implode. An officer came knocking one morning, and in a panic my roommate and I flushed a half pound of weed down the toilet. It turned out he was just there about a complaint of Juice running loose in the yard. Days after that, my house was broken into, and the last few ounces stolen from my room.

I became desperate. I owed my usual weedman money for all the bud I'd just lost. I had some profit left over from what I'd already sold and wanted to squeeze a bit more out of it before paying him back. I called another dealer, a sketchy guy from the other side of town, and asked him to bring as much weed as he could for $1,200. He told me I had to come to him.

When I arrived, he got into the car, locked the doors, and put a pistol on my skull. I'd known the asshole for years and couldn't believe what was happening. He grabbed my cash, my phone, and my car keys, and got back in his Chevy Impala, peeling out of the parking lot next to his scummy apartment complex.

I was rendered helpless, and walked back home with a feeling of defeat. I'd gone from having a few thousand dollars saved up, to being thousands in debt. I sold my black six-string Ibanez from childhood and borrowed money from mom to pay him back. I deserved every bit of retribution that I got that month. All of it was child's play though, compared to what would happen next.

61.

"The treasure is right there on the other side of the dragon. We've got to approach the dragon head on, feel its fiery breath."
-Chris McCombs

I'd gotten the call to fight Kevin Casey. "King," the fighter that had tried to punk me for my seat on the van, the guy I had lived with for seven weeks, a BJJ black belt of the highest caliber. It was nice to finally know who I'd be fighting, a face to put with the crumpling body in my visualizations.

I arrived in Vegas on the Tuesday before the fight. When I landed, a limo driver stood next to baggage claim, carrying a sign with a UFC logo and my name. We waited for Bubba McDaniel before heading to our destination, which was our first round of photo shoots at a studio. The whole thing was reminiscent of my first arrival to *The Ultimate Fighter*.

It had been a few months since I was around anything UFC, and I was quickly reminded of the monstrous scale of things. The promotion was one, giant, well-oiled machine, every cylinder firing on cue. I'd always dreamt of these big league moments, and being back was a great feeling.

I remained in awe for quite a while as we were chauffeured around, doing promotional duties, signing posters and taking pictures. In between my eureka moments of self-actualization, I was trying to take notes on everything I could, wondering if there

HK

was anything that Mitchell and I could learn from them as promoters. It blew my mind, seeing the huge staff behind the scenes, everyone with a job and a purpose. Being on TUF had given me a glimpse into the reality television world, but didn't give much insight into how the inner workings a promotion this large really was.

Besides all the hoopla, I was excited to be competing again. The last time I'd been seen on TV, I was getting choked out by Kelvin Gastelum, and I was entering the cage with a chip on my shoulder. I was heartbroken about not being in the finals, my "Dreams Dashed," the aptly named title of the episode I'd been beaten on. I had a good training camp for this fight and a great group of people with me. I was ready to get my first real win in the UFC.

Tuesday turned to Friday, and it was time to weigh in. For the 19th time in my career, I made the journey down to 185 lbs. The weigh-ins were held in a large area in the MGM Grand, with a crowd to watch. They lined us all up in the back and one by one we stepped on the scale. I looked out into the crowd as they announced my weight, to find my mom and Isabel, which never took long because of how loud my mom was.

I made weight, put my clothes back on, and went to go face-off with my opponent. Dana stood between us as we proceeded with formalities. After weigh-ins, we went to a huge dinner party set up by a friend. Around 50 people had flown and drove from across the country to see me fight, and now we had them all in one room. It was Isabel to my right, my mom to my left; family, friends, and coaches. I did my best to soak it all in. I've always tried to be cognizant of these moments. I knew this would be a special one that I may not ever get again.

My mom stood up for a rare speech, something I'd only ever seen her do at work functions. I'd forgotten how good she was at it. She waxed poetic for a few moments about how my name meant "fierce one," and how she had no idea how true it would be. It was touching, perfectly worded and executed like only she could do.

I feasted as much as I could fit before finally going back to the hotel. The UFC had treated us with a suite at the MGM Grand, one with an amazing view and California King bed. I slept like a baby and woke up as I did all fight days, hungry and focused. Isabel and I walked down to the cafe in the bottom of the hotel before saying our final goodbyes. I wouldn't see her again until after the fight.

"Don't worry. I'll curl my hair," she teased, as if that was all I had to worry about. She put so much work into making sure she had the right outfit, nails manicured, skin tanned; she wanted to look perfect for the occasion, and I felt flattered by it.

I went upstairs to grab my gear and began the trek back to transport. As soon as we got to the arena we were drug tested, and Burt Watson, the UFC employee in charge of the fighters, came by to tell us the exact times we'd be walking out for our fights. Every fight in my life before this one, the walkout time was far from certain, because we never knew how the fights beforehand would play out. This was the big leagues, on live television. Those gaps were filled with perfectly timed commercials, and there was no uncertainty about walk times.

Bruce Buffer, the announcer synonymous with the UFC Octagon, came to the locker room to greet me and ask if I had any nicknames, as well as how to pronounce my last name. I told him no nicknames, but that I'd been waiting for him to announce my entrance forever, and asked him to give me a good one. "I give what I get brother!" He said. "You give me that energy, and I'll give it right back."

I was scheduled to be the last fight on the undercard. I didn't care much where I was in the order, I was just in bliss at finally being there. I couldn't help but move around once we got to the locker rooms. I shadowboxed, stretched, hit mits, and rolled around on the mat for at least three hours before my fight. I was so damn excited.

Finally, finally, *finally*, my name was called to make the walk to the Octagon. I heard the familiar drum beat of the song I'd chosen, "Sympathy for the Devil" by The Rolling Stones. I came out of the locker room screaming, accidentally bumping security

HK

guards, all the way to the cage. My opponent had walked first, and stood inside of it as I arrived, fists clenched, pacing back and forth.

I reached the octagon, got checked by the referee, and took one final look at the crowd. Like at weigh-ins, I tried to find Isabel and my mom, only this time the music was blasting, and the arena was far too loud to hear either of them. I gave up and started looking around the cage for Dana White.

"What are you looking at? Focus!" Cesar, my coach from MMA Masters, screamed over the roar of the crowd. This was the first time he and Daniel had been in my corner. Joe was just standing above the cage, grinning ear to ear that we'd finally made it.

The familiar bright lights shone down on me, only this time much hotter. I made sure again, as I did many times that week, to notice every small detail. Bruce Buffer glided towards me as he belted his signature voice into the microphone.

"...And hailing from Tallahassee, Florida!" It was music to my ears. *God damn right.* I imagined everyone at home going crazy as they heard it.

Buffer finished his intro, and referee Herb Dean stepped in to be the third man in the cage. "You ready?" he said as he looked across at Casey. He stood and nodded, fists still clenched from minutes before, doing his best to look menacing. He wasn't doing a bad job.

"You ready?" Herb looked at me and asked the same question.

Behind my Garnet and Gold mouthpiece with "850" inscribed on the front, I clenched my jaw.

I nodded. The bell rang, and my UFC debut began.

62.

November 7th, 2007

"Come out tonight," Izzi texted. It was a crisp, fall evening, the first cold of the year, and we'd just got home from loading a bale of firewood for the house. We all had fake ID's for years, and would go to bars around town. She and her friends were going to a local club, Chubby's, and she invited me.

A week prior we'd had an incident at my house. It was 3 in the morning, and a friend of hers saw her car in the driveway as she passed by. Izzi had lied to her about where she was staying. She stopped, let herself in my house, and dragged Izzi out of bed. We weren't even doing anything, just watching TV. She yelled at Izzi the whole way out. Izzi and I were both humiliated. I still remember her helpless look as her friend pulled her by the wrist. That friend wasn't with her this night, otherwise she wouldn't have called me. I came running, as I usually did, and dragged Chris out with me.

We were at Chubby's for a couple of hours when my phone started ringing non-stop. It was loud in the club, and I didn't answer. It was my other two roommates calling, and they rang several times each before I went outside to check my voicemail. The first was calm.

"Hey Josh. Uh.. Something happened at the house. You should definitely come home." I didn't think much of it. I listened to the message from my other roommate. His was frantic.

"Holy shit Josh. The fucking house is on fire. The whole thing is on fire. Holy fuck." I grabbed Chris and ran out. We raced home, and I told myself the whole way that it was just a bad joke.

I knew it was real when I smelled the smoke from blocks away. I could see it billowing in the sky before I even got on my road. I swerved into the driveway, nearly hitting the fire truck that was already going to work on the flames rising from the roof. They were 20 feet high. The heat was unbearable. Somehow there were firefighters inside, trying to extinguish it.

Everyone else was out of the house, Juice included. We were all safe, but my mind began to race, thinking of what else was in the house. Money, electronics, and keepsakes, but nothing as valuable as my hand wraps. My fights memories were in those wraps, and they were in danger of being reduced to ashes.

I'd never felt so helpless. It was one of the most traumatizing things I'd ever experienced. My whole life was in

HK

there. I tried to convince myself as I watched that it was repairable, that it would go out any minute and we'd still be able to live in it.

In an instant, the roof collapsed. I burst into tears, the first time since that courtroom a half decade ago. Juice was in the back of my friend's truck, crying the whole time with me. He howled for hours as we watched. For the rest of his life, he wept when he heard sirens.

It wasn't until the sun was up that they'd vanquished the flames. We stayed awake the whole time. I don't even know where we would have gone had we left.

The firefighters called Red Cross for us, and we met them at a Waffle House down the road at 9 am. They gave us food vouchers and clothes, and booked us hotel rooms.

I tried to go to sleep, unnerved. I laid there and stared at the ceiling. I wondered if karma was real. If it was, I didn't know that I deserved that much.

63.

"Everything that you are as a human being gets tested, gets challenged, and ultimately gets exposed in a prizefighting ring."
                                                                    -Jim Lampley

My UFC debut began with Casey trying to kick me in my head. We'd anticipated him throwing a high kick, and I threw a low kick to his leg that was still on the ground. He went tumbling to the mat as his leg crumbled, and I followed him down, something we had not planned. He specialized in ground fighting, and too anxiously I flew, face first into where he was most dangerous.

I became even more aware of my mistake as Casey wrapped his powerful legs around my neck, and began to squeeze. He transitioned perfectly from the scramble into a deep triangle choke and began to cut off the circulation.

Holy shit. I am 20 seconds into my UFC debut, and I'm about to get put to sleep. I flew Isabel all the way to Vegas to watch me fail. My mom is about to see me lose.

I tried my best to avoid letting him have full control and give myself any amount of room to breathe. I began to lose consciousness. It's funny what our brains think about in moments like these when time is slowed down, and the universe affords us the luxury of turning seconds into minutes. Casey was below me, choking me unconscious, and my last remaining sense of fight or flight was fleeting. I drifted off somewhere that was not Mandalay Bay Arena.

I was in the jail visiting room. I saw her behind the glass wall, then on the hotel room bed in Orlando crying. I saw the pictures of her in the dressing room, picking outfits for the night. I saw her in the sauna, with her steadfast demeanor, then her satisfied grin. I felt her stubbornness, and her refusal to quit, and in an instant I felt her coursing through my veins, just as much as I did the adrenaline. It was beyond powerful. All I needed was one of those memories, one of tens of thousands of her. I mustered the last bit of energy I had. With Casey's legs cinched around my neck, I picked him up as I high as I could, and slammed him on his head.

He released the choke hold, and immediately switched to an armbar, beginning to hyperextend my elbow with his hips. This time, I had a better grip on my senses, and while I was done reminiscing, I did think about one more thing. I remembered him behind me in the van, whispering in my ear.

This is a fight show homie. I'll get you sooner or later.

At that point, I made the decision that he'd have to break my arm to win, because there was no giving up. All my years of hard work, all my ambitions and aspirations, everything was in jeopardy. I did the same thing I did when I'd exhausted all other resources in the triangle choke; picked him up and slammed him on his head.

He gave up the armbar on impact, just as he had the choke, but in a split second, he turned the fight in his favor again. He swept me and landed on top, landing heavy punches and elbows. For all of his grappling pedigree and athleticism, I knew that there

HK

was no way he was more conditioned than I was. I sat, and waited, and took his punches and elbows. He began breathing heavily, huffing and puffing with every labored inhalation.

I returned to the fight once I felt him try to take a rest while on top, and dragged him into the position that I'd finished so many of my fights before. I forced my hands behind his head, and pummeled my knees into his body, sucking the energy from him with each strike. Every now and then I'd sneak one to the face. I knew if I didn't finish him in this round, that the end would come in round two.

I came back into the second, and his body language reinforced the notion that he was defeated. I put him immediately back into the same position and attacked with a barrage of knees to the body and head. Finally, he collapsed.

Herb Dean pulled me off, and I grabbed my own head with both hands, in disbelief at what had just happened. I'd finally gotten a win in the UFC, six years and 364 days after my very first fight. An excited Jon Anik rushed into the cage, microphone in hand, ready for a post-fight interview. The crowd roared.

Afterwards, I was escorted to the press area, passing all my friends who'd gotten floor seats. I gave Mitchell and Matt a giant hug and made my way to dozens of flashing cameras and reporters. I did a lengthy interview and finally returned to my locker room.

"You scared us! You motherfucker!" My coaches were waiting. Daniel and Cesar were yelling, grinning ecstatically. I was happy to have made them proud. "Just finish it fast next time," Joey said, accustomed to getting in and out quickly over the years.

"I had to make it exciting," I joked, as if I'd planned to be nearly choked unconscious for the sake of entertainment. We relived the fight several times over and congratulated each other on a job well done.

I showered, changed clothes, and headed back upstairs. 10,000 fans screamed as another fight raged in the background. It was all kind of background at this point, still high from the thrill of a stage that large.

I saw my mom, with Jeff and my grandmother, all glowing, sitting in the place I could hear her screaming from in between rounds. There were a few empty seats next to them, but I couldn't relax and enjoy the moment yet.

"Where's Isabel?" I asked my mom.

"Looking for you!" She replied.

I entered the hallway by the concessions, thick with friends and new fans who'd just watched me win my UFC debut. They were all asking for pictures, and offering congratulations. It was overwhelming. I tried to tune out the chatter and quiet the calls so I could text and make my way to her.

I looked up from my phone to see what I'd been looking for; her standing there, hair in curls as she'd promised, in one of the outfits she'd sent me pictures of her modeling, a sexy white blouse tucked into short black shorts. I felt hypnotized as I always did when I looked at her, the same knees I'd just won with buckling as she ran towards me. We embraced for what seemed like ages. Friends snapped photos behind us to capture the moment. The rest of the world was secondary. None of them knew what it took for both of us to get there, what we'd went through, all the way from the beginning.

We found our seats with my mom, Jeff, and Grandma. I sat there in the exact same position as I was in the night before; Isabel on my right, my mom on my left, the rest of my friends and family closeby, and I couldn't help but wonder if I'd ever had a better moment in my life. I held their hands tightly, riding a wave of euphoria, reflecting on the reality of the situation. Isabel was clutching my hand a little tighter than usual and leaned over to whisper in my ear.

"I'm so proud of you."

There was always something about her whispering to me that gave me chills. Maybe it was her saying things that only I could hear, that were meant only for me. I wanted to tell her it was her that I was thinking about in there, that it was her who inspired me to keep going. I thought it trite, and just gave her a kiss instead. I decided that of the 9,155 days I'd spent on Earth, this was the greatest.

HK

This is it. This is what it's all about.

64.

After my house had burned to the ground, I was hungry for more destruction. I signed up for my third professional fight, and was across the ring from Miguel Shoffner, in my home state of Florida.

Miguel wore a luchador mask during all of weigh-ins and press duties. It was the most bizarre thing I'd seen in the sport. I didn't even know what his face looked like until I stepped into the ring, moments before the fight. I used the same double fisted attack on that face as I did in my last fight, breaking his jaw and orbital bones in a little over a minute.

It didn't make me feel better like I thought it would. I'd lost nearly everything I owned in the fire. Furniture, flat screens, computers, personal belongings; all burnt to a crisp or soaked and short-circuited by the fire hoses. My hand wraps made it out with some water damage, but beyond that, I had to start all the way over.

The cause of the fire was an animal nest in the chimney sweep, they said. We hadn't cleaned it from the year before. I'd never owned a fireplace before. I didn't know, and our landlord had never told us to.

The house was supposed to only be a six-month arrangement. We'd lived there for two years as the commercial construction got delayed quarter after quarter. Due the informal nature of the lease, we had no renters insurance. The owner of the house looked like he saw a ghost when he showed up. He didn't care about the house being gone, he was worried about me suing him. I never did. He collected a nice insurance check from it and sold it to a hotel developer. In a cruel twist of fate, the name of the resort that went up in the place of my charred home was called Candlewood Suites, with a giant flame as the logo.

My roommates and I moved into another home closer in town, but it wasn't the same as Lakeshore. I didn't own all the things in the house. I didn't control the lease, and everything was smaller. I realized how territorial I was over Lakeshore, how much of my identity it had become.

I lost friends that I thought were friends, as the social dynamic changed. I tried to have parties on the same scale, to keep the train going. The house we moved to was not suitable for that. There were neighbors everywhere. One of them was a cop. His name was Cleveland, and he was actually one of the only neighbors that didn't mind the noise. He was a nice guy, reminded me of the dad from *Family Matters*.

We had a party one night while Cleveland was on duty. The cops had already been by once, weeks prior, and told us to keep it down. This time, they were not so polite.

They knocked first, and as soon Chris opened the door, they barged in. Everyone bolted out different exits. I was in my room downstairs, and could see the front door from my bed. I grabbed my weed and tried to hide it, as one cop ran towards me. There was no stopping it.

They cleared the party, then tore my bedroom apart. I had a big bag of weed, and some Adderall that I didn't even know was in a drawer. They cuffed me, and told me I was being charged with possession of marijuana with intent to sell, and possession of a controlled substance.

As they were marching me out to the car, Cleveland came home and rushed over.

"Hold on, hold on. Let's go back inside." They sat me on the porch with my hands behind my back, and went in the front yard to talk. The arresting officer came back and took the cuffs off.

"Cleveland says you're a good kid, that we should give you a break." Relief washed over me like it never had before. It was short lived.

"Although, you're gonna have to do something for us."

HK

65.

"I just want one person I can rescue and I want one person who needs me. Who can't live without me. I want to be a hero, but not just one time."

-Chuck Palahniuk

"I didn't want this weekend to end." Isabel was on the phone, on the other side of the state. She was still housekeeping in Tallahassee but growing frustrated with her restaurant job. I was ready for her to drop everything and pack her stuff anyway. I had the feeling that one of her visits would end up being for good.

She came back down and left her car at my house while we traveled. My truck had 190,000 miles on it but was still running strong. "I want to be there when it turns to 200,000," she said. She liked things like that, made a wish whenever it was 11:11.

We had a Combat Night in Tallahassee, and Isabel's cousin was getting married the same weekend. On the way, we planned to stop and see my mom and Jeff, to stay with them in their humble RV in the woods. They had a small couch that pulled out and slept one comfortably, or two if one person acted like a blanket, as Isabel did.

"You better put your phone down," she said as I answered a text, driving north. "My mom would not be happy with you texting and driving. You have precious cargo in here, you know."

"I know. This shit is going to kill me one day."

"Don't joke like that. Why the fuck would you say that? Give me your phone, I'll text back whoever you're talking to."

It was indicative of my past relationships maybe, my first inclination to say no. I'd never had a girlfriend I was comfortable giving my phone, should they see something they may not like. I thought about it for a second and realized it was a knee jerk reaction, that for once in my life I had someone that I hid nothing from. I handed her my phone and kept driving towards our destination, Ginnie Springs.

She always handled radio duties. I'd never found a girl with such good taste in music. It was another thing I loved most about her. Old school R&B, soul, classic rock, hip hop, I felt like she was reading my mind at times. She liked everything I liked, and everything I disliked she changed before I got the chance to even ask her to.

We arrived at the springs to an excited mom, and sick stepfather. My mom was chatty in, between adjusting Jeff's drip line. He was accompanied by a big metal stand and IV bag that followed him around all day.

I wasn't sure of my mom's condition. She never wanted to worry anyone. If she was in pain, she was doing a good job of hiding it. When we got there, her enthusiasm was welcoming. She had a whole list of activities for us to choose from. We could go eat lunch, or ride the 4-wheeler around the camp grounds, or go in a canoe on the springs, or just hang out and drink.

Isabel's doctor had recommended that we start to curb her drinking in anticipation of quitting entirely for the year that she'd be in treatment. Alcohol sparingly and in small doses was not harmful, although with each additional drink, her liver would suffer, and her chances of success lowered. The possibility that the treatment would fail terrified her only slightly more than the idea of having to be sober for a year. Neither of us enjoyed complete sobriety, and being with her was the only thing besides fight camps that had ever kept me clean.

We decided to forego drinking that day, and take the canoe out on the springs. My mom and Jeff were working part time jobs as hosts of the park, so they were able to reserve and use the facilities' amenities as they pleased.

Mom and Jeff stayed behind as Isabel and I went out on the water. The springs were crystal clear, the weather beautiful. She paddled from the front the best she could while I did work from the back. There were a few mosquitos out, but as long as Isabel was around they bit her and not me. She was too sweet, I told her.

"Being out here reminds me of my brothers," she said of being outdoors, in the woods, on the water. At the time, Owen was

$\mathcal{HK}$

in Tallahassee working as a vet tech for their dad's office, still with Stephanie. Landon was a veterinarian, also in Tallahassee, priming to take over the family business. Wyatt, the middle brother, was the one I took to the most. It was because we were both Pisces, she'd tell me. He was finishing his final semesters at a large chiropractic school in Atlanta. Before all of that, they grew up in the woods, playing cowboys and Indians.

"What do they think of me? Of us?" I asked her. They always made everyone feel liked, and it was hard to tell what their true feelings were. I wasn't sure I'd ever had a full conversation with Landon in my life.

"They know that you love me, and that you make me happy, and I think that's all they care about." I wasn't sure if she was just saying that, or if she even knew how they felt, but I suppose that's all they could've asked for anyway. It was a nice thought, whether it was true or not, that after all these years that I'd finally redeemed myself.

"Things were a lot different not too long ago, remember," she said. I did remember, and I knew many of her family members associated me with her recovery.

"We're going to see them in a few days anyway," she told me. I had no idea that she'd wanted me to be included at her cousin's wedding. The idea of her whole family at once was intimidating. She made fun of me for being nervous, never realizing what a daunting task it was to make a good impression.

"I love your mom," she said, changing the subject. "And Jeff. And them together. They are cute." I didn't know if "cute" was the word I would've chosen to describe their situation. I was scared for her, thinking he was going to drop dead at any moment.

"He's going to be fine," she said, optimistic as always. "Your mom takes good care of him." She did, and I knew she found purpose in it.

"I want us to take care of each other like they do," she said. "I want us to be old one day, and have lived through everything that we already have, and more. Can we..?"

66

The officer that had raided my room sat me down in the kitchen. He'd called another cop, the head of the vice unit, who was sitting across from me at my own table.

"My name is Detective Pender."

He explained he ran a squad that used confidential informants to arrest drug suppliers in Tallahassee. He knew I wasn't a large dealer, and he wanted to use me to get to people that were. He asked where I got all the weed from. I didn't give him an answer. He acted as if he was going to re-cuff me, and the other officer came to the rescue.

"Let's give him a week."

I don't know if that was a tactic they used, or if I was really on the verge of being taken to jail. They knew I'd been drinking, they told me, and couldn't make a good decision right now. Detective Pender agreed to give me a week. He left me with his number and said that if I hadn't called by next Saturday with a name I was willing to implicate with a wire, that they'd arrest me, and I'd become a felon.

I avoided the concrete bed that night but woke up the next day with an uncertain future. The first thing I did was call the guy I'd gotten the bud from, and told him what happened. I'd cycled through several dealers by this point, some friends, some not so friendly. This one was somewhere in the middle. I owed him a couple thousand dollars, and he wouldn't be getting it for a while. I wasn't close with him, but I didn't have it in me to set him up.

He called the next day to tell me he thought I was lying. He said he had a friend in the department, who told him that there was no pending case on me. He made vague threats. I gave him Detective Pender's number and told him he could call and ask if he'd like. I didn't hear much after that.

I got him off my back but didn't know what to do about the police. I thought about trying to somehow give them the thug who'd robbed me at gunpoint. I hadn't seen him since and didn't know where to start.

HK

The days passed, and the deadline grew near. I prepared myself for life behind bars. I'd been through it before. I wasn't afraid.

On Wednesday, May 7th, 2008, a terrible thing happened. FSU student Rachel Morningstar Hoffman was killed in a drug sting gone wrong. The dealers targeted in the bust found the wire in Rachel's purse, and shot and killed her.

The tragedy was the talk of the town. The city was outraged, and TPD came under scrutiny for the operation. Detective Pender was fired, and the vice unit disbanded. I never heard from any of them again.

Rachel and I had a number of mutual friends, and I'd never been in such a moral dilemma over how to feel about something. I was spared from a jail sentence, at the cost of someone's life. I'd have rather gone to jail.

Izzi and my roommates were the only ones that I told. The event rattled her. "That could've been you," she reminded me, more than once. I tried not to think about it, to pretend it never happened.

Around the same time, Izzi had her own run-in with the police. She was driving home from a party, and gotten a DUI. I remember the relief I felt that it wasn't my place she was driving to, or from. That was one of my biggest fears, something happening to someone coming from my house.

Whether it was coming from my party or another was irrelevant for her. She was still a senior in high school, months away from graduating. She got her license revoked, and had to rely on friends for rides everywhere.

It wasn't just a matter of convenience that was our undoing. After her DUI, things changed. Just like I had done several times in my life, she cut out the people that she thought were the source of her problems. For years, she used me as a way to rebel against the things that were expected of her, and she didn't want to rebel anymore.

67

"Heaven isn't some place you go to when you die, it's that moment in your life when you actually feel alive."

-*Eyedea*

Back in Tallahassee with Isabel, I woke to a text from my old roommate, Chris. He echoed the sentiment that many others who had known me for years expressed. "Proud of you man. It is crazy, how you said you were going to do all this stuff years ago, marry that girl and fight in the UFC."

Isabel and I hadn't talked about it yet, but considering the circumstances it would've been hard for anyone to argue that we were in it for anything other than the long haul. Until then, we'd remain guests at the wedding.

That's where we were, at her cousin's wedding. We sat next to her oldest brother Landon, and his wife, Savannah. They'd been together since I met Isabel, and their story mirrored that of my stepmom's sister that I'd grown up with visiting Mississippi as a kid. Like Aunt Charlotte and Uncle David, Landon and Savannah had been high school sweethearts, and the way Isabel told the story, they didn't know what it was like to be with another lover. Savannah favored Aunt Charlotte, an assertive personality with southern belle beauty. She was pregnant, and due any day now.

Savannah had been around since Isabel was small, and helped raise her, alternating between motherly and sisterly roles. Isabel said that she was the only girl who didn't care about being nice to her to get closer to her brothers. Her relationship was one of the few that suffered most when Isabel began getting in trouble, and she was excited to have Savannah take an interest in her life again.

Being a part of a big family was something that fascinated me, deep rooted into my childhood days. Isabel teased me the whole morning about being nervous to meet everyone, though I knew it was important to her too. I hadn't met most of them yet

HK

and didn't realize until I got there that it wasn't even her dad's side of the family. Her mom's side was just as large.

I could tell many were curious to see who it was Isabel had been driving back and forth across the state to see. Her cousin's groom, Jason, was a huge MMA fan and was beside himself that a cast member of TUF 17 was at his wedding. His enthusiasm spilled over into the rest of the folks, and their welcome was warm.

We had another trip planned, back to Vegas, and to California for her first time. Matt had tried out for Season 18 of *The Ultimate Fighter* and had been chosen, with the help of calls to a few friends I still had at the show.

"That's so cool that he's following in your footsteps. Everyone in Tallahassee is going to love that." Isabel was excited when she got the news that we'd be going to watch him fight. She and I were his guests, along with Mitchell.

"He's gotta win first," I reminded her.

One of my local sponsors, Lance, had helped with the tickets to Vegas, and we were going to eat dinner at him and his wife Connie's house after the wedding. Lance was an old timer who owned a successful plumbing company, and had been largely responsible for helping bring MMA to Tallahassee. He lived outside of town, with a huge plot of land; deer and wildlife running free in the backyard. We got there, and Isabel lit up.

"This is what I want," she said, squeezing my arm. She was seduced by the idea of creating what Lance and Connie had, raising a family in the woods. Connie was an ultimate housewife; cooking, cleaning, gardening, raising their granddaughter. She made her feel at home while Isabel took notes and stole recipes. Stuffed mushrooms were the appetizer that night.

Lance and I caught up while the ladies played in the kitchen. "Man, what you doin' bringin' sand to the beach anyway?" he joked, about me taking Isabel everywhere in Vegas and Miami. She was in on the joke. "Sandy" was his nickname for her. It reminded her of her evil stepmom from early in life, with the house cleaning business. It reminded me of that stupid hurricane that left everyone at home while Veronica and I were stuck on the bed, filming the first scene of TUF. We laughed about it over dinner and went home to get ready for an early flight.

"Can we go play in the mountains?" she asked, looking down and pointing as we flew over the rocky Nevada landscape. Some of Isabel's fondest memories she talked about were being at her Aunt Jo's mountain house in North Carolina. She was anxious to explore the different terrain of the west.

It would be the first thing we did the next day, something the boys and I had promised ourselves we were going to do almost a year ago; get to the top of Red Rock. Bubba and Gilbert from my season were going to Vegas to watch some of their friends fight as well, so they met us there.

Isabel was athletic, but I wasn't sure how difficult it got towards the top because we'd not been allowed to get that high last time. We neared the peak and the difficulty increased, enough that I was willing to forego the summit. She sweat through her garnet and gold Combat Night shirt. "Reppin'," she called it.

"Shut up, keep going," she said, huffing and puffing when I asked her if she wanted to continue. Gilbert had tried to quit and turn around several times. Isabel made fun of him to our amusement, a 5' girl calling a giant black guy a sissy.

We got to the top. "I told you I could do it," she said with a triumphant look on her face. I felt silly for thinking otherwise. The grand prize for our efforts was revealed; a view of the vast mountains and valleys beneath us, red like the name of the park, with the whole city of Las Vegas in the horizon.

I thought about what Chris had said earlier in the week, about him and everyone else who knew us from years ago, and watched as an outsider as these things materialized. It wasn't like I'd been waiting on Isabel to come back the whole time. I was just looking for someone who compared, and it never ended up happening.

After years of thinking I'd grow to be old and alone, I was no longer afraid. I finally had someone who opened doors for me, who kicked through them with full force. On top of that mountain, I held a celestial being, one who ripped open my jugular of passion, who could paralyze me with a touch. I had a woman with

HK

the youth and beauty of a 22 year-old, and the wisdom of one twice her age. I had someone who'd seen many of my struggles from the beginning, and vice versa. I had someone who'd been through similar life situations, in the same hometown even. I had someone who knew what it was like to battle demons, to know pain and struggle. I had someone who'd seen the light and the dark, peeking highs of shining moments, and staggering lows to the depths that few understood, with all her own layers of intricate complexity.

We sat there for hours. The rest of the group had trekked down long ago while Isabel and I stayed up. It was symbolic, being there at the top of this mountain with her, looking down on the mecca of the MMA world in Las Vegas. I felt like I'd conquered the world. Even with her sickness and difficulty ahead, I couldn't have been happier, and it was having her next to me that was my proudest achievement. I was no longer without a deity. She was God to me, and I was just an Earthling that had finally reached my Zion, my Valhalla, complete and total bliss.

There was something that felt so right about the whole thing. Much like the moment we had last time we were in Vegas, I felt triumphant at last. I'd done everything I set out to do. I envisioned a life traveling the world, winning fights in front of millions, the girl of my dreams on my arm. In my mind, we had nothing but fairy tale endings in front of us.

68.

Early Summer, 2008

I don't know if you're good for me.
Izzie said "good," but I knew it meant "good enough." She'd woken up that day and decided she wanted to ruin me. I'd developed Atelophobia, and she set her sights on it.

When I look back, I see this as the moment it all changed. The novelty of being a bad boy had worn out. The whole thing was a brutal crash course in the importance of character.

You try too hard. I'd never had a girl tell me that. We had chemistry, but the connection wasn't enough. I wanted more. Of all the things that had rocked me, nothing had the force of this 18 year-old girl.

You teach people how to treat you. Telling a girl "I'm yours" wasn't the smartest courtship tactic. She'd begun to use me for attention, or to make jealous whatever high school fling she liked at the time. I realized she wasn't mine the way I was hers.

You just like me because I'm a challenge. Maybe there was an element of conquest that did beckon me. If I was being honest, she was the most challenging thing I'd ever embarked on. People asked what was going on with us.

She'll come around. It wasn't just wishful thinking. I believed it.

Stop telling people that. Maybe she would, but it wouldn't be any time soon.

What is it you expect from me? I didn't know what I expected, but I knew I wasn't getting it. Izzi never gave me a title in the sense that I wanted. I'd become just a guilty pleasure.

I can't even sleep over without someone coming to drag me out of bed. I was public enemy number one. I'd been selling weed for years, and had nothing to show for it but an old hot tub and a lousy reputation. Bad things I'd done lent credence to worse rumors.

Do you take steroids?

Really, that's what you think? You too?

Sometimes I wonder. She was laying it all bare, questioning me on all the nasty things anyone had ever accused me of.

Have you ever given me something without me knowing?

It was the most hurtful thing she'd ever asked. I'd done deplorable things in my life, but never in a million years would I have done something like that. We lashed back at each other, hard.

Really? You drug yourself just fine.

Fuck you. She was stabbing a knife in me. *Do you think you're a good person?* Her tone was so hurtful, the only time she'd ever talked to me like that.

HK

Are you someone you would want your sister with? She said harsh things to get the point across, and succeeded.

I was so embarrassed. It all felt so public, my inadequacies on full display. I wasn't good enough, and a simple solution to not being good enough was to get better, to do better, to *be* better.

Most my life I'd felt like the villain, and I was tired of that. I wanted to change a lot of things about myself, to retire the red lightsaber.

She'd call later to try to apologize, but the damage had been done. It would be years before I ever forgave her. She never realized what a life changing moment it was for me. The impact was profound. Izzi made me want to become better at everything because I needed the approval of her, and her brothers, and I didn't have it. I'd never wanted anything so badly in my life. I never wanted to feel like that again.

I'll show them. My existence became a game of it, trying to shed the image I'd solidified over 20 years. It wasn't one that would go easily, but the seed had been planted.

69.

"The greatest thing you'll ever learn is just to love and be loved in return."

-Eden Ahbez

"So what are you doing with this guy?" Gilbert joked the next morning over breakfast.

"It's a long story," she said, looking at me. Long story was right.

"You guys sure have some loud PDA," he said as he chewed. I realized how close we were sitting to each other, hands intertwined under the breakfast table. If she didn't match my physicality, she was close. She was always in pictures with friends and family clutching loved ones tightly.

Matt's fight wasn't until the following afternoon, and I'd rented us a car to drive to Los Angeles to see my friend Gerard, the producer from TUF. The drive was only four hours and was one of the more scenic routes I'd seen. Anything was better than driving on flat, boring I-75 in Florida.

I drove for an hour or so before asking Isabel if she'd take over. I had put our destination into my phone's GPS, and she used it as I dozed off in the passenger seat. When I woke up, we were in LA.

"Why didn't you wake me? You didn't have to drive this whole time."

"I didn't mind it, actually. It's beautiful out here. Can we go on more trips like this?"

I'd forgotten how enchanting everything so far from home could be. To her, I was helping show her the world, but to me I was showing her *to* the world. She was the prize, the treasure, the beauty of this whole experience. I loved taking her on trips with me. It was my way of saying *Look, look at this glorious life partner I've found. Look at how I've won the soulmate jackpot.* I didn't tell her any of that, I simply replied, "Yes. As many trips as you want."

We got to Gerard's and proceeded with introductions, as he and his wife had never met Isabel. We left his house and headed to Venice Beach, one of my favorite places to be a tourist. It was a place I knew she'd appreciate. The streets were lined with performers and artists. Isabel spent the whole time walking the boardwalk with a look of awe on her face, unable for even a moment to stop taking pictures, picking up and putting down all the souvenirs of every stand she passed. Her enthusiasm and wonder were captivating. It held the same magic for her as it had for me years ago. She found a street vendor with an assortment of handmade jewelry, looking the table over until she found one that spotted her eye.

"Will you buy this for me, please?" It was a leather-strapped bracelet with a silver charm in the shape of a tree. "It reminds me of the one from The Fountain." Her mom had given her a similar charm when she was a child, she said, and the tree had symbolic meanings for her. She was always drawing them, trees and feathers. She never asked me to pay for anything, but wanted this to come from me.

HK

I bought it, and she immediately put it on the wrist that bore her one and only tattoo, *Believe*. Coincidentally, *Believe* was the shared mantra of Evan Tanner, the man whom Gerard had made his documentary about. I told her about it and promised her we would watch it when we got home.

One performer we passed was singing Nat King Cole's "L-O-V-E." Isabel squeezed my hand three times to get my attention, her code for saying *I love you* if she thought maybe the situation wasn't appropriate to say out loud. I smiled and squeezed back, knowing it was the song that she was getting my attention for.

We had to get back to Vegas for Matt's fight, and we left early the next morning. I made sure to stay awake the whole drive this time. We met Mitchell back at the hotel and transported to the UFC training center that I'd become so familiar with.

It was a wild experience being on the outside looking in, taking Isabel to the same building that my dreams were made and broken in. It was the first time I'd been back, and I felt all the memories of my experiences rush in as we got to the large warehouse. I was able to talk with Matt for a moment before Mitchell, Isabel, and I all took our seats next to the cage.

Matt was fighting some schmuck from the midwest. The fight started well, with Matt winning the first stanza, and looking like he was well on his way to winning one more round to make his own dreams come true.

Then something happened. He began to crumble. Mitchell and I were taking turns screaming instructions at him, and he just stopped listening. By the middle of the second round, he was going for sloppy takedowns. His attempts were getting stuffed, and he was getting punished for it. By the end of the third, he had all but guaranteed his loss. The judges saw it as we did, with him walking out of the cage, dreams left behind him. I couldn't find the words to console him. I was frustrated.

The most important fight a fighter at that level could have was the one to get in the house. That was the one that determined whether he would join the TUF alumni, whether or not he would be broadcast out to fans and viewers of millions for 13 weeks. Mitchell and Isabel were just as disappointed as I was.

After the fights, they let Matt go, and we all went back to the hotel. I got to see the other side of the spectrum from the one I'd been on, the night of TUF entry fights. It had taken me several tryouts to get there, but when I did, I'd at least won my first fight to get on the show. I didn't know what it was like to have gotten so close, and have it slip through my hands.

It was a sad sight, those that came up short all at an Irish pub, drinking their pains away. Neither Isabel nor I were comfortable with the mood and weren't interested in staying long. To make things worse, Landon and Savannah had delivered their son while we were gone. Isabel had wanted badly to be there for it, and it troubled her when she missed it. We said our goodbyes to Matt, who was having a hard time accepting the loss. We went back up to the room and got ready to return home in the morning.

70.
Summer, 2008

It wasn't just run-of-the-mill teenage rejection. Izzi's slap in the face made me want to change in a way I never had before. I felt insufficient, and it had a huge effect on my psyche.

Getting my feelings badly hurt was a good way to make me strive to do great things. It may not have been about her brothers at all. That may have been a defense mechanism for a shaken ego. Either way, **I'd been a menace most my life before I met Izzi, and I wanted to be anything but after.**

I learned what my dad had tried to teach me for years, that reputation was important, and quality of life depends on self-image, which is often influenced by people's perceptions. No matter how I tried, I couldn't go through life not caring what others thought of me.

I had so much anger, and used my bitterness as motivation. I wasn't doing it to get her back. I did it because I didn't ever want

HK

to fall in love with someone again and have to deal with having a toxic social status.

We were headed towards separate paths. Despite her best efforts, she was going towards more darkness. I was en route to something brighter, in a vehicle gassed by fumes of failure.

I wanted to distance myself as much as I could from the person I was, and a way to help do that was all new everything. I moved out of the house I was in, into a small house by myself where I was free of distractions. I proved I could make a living not selling weed, as I stumbled through odd jobs and security gigs at bars down by the beach. I got a stint bartending, and training people at the Gold's Gym I worked out at. Being a personal trainer was gratifying, knowing I was helping folks improve their lives by getting healthier. It was the first thing I'd felt good about in a while.

A new house and job weren't enough. I tried to find a new girlfriend, and hooked up with chicks from the gym and clubs I worked at. Tallahassee was a revolving door of sorority girls. Part of the new me meant trying to be good to women, and I did my best.

The last piece of the transformation was a new gym. Orkin was an attorney, and the academy was only part time for him. I had surpassed everyone at our little dojo, and I wasn't getting the training I needed to improve. That was the whole point of this, to get better. It was time to get focused on a career, to take it seriously if I expected others to.

I sought out other training partners and coaches. I'd found one in Jacksonville that I began learning from, named Roberto. He was a brawny Colombian, a talented black belt, but not enough of an MMA coach for me to move there. I resorted to making the commute every weekend.

I needed someone to help with striking fundamentals, and amidst the search, one fell into my lap. One of the owners of Gold's had heard I was a pro fighter. He told me he and his brother also trained, with an older boxer named Rodolfo Aguilar, a former contender to Julio Cesar Chavez.

Jim and Joey Burtoft were their names, and together all of us began training in the warehouse across from Gold's. It was a cheerleading studio, and although there was humor in a bunch of meatheads punching each other with tumbling mats right next to us, it was what I needed.

I'd taken another fight since the luchador-masked man. It was in North Carolina, at Camp Lejeune. I lost the bout, but had entered it with injuries, and didn't beat myself up about it. Rodolfo came and went, but Jim and Joey stayed. I thought I'd be in the UFC by this time, and with each passing fight that I didn't get signed, I became hungrier.

Orkin had mentored me, but the Burtofts were the first to show the kind of enthusiasm that made me believe I wasn't completely crazy to go for broke. There's something to be said about the perfect storm of events that make someone who they are. It was a nice whirlwind that removed all doubt from my mind. I would make it to the UFC.

71.

"To have a writer fall in love with you is to never truly die."
-Mik Everett

Isabel and I were back south for Brian's birthday. South Beach was lined with nightclubs, but the nicest were in the luxurious hotels that provided exclusivity to high profile customers from around the world. LIV was the name of the club we were going to that night, inside a hotel called the Fontainebleau. It was commonplace for pop culture stars and athletes on a regular basis. and the place itself was ridiculous. Admission could range from $50 - $250. Once inside, the drinks started at $20 a beer, with bottle service in the tens of thousands.

There wasn't a single file line outside the club, as with traditional establishments. Instead, a large circle was roped off, with patrons crowding around outside, all vying to get a bouncer's attention. Once noticed, the bouncer would decide if the patrons

HK

were attractive enough to be let inside. And this is how people were chosen, all night long. Sometimes we'd go at midnight and come out hours later to see the same groups of people still hugging the ropes, waiting to get inside. It was so silly.

I was friends with a promoter of the club, otherwise we wouldn't have been going at all. She'd heard about the place, and I told her I'd take her, so she could see what the buzz was about. The design of the club was extravagant, a giant rectangular room with lights, lasers, confetti, every assortment of sensory stimulating effect imaginable.

Inside, girls filled the place with silicone and makeup, fakes tits and asses, rubbing on the occasional celebrity at a VIP table. South Florida was a lot more fun, or a lot more tolerable maybe, when remembered that it was all a big circus. She was so tickled, as I was, that people would pay that much, or wait that long, just to say they were partying at some club.

It was a stark difference from our quaint Tallahassee upbringings, and for me it was great having her with me, my little piece of home, reminding me where I came from, among a sea of strangers. The last few times I'd been, I had my face in my phone texting her anyway.

It was one of the last weekends Isabel had before she started her treatment, and she wanted to go out with a bang before we had to stop drinking for the year. I'd promised I'd quit with her. We were both social creatures, and it would've made things much more challenging had she done it alone.

Everything in South Florida started later, because it ended later. While last-call in most of Florida was 2 am, Miami closed shop around 5 am, with many 24 hour districts and after-hours joints that served alcohol all morning. That night we were determined to stay awake until sunrise, and go to Hollywood Beach before daybreak. We got there just in time, bringing blankets, and a cheap bottle of wine. She snuggled up, and asked me things that were on her mind.

"What else do you want to do in life?" she asked.

"What do you mean?"

"I mean what else do you want to do? What are your goals?"

"Like a bucket list?"

"Just like a bucket list."

I pondered for a bit. I guess I did have a list of things I'd thought about before.

"Well, I want to learn another language." I'd always wanted to be bi-lingual. I planned on learning Spanish before my move to Miami, but when I came down, all my training partners were Brazilian, and I heard Portuguese more than I heard Spanish. I got overwhelmed and decided I'd tackle that quest later on.

"And I want to make Combat Night bigger."

"We will." I liked her saying *we*.

"And I want to headline a UFC card, to be the main event on the biggest stage in the world." If I had a clearly defined goal for my personal career, it was to be the marquee fight at a UFC event. *Samman vs. Whoever.*

"You will," she said confidently.

"And I want to rebuild my house that burnt down." Some of my fondest memories were in that house. I was always infatuated with the idea of building a replica to walk through, and live in once more.

"Really? I didn't see that coming. I like that idea." She was synonymous in my mind with that house, where I first remember being crazy about a girl.

"And I want to get married, and have a family," I told her.

"We will," she said, turning to face me, "won't we?" She didn't ask often, but was always wondering where she fit in. This life of mine was quickly becoming ours.

"Are you proposing to me?" I joked. I'd thought before, about how I would ask her when the day would come. Big Sur, maybe. That was one of my favorite places, and somewhere she dreamed of going.

"Who's going to be in our wedding?" she'd ask. I told her Matt would be best man. She reminded me I had to leave room for her brothers to be groomsmen.

HK

"And I want to have kids, sons," I told her.

"Am I going to have your sons?" Something about the way she worded it gave me chills. Isabel had a touching idea she wanted to do with her sons when she had them, she said, to paint Lynyrd Skynyrd's "Simple Man" lyrics on their wall.

She shared stories with me of how her mom told her all the ways she loved her dad, how Sue wanted to have all the babies Dallas wanted. "I can't wait to have grandchildren," she'd say on more than one occasion. I reminded her that we had to start with regular children first.

"I think you will have my sons. And I think we'll make attractive babies," I said. She agreed. "And last, I think I'd like to write a book before I die."

"What kind of book? Like a storybook?"

"Like a fiction? No.. I've got enough real things to share before I have to start making them up." She was always telling me to write more, to tell stories. I'd promised her I'd never go through her journals, though I suspected she'd gone through many of mine.

"Well, do you think I'll be in your book?" she asked, with genuine curiosity and naivety.

"Darlin', if I had to guess, I'd say you'll be the whole damn thing."

72.

Spring, 2009

I was 21, and with each fight I grew and yearned for the next level. Jim and Joey Burtoft agreed to invest financially in my success. The UFC was holding a casting call for *The Ultimate Fighter*, Season 10, and the Burtofts ponied up the money for my hotel and flight to Seattle.

I'd won another fight in the meantime, against a guy named Ryan Hodge for the middleweight championship of a rinky-dink Florida organization. At the fight, the promoter had forgotten to print ring cards and gave the ring girls cardboard pizza boxes with the number written in sharpie. Competing for local promotions was not a pretty business. It was little pay, unreliable opponents, and dubious promoters. *The Ultimate Fighter* meant a way out of the pizza box ring cards.

I had to impress to make it. I trained for it like I did a fight, staying in shape after the Hodge bout. During those months, I started to push my limits of distance running. Often times I wouldn't plan on going as far as I did, and sometimes I'd bring Juice.

It was April in Florida, and getting hot. We were on mile nine, a half mile from the house, when Juice laid down. He started panting hard, and wouldn't get up. I tugged a couple times, before realizing something was wrong. I panicked, and frantically waved down an old couple to give us a ride back home.

I had to pick Juice up to get him in the back seat. I told the lady where I lived, and thanked her for helping us. Juice was in my lap, breathing heavily in my face, when he started shitting all over the back of the car. I freaked out, and told the poor couple up front to stop so I could carry him the rest of the way home. They drove faster, taking me all the way to the house.

I called my friend who worked for animal control and knew several veterinarians. He called one he liked, Dr. Ohm, at a place called Animal Aid. He said to take him there right away, and we did. It was awful. Dr. Ohm stated that Juice had a heat stroke, and would need a plasma transfusion to live. I couldn't afford it, and Joey covered the costs until I could pay him back. The operation was a success, and Juice was back to his old self within days.

When I went to pick him up, a surprise greeted me at the door. It was Izzi's mom, Sue, at the desk. I knew their dad was a vet but didn't realize Sue worked in the same field. I'd met her a few times. *At least my mom has a crush on you*, Izzi had once said. I remember because she'd said the words *at least* as a dig.

I told Sue about my upcoming tryout for *The Ultimate Fighter*. She didn't quite know what it meant, but was excited for me. She hadn't the slightest clue that it was her daughter who set the events into motion.

HK

We talked about Juice for a bit. She told me to avoid any more crazy runs and to keep his hair short when it got hot. I was able to take him home before I left for Seattle.

When I landed, it was pouring rain. I tried to fight the feelings of gloom. I had no idea what to expect. They briefed us on the process; two minutes of grappling, two minutes of striking on pads, then a brief interview. There were a few hundred participants, and there would be cuts after each segment.

The grappling partners were chosen at random. I got matched with future TUF 17 castmate Zak Cummins. I performed better than many of the folks there, submitting him twice within the short allotted time. I had a good feeling I'd make it to the next stage, and walked off the mat happy.

As I cooled down and waited for the names to be called, my thigh began to hurt. I thought I'd pulled a muscle, and paid it no mind. After an hour, it was severely swollen. After two hours, it became difficult to walk. The paramedics were unqualified. One told me to go upstairs and take a hot bath. The other told me to elevate it and ice. I tried both.

They phoned my room to tell me I'd been chosen to advance, and I went back downstairs for the next phase of tryouts. I explained to UFC matchmaker Joe Silva that I was injured, but wanted to continue. He said to not worry about kicking, and just show him some punches. I did, and he cut my time short before 30 seconds had passed.

By this point, I was in pain too severe to hide. Folks around me told stories of similar injuries and tried to guess diagnoses. I had no idea what was going on but knew my grit made an impression. When I finally sat down for a final, Joe Silva shared the concern of many in the room.

"You did good, kid, but I think you've hurt yourself. It's possible you have a blood clot. I've seen stuff like this, and it doesn't end pretty. I think you need to go to a hospital."

I didn't take his advice. I asked only whether or not I'd made it.

"You may be hearing from us."

And that was that. I went back to my room, drank a small bottle of vodka to ease my pain, and tried to sleep until my flight the next morning.

When I woke up, my leg was no better but no worse. I wrote it off again and told myself I'd go to the hospital when I got home. I had a five-hour flight before I'd get there.

Once in the air, I became alarmed. With each passing minute, my leg got worse. It grew before my eyes, doubling in size, and was hard to the touch. I alerted a flight attendant, who consulted with the captain about an emergency landing. I told them I was fine and to just get me home.

Once we got to Tallahassee, I got in an ambulance from the airport to the hospital. They rushed me to the operating room, and within 10 minutes of being there, I had a gas mask in my face, doctor hovering over.

"Josh, you're in serious danger of losing your leg. We need to operate immediately. Relax, and count backwards from 100." He slipped the mask over my mouth. I'd never been more terrified.

73.

"Can you think of anything more permanently elating, than knowing that you're on the right road at last?"
-Vernon Howard

There would be no more crazy Vegas trips for the next year, no more late nights partying and watching the sun come up. Isabel was scheduled to start her treatment on a Wednesday, which coincided with her doctor's appointment explaining dosing schedule, and a demonstration of how to self-inject the interferon. She didn't need any help with that and took the liberty of pointing it out.

She was having mixed feelings about it; excited to get the thing over with, nervous about what side effects she'd experience. "What if it never grows back?" She said of her locks. I assured her they would. I didn't know one way or another.

167   *HK*

Wednesday came, and she went to the office to find that the doctor had double booked her appointment. She'd have to wait until Friday to reschedule. She was not happy about it.

"It's only two days, what's the big deal?" I asked.

"It just is. I've been having a lot of anxiety and I wanted to get it over with. I prepared myself for today."

She went back to the doctor Friday and took her first shot at the office. I realized I should've been in Tallahassee for this, and felt like an asshole for not making the trip.

I'd asked her once before if she wanted me to go to the doctor with her. "My dad likes to be the one to go with me," she said. I suggested the three of us go. I figured it was something we were all suffering through together, and I wanted to let Dallas know I was there for her.

"I'm not sure that's the time for you two to meet," she said. I'd made other efforts to meet her dad on occasions. She was content with only her mom and I having a relationship.

"How do you feel?" I asked, after her first of 47 treatment shots.

"Tired. And kind of nauseous."

"Hair all still there?" I said, trying to make light of it.

"Not funny. You're not being sensitive again."

"I'm sorry. Just trying to help."

"I'm gonna nap. I'll call you later." She didn't sound good.

I didn't hear from her the rest of the day. I hoped it wasn't an indication of things to come. We finally spoke late that night. She told me she wasn't feeling well and began asking strange questions.

"Do you still think of Karla?" she asked. Karla was an ex, my rebound after Isabel, when she was still Izzi. I'd always assumed Isabel was immune to jealousy, but this wasn't the first time I'd heard Karla's name. She brought her up from time to time and compared herself in ways. If I bought her a perfume that I liked, she would ask if I'd done the same for Karla.

"Sure. Sometimes." I didn't blame her if she was jealous. I understood perfectly. I hated every guy who'd ever touched her, resented if I was ever forced to make small talk with them around Tallahassee. I told her so, too.

Because she compared herself with Karla, I sometimes did the same. This was around the time Facebook began implementing algorithms, narrowing down news feeds to pages visited most often. When Karla was scrolling through her news feed, it was always a ton of guys, most of whom I was already suspicious about. Years later, when I'd see Isabel on her feed, it was never anything but family members, a few close friends, and me. Infidelity was never a thing I worried about with Isabel, not even once.

"Did you guys ever live together?" The interrogation continued.

"I stayed at her house for a few weeks in between moves. Does that count?"

"I don't know," she said. We'd discussed her moving down, but she told me she couldn't leave her dad, so I stopped bringing it up.

"You haven't mentioned anything about us living together in a while," she said, "do you not want to anymore?"

"I didn't want to keep bothering you about it. Where is this all coming from?"

"I don't know. Sometimes I just worry about being the girl you thought you wanted." She found the right words to cripple me.

"Pack your shit and come on then."

"You don't mean that."

"Of course I do."

And that's how it happened. Before I knew it she was in my driveway, car packed full of stuff. The next chapter was starting.

74.

Late Spring, 2009

When I woke up in the hospital, I was surrounded by familiar faces. Roberto, Joey, and my mom, all looked for a first

HK

reaction of how I felt. I felt like shit but was relieved to look down and see two legs. I'd nearly killed my dog and lost a limb over the course of weeks. I made it out with both, but landed myself in the hospital with a pain unlike any I'd ever felt.

On the right leg, gauze wrapped all the way from my kneecap to my hip. The outside was soaked in blood, and there were two tubes inserted in the front of my thigh, attached to a vacuum system, sucking out dried blood in sporadic increments. I looked like a science project.

The doctor was also in the room and explained what had happened. I tore a muscle grappling, and exposing it to altitude forced a blood clot, causing a deep vein thrombosis. I'd had a history of blood clots in my family, and by the time the doctor had removed it, he said it was the size of an orange.

Underneath the blood-soaked gauze, they still had my leg open, with clamps I couldn't see. The metal would remain there for a few days until the tubes could be removed, and my leg fastened shut. When it was all said and done, I'd received 200 stitches, three layers deep, and 40 staples on the outside. I'd been in the hospital for nearly a week when I got the call.

"Hey Josh, this is Jamie Campione with *The Ultimate Fighter*. We'd like you to come back out next week." I was doped up and told her I'd be there as soon as I got out of the hospital.

"Hospital?" She said.

"Yeah, everything's gonna be fine though." I told her what had happened, that Joe Silva had been right about my leg. She offered her condolences and told me I'd have to try out another season.

It was a powerful feeling of disappointment, thinking I'd been that close, and blew it in a freak accident. When it was all said and done, YouTube street fighting sensation Kimbo Slice signed onto the season, and my weight class wasn't even showcased. The whole roller coaster of emotion, pain, and disfigurement was all for nothing. Nothing but a scar and a story.

I was bedridden for weeks. I couldn't walk for months. I had to use crutches until the bottoms wore thin several times over, slipping and sliding with every stride. The whole thing was scary and happened at a young age. It was the worst injury that I'd seen anyone have, and it was hard to not wonder *why me?*

I called girls that I knew liked me enough to help. I hadn't spoken to Izzi in months, and wouldn't have asked her for assistance anyway. I didn't want to be seen like that by her. I also didn't want to rely solely on my mom. I phased through them until Karla came along. She made things easier for me, carrying piss bottles to and from the bed, like my mom when I'd broken my leg. Karla was helpful, and brought over food. She believed in me. It was nice to have people do that again.

She was strong enough to keep me from running over her, but I was always hesitant to commit. I met her at a point in my life where I saw girls in two categories: Izzi, and not Izzi. It was hard to break that pattern of thinking, and Karla got caught in it.

They gave me lots of medicine. I didn't abuse any of it. I detested it, with pride. The worst part was the self-injecting blood thinners I had to use once a week. I never liked needles and dreaded the task every time.

The Burtofts continued to support me, in recovery, and mental coaching to keep a positive state of mind during the ordeal. We all knew I'd gotten close to succeeding, and that things like this were a risk in the sport. To roll with the punches was the motto for all of us, and they doubled down on me being able to do that. Joey came one day, with a proposition that would give me something to look forward to while healing up.

"We'd like you to become a partner with us. We want to open an MMA gym, with you as the coach. We want to promote fights, and for you to be a part of that too. We want to you to be the face of it all." It was a fantastic compliment, and a slingshot to opportunities I'd never had possible. I agreed, and we began buildout right away.

HK

75

"It seems right now that all I've ever done in my life is making my way here to you."

-The Bridges of Madison County

Piece by piece we'd let each other into our own little worlds of insecurities and peculiarities. When we began living together, it was the definitive joining of my life and hers, into ours.

Before she came, I surprised her by having the house painted, including our bedroom, the same garnet that she'd had in hers growing up. She brought an assortment of items from her house. Many were hers, many her roommate Stephanie had given her, a nice parting gift for the sudden move. She'd likely seen it coming.

Among her most prized possessions was a cairn from her Aunt Jo, a stack of stones to symbolize the things she'd been through in life. She brought the dried petals from the first dozen roses I'd bought her, still intact, in a small glass container.

The last thing she pulled out of her car was a framed photo she made, a quote from *Alice in Wonderland*. She was always doing that, taking screenshots of verses or lyrics that she liked, or pictures of places she wanted to visit on our next trip. She'd send me at least a dozen a week. Many are the same quotes used to begin these chapters.

"Have I gone mad?" The frame read, quoting the Mad Hatter as he asked Alice.

"I'm afraid so," Alice replied. "You're entirely bonkers. But I'll tell you a secret. All the best people are." It was perfect.

I gave her half my closet and several dresser drawers, and we spent the night settling her in. When woke, it was with the comfort of knowing that the rest of our days would be spent like this. No more back and forth with long weeks apart.

"Let's go play," she said. It was always play this and play that. Most mornings she would want to take Juice to the park, or go play soccer on the beach.

"I thought you wanted to go house shopping?" I asked her.

"Well, if you insist," she said with an impish grin.

We'd discussed it prior to her coming down, although I didn't know what I was getting myself into. We went to IKEA, the mecca of home furnishings. What we thought would be a quick trip for some knick knacks turned into three shopping carts full of stuff. We bought *everything*. Lamps, rugs, candles, throw pillows, wall canvases, picture frames, shower curtains, indoor plants, outdoor plants, dinnerware, tiki torches, I mean *everything*. And I loved every second of it. The trip was so exciting for the both of us, such a significant moment as we shopped for our shared home for the first time.

She was having a blast, driving around exploring her new home, finding obscure shops around town. Isabel was the first girl I'd ever trusted with my credit card, and I let her have at it. She found a little used CD shop that sold all sorts of neat stuff, and bought me a poster of Albert Einstein riding a bicycle. She was the first one to tell me that he and I shared a birthday with my mom. She found a pet store for us to buy Juice a new doggy bed, and special Burt's Bees dog chapstick for his nose. She even went to the store and found the brand of deodorant that I wore as a teenager. I had no clue how she remembered.

She kept receipts of everything we purchased, in a little folder. "What's this for?" I asked when I saw it.

"Your mom told you start keeping all your receipts for your taxes next year. You didn't listen, so I'm doing it for you." I didn't remember my mom saying anything about receipts, but it was another good example of her learning what she could from the women in my life.

We crawled into bed after a long day and laid in our typical position we'd grown accustomed to sleeping in, both of us on our sides, her head resting on my left arm. Her backside pressed firmly against my belly and lap, sandwiching my leg between hers as she would a pillow. My right arm laid underneath hers, draped around her torso. She held onto it tightly. My head rested right behind hers, positioned for neck kisses, or to peek over her shoulder if I wanted to see her face. Every night she nestled and

HK

wiggled her way into my arms like two pieces of a jigsaw puzzle, forcing me to spoon.

She had the remote and was flipping through channels on the television. She stopped on the Science Channel to appease me. The program on was on the science of love, which made her want to keep it there. It was explaining what happens to the brain when we experience what humans know as being in love. Heart rate fluctuates, pupils dilate, and pleasure endorphins are released, that let us know we're in the presence of someone special.

These were all things I'd read about before, but Isabel was fascinated by it. She had it all explained, finally, the things that she felt when we were together, she said.

Isabel had just discovered F. Scott Fitzgerald, and had been texting me quotes from him that she liked. The program on TV reminded her of one she'd saved, but not sent. She scrolled through her phone's pictures. She didn't say anything, just motioned for me to read as she handed me her phone. She had a sly grin, pleased with herself that she had something relevant to what we were watching.

The quote read, "Her heart sank into her shoes as she realized at last how much she wanted him. No matter what his past was, no matter what he had done. Which was not to say that she would ever let him know, but only that he moved her chemically more than anyone she had ever met, that all other men seemed pale beside him."

"That's how I feel, like it says here," she said. "Like you move me chemically, in a way no one else can."

My heart melted through the bed. They were the sweetest words ever spoken. In one sentence and gesture, she'd managed to encapsulate exactly how I'd always felt about her. Something I'd always struggled to express, she was now explaining to me. Isabel was the only one that could tickle my brain's amygdala like she did, but I didn't know how to tell her that without cliches. We were always looking for new ways to say "I love you," and she'd just knocked it out of the park. Maybe the acknowledgement that love was a chemical reaction rather than an act of God got her wheels turning.

"Why don't we ever talk about God anymore?" she said. "We used to talk about it all the time. Now you never bring it up." Gone were the days of our ideological debates, for plenty of reasons. While the height of my religious rebellion was when I last knew her, I no longer cared. I'd given up my atheistic crusade, learned to let people just believe what they want to believe if it wasn't hurting anyone. Most importantly, I wanted Isabel to use whatever tools she had at her disposal to help get through the things she'd gone through, and was still going through. Her faith was one of those things.

I was in love with her wholly, not partially, and that meant loving everything about her, including her beliefs and all else, good and bad, as she did me. Her convictions were something that defined her, and I didn't want her to change a thing. We had different feelings about our spirituality but respected each other's notions. She finally coerced me back into a conversation about it, picking up where Kevin Casey and Jimmy Quinlan left off in the kitchen of *The Ultimate Fighter* house, almost a year prior.

"I just still don't understand how you can think we're all just a random happening, that there isn't a reason we're here," she said.

"Just because I think we're here by coincidence doesn't mean I think there's no reason," I told her. "I'm here to feel all those chemicals we just talked about." They were the ones that told our ancestors who to start tribes with, the ones that pointed the way to who was worth living and dying for. "I think the reason we're here is to do what we're doing, right here and now. People look their whole lives for something like we have." Those were *my* convictions, strengthened by her. She made me understand life, and I didn't think our paths were pre-determined. I believed we chose our own purpose, our own destiny, and Isabel was my fate.

"Well, I think God brought me to you. You're my silver lining. I had to go through all those things that I did, to get to where I am now, with you. And it helps me when I think like that."

HK

76.

Later Summer, 2009

The Burtofts and I had set up shop in Tallahassee, to Orkin's chagrin. He and I gloved up one last time and parted ways with a final sparring session at his gym. It was our attempt to end things amicably.

The new school was called Tallahassee Combat Sports. We'd gone through a few warehouses before we found the right complex. When we finally did, it was complete; two rings, mats, cages, and amenities and features that no gym within 100 miles could boast.

The Burtofts invested serious money into it, and their experience with the fitness industry helped in a lot of ways. Joey became more involved in the coaching side with me. He'd watched Rodolfo in detail. He knew he wasn't sustainable, that if we wanted to build something, we had to rely on ourselves to do it.

The nature of MMA was that it was so new, everyone was forced to learn primarily from people who were still learning themselves. I was the most experienced fighter that anyone in Tallahassee had access to, the only one in town that had made a career of it. We wanted to build a team of fighters with the same dreams. Folks came from all over, Mitchell and Matt included. Matt had sworn one drunken night that he was going to become an MMA fighter. Lots of drunk people said that, and I wrote him off. He was there the next day and never left.

We didn't try to poach from Orkin's gym. Many came without asking. I had men that were older than me, calling me sir, asking for advice on fighting and otherwise. It was all new to me, being in a position of leadership.

I mimicked Orkin in coaching style, striving for structure and method, with a hint of big brother bullying. I took things that I'd learned from Roberto, and Rodolfo, and every other training partner along the way, and tried to implement curriculum. Most importantly, I took my own experience in constructing training camps for fight preparation, which I felt was my biggest asset.

HK

I taught MMA, and we hired other folks to teach specific classes. They were mostly kids my age that we'd grabbed from the university. Our wrestling coach had placed nationally in high school. Our boxing coach had once been on the Junior Olympic team. Our grappling instructor did a few tournaments here and there. We were all absorbing what we could from one another.

We were taking our amateurs to Georgia for all the same events that I came up in, while the wheels were turning in Tallahassee to put together a show of our own. Orkin had always told me that live MMA would never work there, that folks weren't ready for it. He became another person I had something to prove to.

While I'd left most my old friends behind in the wake of aiming to be a better person, I still had plenty links to my past. I still went by Animal Aid to see Sue and ask about Izzi. *She's, well, you know.* I didn't know, but I'd heard. I told Sue I'd be fighting in Tallahassee soon, and she promised to try to make it.

The Burtofts and I partnered with an old boxing promoter, JC, and a local club owner, Scott Carswell. JC was European and insisted on calling the new promotion *Ubersmash*. We didn't care what it was called, as long as we were able to use his promoter's license.

The mission was to showcase our hard work and to test our up and comers. I'd reached main event status of the regional promotions. It wasn't quite the UFC, but it gave others something to strive for and showed them how long this thing really took to get to the top. I had responsibility, and I was proud of it.

77.

"Take a lover who looks at you like maybe you are magic."
-Frida Kahlo

We both had several sides, but more than any, I was in love with Isabel the Housekeeper. Maybe it was from her years of practice, maybe she just held an eagerness to please, but she was

HK

a domestic goddess. Isabel had an innate ability to turn a house into a home better than any girl or woman I'd ever met. She was what every housewife in the world strived to be. I thought I knew how good she was. Until we lived together I had no idea.

She had tricks for everything, and kept the house immaculate. She could turn a dirty pile of clothes into a neatly folded stack in no time, could clear out a sink of dishes into ready-to-eat-off plates and silverware in minutes. She could put a duvet on a comforter, and make the bed with fitted sheets in a matter of seconds. She could tell me where anything in the house was without having to think about it.

She had my suits dry cleaned and pressed before I even knew I needed them done. She pleated pants with precision and knotted ties to the perfect length. She hemmed clothes and sewed on buttons. She could do any and every thing imaginable around the house. She joked that her brothers had trained her well, that Wyatt told her one day she'd be the best wife ever.

On top of that, she was just so much fun to live with. She was always doing silly things, hiding behind doors trying to scare people, or convincing us to jump off the roof into the pool with her. If anyone at the house was ever playing video games, she'd always want to join. She jumped up and down as she played. Half the time I wasn't sure she was even looking at the right screen.

She always had music on. It flowed through her, she oozed with it. There was hardly a time when she wasn't dancing or singing, never one for idle ears. She didn't like any of her senses idle for that matter and was an expert of avoiding such. Always candles burning and music blasting and coffee brewing and touching and kissing, new hot sauces and recipes being tried. She was the perfect counterpart for me, companionship and compatibility embodied. She truly was the epitome of sensational, a spitting image of life being lived to the fullest.

There was something beautifully fulfilling in not just having someone to take care of me, but someone to take care of as well, like we'd talked about on the canoe ride. I may have been supporting her financially, giving her a place to live, but it was largely her that was taking care of me. I wasn't an easy person to be with, I'd learned from numerous failed relationships with friends and lovers. She managed it with ease.

It wasn't just me she took care of, it was all of us. She'd lived with men her whole life, and it showed. Several times I'd have to tell her to stop doing Brian and Matt's laundry, to stop cleaning their bathroom. She would bathe and comb Juice, clip his toenails until he was perfectly groomed. He followed her around the house wherever she went. She was motherly beyond her years, and we were all smitten by it.

By this point, Combat Night had become all of ours; Mitchell's, Brandi's, Isabel's, and mine. It was the venture that made it possible for us to have no other obligations but each other. It was one of her favorite things, the four of us together. Mitchell and Brandi had moved to Orlando, and we stayed at their house while there.

Combat Nights were Isabel's time to get dolled up, a chance to go to the mall and buy us both new outfits and accessories. Before we went on trips she'd have our bags packed, truck gassed, everything done and ready. She was always on top of everything.

She loved visiting old friends that had moved out of Tallahassee and gone to college in the towns we went to. Many of her friends hadn't visited with her in years and were so happy to see her doing well. I decided it was time to fly my dad in, and show him what I'd been doing with my life, romantically, and professionally. "Don't fuck this one up," he said, after meeting her.

My dad enjoyed chatting it up with our employees while he was there, learning more about what we did. One of them he liked was Larry, our referee for Combat Night. Larry might've been the baddest dude on the planet. He was the on the S.W.A.T. team, worked with an anti-terrorist unit, and had a brown belt in Brazilian Jiu-Jitsu. While Isabel was in jail, she was part of the work camp that cleaned the Sheriff's office. Larry recognized her but kept it a secret.

While Combat Night used Larry as the same referee for every event, we hired different ringside physicians for each town. At the same event my dad came down for, the doctor asked me

HK

how long my fiancee' and I had been together. He said his assumption within earshot of her, and she darted her eyes towards me, flicking her eyebrows up and down.

I like the sound of that.

Wyatt had told her he was thinking of proposing to his girlfriend, Lauren, and it'd been the topic of conversation lately. I asked her what it was she wanted to do if we got married. "Am I not doing a good enough job of being your housewife?" She joked. Some folks look down on traditional gender roles, but Isabel relished in them. The single thing she wanted most in life was to bear children.

Being a mother meant the world to her, but that wasn't all she wanted to do. Her dream was to own a coffee a shop, she said. That was another of her impeccable skills, the little barista. She had her own heavenly combination of Splenda and sugar and milk and cream and hazelnut and French Vanilla, a whole recipe perfected over thousands of cups of practice.

She enjoyed making coffee as much as she liked taking pictures. She'd asked me for a nice camera for her birthday. She was always taking photos, and reminded me once that there were years of her life that she felt like taking none. She said it felt good to feel pretty again.

She was always asking questions when we were watching fights, trying to get a better understanding of what was going on. She'd gotten good at it. She liked seeing emotion in the fighters, catching them on some of the best or worst nights of their life. MMA had a way of chewing people up and spitting them out, she said, phrasing it perfectly.

Everything was moving at a mile a minute. I'd managed to create a charmed life for myself. I was living with my best friends, and doing what I was passionate about with the woman of my dreams. Life was great, and I thought there was no end in sight.

78

Spring, 2010

The Burtofts and I were firing on all cylinders. I had access to a gym day and night, a team built around me, and a whole operation geared towards my success. TCS was gratifying, but outside the cage, the promotional side of MMA was what intrigued me most. Having new fans share my enthusiasm for the sport was what turned my gears.

I became immersed in it and wanted to control everything. I insisted on sitting in on every Ubersmash meeting. I wanted to learn as much as I could about the business, from the inside out.

I was coaching the guys on the card, so conflict of interest prevented me from being a matchmaker for Ubersmash. I got a license for it anyway and worked with other promotions around the state. I got paid for that, as well as a percentage of winnings from the folks I coached, and a cut from the gym fees. Between those revenue sources, my own fight purses, and personal training, I was making a good living off of something most never thought possible.

I met many of the sponsors that supported our events. My favorite was Lance Maxwell. He coached little league teams around the city and was as a leader in the community. He helped serve as a male influence in Orkin's absence.

I moved into a new house with some of the coaches and fighters from the gym. Karla stuck around and was a nice addition to the things I had going on. Training camps were easier when I had a team and a lady to go home to.

While fighting in front of 1,000 screaming fans in my hometown was a great experience, my goal was still the UFC. Since my last TUF tryouts, the UFC had held two more casting calls. I went to both, one in Los Angeles, the other in Vegas. It was the first time I'd gotten to fully experience Hollywood Hills, Venice Beach, the Vegas Strip. They were all such eye-opening adventures.

I got to train with people across the country outside the confines of the Florida Panhandle. It gave me an idea of just how

HK

many people were chasing this dream. I was obsessed with getting on *The Ultimate Fighter*. It wasn't about the reality show for me. I just wanted to finish what I had started.

I wasn't loud enough the second time. I should've been more vocal. I should've told them what I'd been through en route back to them. I assumed I would be a shoe-in, that I'd be ushered to the front because of what had happened. I was wrong.

When I went back a third time, I took pictures of the surgery with me. I made sure to find the producers, and make them know my story. *Well why didn't ya tell us last time?* They invited me to be on the show. *Of course, no problem*, they said. *Just do us a favor and make 170 lbs.* They'd held casting calls for several weight classes that season, and just like the first time I'd went, they dropped middleweight. There was no way I'd ever cut to 170 lbs.

While I went home for a third time disappointed, it was also with a knowing that I was close. I took my experience back to Tallahassee and used it to keep helping the ones coming up underneath me. I was still the only person in town that had ever gone across the country for face punching. From time to time, I'd think about how I'd started a pro career just to impress a girl. It was a crazy thing, fantasizing about how far MMA could take me. Until then, I kept my head down and continued grinding.

79.

"There is a sense that we are all each other's consequences."
                                          -Wallace Stegner

Isabel answered my phone as it rang one morning. It all started with that call, months in the making, that set into the chain of events that would be my unraveling. Before that call, it began with a man named Dzhokhar Tsarnaev, and his brother Tamerlan. The Tsarnaev brothers were Chechen natives that planned and executed the Boston Marathon bombing. Because of the recent terrorist attack, Massachusetts increased the difficulty with which visas were given to immigrants before entering the country for work. The effect, as would it would ripple in my life, would be the withdrawal of Canadian UFC middleweight Nick Ring from his bout, against TUF castmate Uriah Hall. Naturally, I got the offer to replace Ring and was asked to fight Hall in Boston on August 17th, 2013. I accepted and began training camp immediately.

I'd had knee surgery in Spring of 2012 before TUF, and it had never felt right since. I thought I could make it to one more fight, and did my best to push through. The clicking in my knee was always present, but one day started to get louder. It became painful, and my patella was beginning to shift. One day while wrestling, I felt a final pop that was not the same as the others. It swelled and put an end to my training.

A prominent storyline that the producers had beset from the beginning of our season circled around the fact that I'd chosen other fights besides Uriah during the tournament. I'd done my best to advance as far as I could using the tools I was given, like Chael had encouraged. I wasn't scared of Uriah, or anyone else, and didn't want the public to think that was the case when deciding whether to pull from the fight. I had never withdrawn from a bout before, and it didn't sit well with my ego.

I reached out to the coach from the show that I was closest with, Frank Mir. We kept in touch after the season from time to time, although he favored brevity, so I spoke accordingly.

"Torn meniscus.. Could maybe fight, but not sure if it'll get worse." I texted.

"Do you need the paycheck?"

"No." Combat Night was becoming bigger every day, and we still had money in the bank from the Casey fight.

"Live to fight another day." Short and sweet.

And that's how the decision was made. I thought I had made it to the point in my career where it was time to take injuries seriously, and not just ignore them as I had many fights on my way to the UFC.

I bowed out, planning the surgery that would hopefully once and for all fix the problems plaguing my knee. My orthopedic surgeon lived in Tallahassee, and that's where we

HK

chose to do the operation. Isabel and I headed north, and were planning on staying at Stephanie's house to recover. It would be a few days before I was able to sit in a car long enough to drive back home.

When we got to the doctor's office, we were surprised to find her aunt as the nurse. It was the same aunt whose daughter's wedding we'd gone to months earlier. We chatted for a few minutes before Isabel left to go the bathroom, and had a few moments to ourselves. Her aunt gave me words of endearment.

"Thank you for being so good to her," she said, taking me by surprise. I wished I had more time to explain how anything I'd done for Isabel had been reciprocated several times over. I thanked her and assured her it was mutual. Both Isabel and the doctor returned, and wheeled me towards the operating room. The doctor put the mask on me.

"Take some deep breaths and count backwards from 100."
That damn line.

It never took 100 seconds to go out. I woke up hours later, feeling sedated, with a dull pain in my left knee, Isabel to my right.

"You survived!" She wasted no time cracking jokes. "You wanna drive home?"

I chuckled a bit, still inebriated, and asked her to hand me one of the cold Gatorades she'd had waiting for me when I woke up. She wheeled me back to the truck and drove us to Stephanie's. I woke up to a text from my mom later in the afternoon.

"How you feeling?"

"Fine. Drugged up."

"Good. Make sure you're being nice to Isabel. She's been in touch with me. You're lucky to have her around." She wasn't telling me anything I didn't know. I wondered what I would've done without her. She waited on me hand and foot, getting mad if I tried to use my crutches to get anything for myself. Finally, I'd had enough, and convinced her I was well enough for us to drive home.

I thanked Stephanie for letting me stay while Isabel packed our stuff into the truck. We were both anxious to get back. I was in the passenger seat on the way home and was in pain, and reached into the back to grab my bottle of codeine from the doctor.

"You're not worried about leaving all those pills around me?" She asked.

"What? No. Why, are you tempted?" I hadn't even thought twice about it. Her doctor had written her a prescription of Klonopin for some of the side effects of her treatment, and she'd yet to take a single one. *I don't even want to start that game,* her exact words when I asked her why she hadn't been using them.

"I'm not tempted," she said, "that's just a big bottle to leave around someone who's had drug problems." I should've been more considerate.

"That's all behind us, right?" I asked.

"Yes. I think I was just trying to say I appreciate you trusting me." I did.

Our conversation was interrupted by a loud noise from underneath the truck. With every wheel rotation, another crack emanated from the axle.

"What the *fuck* is that?" She said, pulling off the road.

"I don't have a clue." It sounded terrible.

I called AAA and got a tow truck to the scene. We were near Orlando, so I had the driver take us to Mitchell's house, and the truck to a shop nearby. I got a call from a mechanic, hours later.

"Looks like your front differential. Gonna be a couple grand and a little wait before I can get it fixed." I asked him to make it as quick as possible, while Isabel and I buckled down for another few days away from home. Within the course of a week, I'd gone from training for the biggest fight of my life, with a comfortable amount of money in the bank, to being broke, sedated, and handicapped, relying on my girlfriend to do everything for me. I thought that I had it bad. There'd be more to come.

HK

80.

I'd seen some weird shit in the sport, but nothing was stranger than the return of the masked Luchador man.

JC and the Burtofts were hesitant to give the hometown hero a tough matchup in our first Ubersmash event and had paired me with a can, combat sports lingo for a low-risk fight. The following three opponents were stronger. One was a TUF vet, Dave Baggett. Another was an eventual UFC vet, Chris Cope. Finally, I rematched the last guy to have beaten me, John Walsh.

I won all four of fights in the first round. Three of the four had gotten double punched, which fans around Tallahassee affectionately named the Samman Smash. I didn't care for the moniker; double punch was fine with me, but at least it got people talking.

Amidst our events at home, I'd gotten several emails from folks wanting to get involved in guiding my career. At the time, I was managing all the guys on the team, as well as myself. There was no need to sign with anyone, unless they could get me into the UFC, and that's what Michael Schaffner promised to do. All I needed to do in return was sign an exclusive management contract with him.

It wasn't until he sent me the terms that I got suspicious. I did a background search on the guy and found nothing. I wondered why his name sounded familiar. Finally I realized; Michael Schaffner was actually Miguel Shoffner. He'd changed his name, not disclosed anything about being the same masked man whose face I'd broken years ago, and tried to sign me to a restrictive five-year contract.

The whole thing was disturbing and made me want to talk to a lawyer about what had happened. There wasn't any possible recourse for what he'd done, but a friend recommended I get in touch with a real manager if I wanted to get to the next level, and ensure that stuff like that didn't happen again.

An old friend I trained with who'd moved to California introduced me over the phone to Gary Ibarra. He was the owner of a management group out of San Francisco called AMR Group. Gary told me I'd been on his radar, and while the middleweight UFC roster was full at the time, he could get me into a league called Bellator, the second most prominent MMA organization in the world. Bellator had just signed a contract with MTV and was offering $100,000 to the winner of their tournaments; three fights over the course of three months. To enter, I had to win a qualifier, against a guy named Dan Cramer.

Gary flew me to San Francisco to meet his family, and some of the other clients he represented. Also signed to AMR Group was Cesar Gracie, who coached MMA superstars Nick and Nate Diaz, as well as Gilbert Melendez, and Jake Shields. Nick was the team captain, armed with a bag of weed and a chip on his shoulder. He was my favorite fighter, and it was surreal to share a training room with him.

I traveled to several parts of California while there. I went to see Big Sur and other state parks. The city of San Francisco was stunning and was the first time I'd thought about moving out of Tallahassee. There was just so much more to offer elsewhere. I wasn't sure about the details of getting out, but I knew that signing with Gary was the next step. I agreed to join AMR Group and enter Bellator's tournament.

The fight with Cramer would be in Miami, a city I'd come to love after several trips with Karla. She knew I wanted to get out of Tallahassee, and she wanted to move too. She'd gotten an offer for an internship in Tampa, and accepted. It took me by surprise.

She complained that I was vacant, that I'd never love anything like I loved MMA. It was a source of most of our arguments. I was obsessed, and spent too much time on forums and fighting websites, she said. I was focused on my career when she wanted me to focus on her. I had love for Karla but realized she was right when it wasn't hard to say goodbye. We agreed to spend the last few months together and try to have a clean break. My fight in Bellator would be the last we'd see as a couple.

As Karla was on her way out, my mom had a man coming in, named Jeff. I gave him a hard time when we first met, as that's

HK

what sons are supposed to do when they're introduced to stepfathers. I liked him just fine, I just had to test him a bit first.

I went down to Miami for my Bellator debut, and lost a hard fought decision. While I didn't win, there was much to be gained from it. I was reminded how it was to fight away from the comfort of home. I got a glimpse of how world-class organizations worked and had my first brush with national television. Most importantly, I met Daniel Valverde and Cesar Carneiro, the coaches from MMA Masters. We shared a locker room as they prepared fellow Bellator veteran Luis Palomino for his fight that evening. They invited me to come train with them. I told them I'd take them up on it one day.

81.

"We gravitate to where we feel most important."
                                                        -Isabel Monroe

Isabel loved rainy days. I couldn't stand them. Cuddle weather, she called it, but I didn't feel like cuddling. I hadn't even recovered from my knee surgery before I was bedridden again. I was laying there, sweating a storm, with pain in both my sides, worsening at an alarming rate. I couldn't stop aching, and it'd been going on for a couple days. Isabel was begging for us to go to the hospital. I had limited health insurance and insisted we play internet doctor.

Armed only with a list of symptoms that I had, we narrowed it down to what we thought was a kidney infection. Isabel managed to find a bottle of antibiotics that she had left over from last winter, and we hoped it would work. In the meantime, she was on nurse duties, making every combination of lemon and honey green tea that she could find. She changed the sheets every few hours after I'd soaked through them with sweat.

Isabel was trying to cure me, and came in the bedroom to shower me with what always made me feel better, affectionate hugs and kisses. I asked her to stop. I wasn't in the mood. It upset her, and she lashed back.

"Stop being mean because you don't feel good. You may miss these kisses one day." She'd said the same thing once when I was trying to shoo Juice away from licking my face.

"What the fuck is that supposed to mean?" It was reminiscent of her response to my morbid jokes of texting and driving being the death of me.

"It means you never know what's going to happen. I'm lucky to still be here now, you know." I sometimes forgot.

"I get it, but you can't say stuff like that." We argued until she didn't want to talk anymore, and left the room mid-conversation.

"I'm going to get you some more medicine." When she came back, it was with a thermometer. She opened the package and motioned for me to open my mouth, like I was a child.

"104.3. You're being fucking stupid, and we're going to the emergency room." There wasn't any arguing after that.

For the second time in a month I was in a hospital bed, Isabel by my side. I laid there, miserable and delirious, as she explained to the doctor everything I'd been feeling, all the medications I'd taken in the last 30 days, answering questions about food and drug allergies. She told the doctors things about me I didn't even know she knew.

He said I wouldn't be getting out that night, or the next, or any foreseeable night in the future. I indeed had a kidney infection, a severe one, that could've been prevented had we got it treated days ago. He scolded us for trying to diagnose and medicate ourselves, to which Isabel gave me a very stern look.

I'd have to stay at the hospital to be monitored, and undergo intravenous antibiotics as my stepfather Jeff was still doing. I'd been trying to kick the thing all week because we were supposed to go to Boston, to watch the event I was originally scheduled to fight Uriah Hall in. We'd already bought our flights. We wouldn't be making it to Boston, and I went from being a participant in the event, to being a live spectator, to laying in a fucking hospital bed with no cable TV.

189

ℋ𝒦

My mom sent me a text, similar to the one last time that we were surrounded by doctors and nurses. "Isabel's been calling me. You need to be thankful for her. I worry about you less when she's there."

For almost a week Isabel slept on the recliner next to my bed. The hospital we were at was right down the road from my house. Every night I told her she could go sleep in our bed and come back in the morning, and every evening she told me to stop saying that.

"Wild Horses, baby," she said, quoting the Stones' song. I knew just what she meant.

82.

Winter, 2011

Mom, Jeff, Grandma, and I were all at an awards banquet, where mom was winning "Leader of the Year" in Tallahassee. It was a proud moment for us, recognition for her life of social work in the community. It was sometimes a thankless job, and it was nice to see others acknowledge her diligence.

It also served as a goodbye from her to the field of work. She and Jeff had gotten engaged. I never thought I'd live to see my mother married again, but she did, and planned on leaving for the west coast in months. They put their house on the market and left their jobs. Neither of them were in great health, but I was comforted knowing that they had each other for the road.

Her plans to move made it easier for me to do the same. I wasn't quite ready yet though, and had agreed to run another gym in the meantime. Coaching had become a part of my identity and was hard to let go of. The Burtofts had to let go of the business for various reasons. Joey got married, and Jim went through a divorce. While Joey I still trained together, he left the coaching to me.

I added another feather to my cap, picking up where the Burtofts had left off. My new gym was called Capital City Combat Club, C4 for short, and was owned by myself and a Tallahassee landowner who thought he wanted to be in the fight game.

As C4 was to TCS, Combat Night was to Ubersmash. The new promotion was the brainchild of Mitchell and I. We'd gotten the idea while driving home from an event in Port St. Lucie, near the end of 2011. I'd made promoters plenty of money, both as a fan and a fighter, and it was time to earn from the other side. I knew the industry and had established connections all over the state. Our first show would be in January of the new year.

We built everything from the ground up. It was a grassroots campaign, that was made possible by the local supporters I'd collected from Ubersmash. It was something that continued to serve as a way to showcase guys that I was training. Our new facility was larger and provided space for more members and classes. Teammates from TCS followed me, and more from Orkin's.

The investor who I'd partnered with didn't realize how challenging the industry was, and lost interest quickly, leaving me with the brunt of the work. It was a lot of fun, being the sole leader, but I missed having Joey around. It taught me that there are no perfect situations, only best case scenarios.

We asked for a release from my Bellator contract after the loss. If I wasn't in the big money tournament, it was not worth sticking around. They obliged, and I was again a free agent on the market.

I got approached by an organization called the XFC. They were based out of Florida, and I had frequented their shows. They traveled around the country occasionally, and offered me a fight in my one time home of Knoxville, Tennessee, against Mikey Gomez.

Gomez was an instructor at an affiliate of Roberto's gym, who I was still training with. Roberto was forced to choose his loyalties, between coaching me for the fight, or conceding to his higher-ups. There was a lot of politics involved, and he made the business decision to stay in good graces with Gracie Barra, the BJJ lineage he'd committed to. I understood, but it spelled the end of relying on him for training.

Besides one coach leaving me high and dry, and the other focusing on his own projects, I'd torn my meniscus preparing for

HK

the Gomez fight. Even worse, it happened it doing yoga. It's a silly story in retrospect; a big goon injuring himself in a Toe Stand Pose, trying to keep up with the instructor. A Padangustasana is not meant for people over 200 lbs. It was not funny at the time.

I flew to Tennessee, more nervous than usual. I'd gone into fights with injuries before, and it hadn't turned out well. I was coming off the Bellator loss, and if I wanted to be taken seriously in the eyes of the UFC, I couldn't afford two losses in a row. I was feeling the pressure.

83.

"He loved her, of course, but better than that, he chose her, day after day. Choice: that was the thing."

-Sherman Alexie

I'd finally made it out of the hospital, already wondering what disaster was going to happen next. Isabel was a few months into treatment, and the effects were worsening each week. Her shots were on Fridays, and I'd learned to let her be until Saturday evening when she'd start to feel better.

Her body's reactions were wearing her down. There were so many ways that this thing had seeped into our lives. We brought her medicine around with us wherever we went, three pills at 10 AM, and four at 4:30 PM, every day. Because she was worried about taking them late, or missing one altogether, we kept doses everywhere. We had a bottle in my car, several in her car, some in her purse, and the rest at home. We'd both gotten used to the daily alarms sounding on our phones to remind her to medicate. Sometimes they'd go off and she wouldn't have anything to drink, having to choke them down dryly.

The interferon shots had to be kept below 40 degrees or they'd go bad. We had to pack that poison, all those needles, into a lunch box with ice packs in it every time that we went out of town. She was so embarrassed, and tried to avoid having anyone ask questions about it. No one knew of her illness except those that had a right to know. Stephanie, Brian, and Matt, because we'd all lived with Isabel. Her family knew, but not all of them. Mitchell and Brandi didn't know, my mom didn't know, no one else had a clue. It was our secret that we hid from the world, and she was beginning to feel dirty about it

Besides the secrets, ice packs, and random pills everywhere, there were always so damn many band-aids, around for when either of us would get a cut or scrape. It happens more than one would think once you start keeping track of them. She was terrified of getting me sick. I was too, more than I'd anticipated or let her know. Every month I'd go to the lab and get a blood test. I never told her about it. I didn't want her knowing I was worried, or for her to feel more burdened than she already did.

Isabel had all but quit drinking entirely. We had occasional nights where we'd try a new beer or two, but when we were out, especially at Combat Nights, she would drink just soda, no whiskey. She'd put it in a rocks glass with lime so no one would ask questions. She carried a large water bottle around with her, per doctor's orders, and complained about having to pee non-stop.

She worked out daily, except for on Fridays, when she took her shots. Those days we laid in bed and read books. I headed out one Friday to go grocery shopping for us. She asked me to wait as she crawled out from under the sheets and put clothes on.

"You feeling alright?" I asked her.

"No, I'm not, but I'm tired of laying around." It'd been a miserable couple of weeks.

Outside the supermarket was a Red Cross blood drive, collecting donations. I saw the disaster coming from a mile away, and tried to walk past the truck without making eye contact with the lady collecting donations.

"Hey guys, would you like to help some folks in need today?"

"You don't want my blood," Isabel said venomously. She tried to play it off as if it didn't bother her. She dragged her feet as

HK

she walked down the aisles of the store without her usual pep. She stopped in the beauty section and looked for a new hair brush. An episode was looming.

The treatment weakened hair follicles at the root, and while it was almost always partial loss, it sometimes never regained full thickness. I'd seen the frustration on her face as she tried to curl her hair as she had before, with less bounce and body every time. She tried to reassure me that she didn't mind, that it was easier to manage, but she was washing her hair less, and would stop me from running my fingers through it when we laid in bed.

Finally, her worst fears became a visual embodiment, in the form of a large hair clump at the bottom of the shower drain. She wept and cried as she tried to unclog it. It was the most heartbreaking thing I'd ever seen. I pleaded with her to stop, to dry off and go lay down.

"I don't want to do this anymore," she wailed, more upset than I'd ever seen her. "I don't like the way it makes me feel. I hate it. We don't even know if it's working." I questioned if she was even doing it for herself anymore.

The truth was she was right, we didn't know if it was working. She had an appointment in two weeks, the most critical one, where her doctor would decide whether or not to continue her medication. Blood tests revealed her viral loads were not dropping at the rate that they should've been.

As time went on, the possibility of unsuccessful treatment increased. If that happened, everything would be for naught, leaving us desperate for another medical breakthrough in Hep C treatment. What terrified her most was another option not ever emerging. She correlated the disease with an inability to give birth, and the thought of never reaching motherhood crushed her.

Some studies suggested transmission rates from mother to child as high as 40%. It was something we discussed often. It was her one true calling, she felt, to be a mother; her most primal need, the one thing she was destined to do.

"I know you," she continued in the shower. "I know what you do to people. You just up and leave them when it's not working. I've seen you do it so many times. Is that what you're going to do to me?"

"Of course not. Please stop. Please calm down." We were both in tears. She was near hysteria.

She was right, in that a choice had to be made if she remained sick. My career as I knew it was contingent upon not having Hepatitis, and not having a partner that put me at risk. It was a threat, becoming ill, but what weighed on me most was the risk that it bore on those I trained with. When getting ready for fights we sweat, and too literally, bled with those around us. It would have been unethical for a gym to have a competitor that was Hep positive, and it wouldn't just be the end of my career, but the end of martial arts as I knew it. I would've never been able to forgive myself, had I unknowingly gotten sick and infected someone else in the process.

The nature of the two things made them mutually exclusive. It was painfully sobering, having to choose between the goals I'd dedicated my life to, or the person from whom I drew inspiration for those goals. It was a choice between the thing I always wanted to do most, or the person I wanted most to do it with. My struggle was always internal because nobody knew what we were going through, I had no one to talk about it with.

I'd already made my decision, of course; that of Isabel vs. career, if it came down to it. When God sleeps in your bed, you don't kick Her out. I hadn't done a good job of addressing it, otherwise it wouldn't have been a concern for her. The choice was easier than many would've thought. I don't think she realized how many times I'd been at this juncture before, to go the same way every time. I was upset with myself for not having instilled the confidence in her that I should've.

"We're here for a reason," she cried. "The two of us are together for a reason. We are supposed to be." If ever there was a convincing argument for cosmic destiny, it was standing right in front of me. Everything we'd been through stiffened the belief that it was meant to be, that after wandering all this time through life, I'd finally found one concise path.

HK

Isabel gave me something no one else ever did, added a depth and color to life I'd never known. She brought out the best in me, my own magnifying glass with which I could set the world on fire if just held correctly. Isabel was my own delectable dose of sugar and spice, making everything sweeter and more savory than it really was. She was the most powerful soul I'd ever encountered, the most cognitively fruitful and physically satisfying thing I'd ever experienced. She pierced my soul, and spun me on my head.

Deep down, at the end of the day, we are what we contribute; a lens for others to look through, painting pictures for the viewer. Isabel was my "La Vie En Rose," my life through rose-colored glasses, and that was never going to change.

84.

Summer, 2012

"One year," I told Lance, pointing to the octagon below. "You'll see me there in a year." We were in Las Vegas for Fourth of July weekend, watching two of the greats; Anderson Silva and Chael Sonnen, in one of the biggest middleweight title fights in history.

It was my first live UFC event, and I was awestruck. I hadn't yet heard about TUF 17 tryouts. I didn't know how I would get to the UFC. I just knew I was close.

I'd double fisted my way through Mikey Gomez, with my yoga knee injury, and would soon be getting surgery on the torn meniscus. It was common practice to wait until after fights to repair limbs so that the promotion could cover it under insurance. We were on one last vacation before I'd have to spend a couple months recovering.

The first Combat Night delivered with a bang, and we were already planning more events. We'd conceived a vision, and began laying the groundwork to take our promotion across the state.

In the meantime, I got my meniscus repaired, in yet another surgery that would leave me bedridden for weeks. By now

I knew the routine. The recovery was worse than I thought it'd be, but I was hopeful that it'd all be worth it.

Once I could finally move around again, I got back to training people. I couldn't work out yet, but it was a nice reprieve from being pent in the house all day.

I was eventually able to walk without crutches and began to get back out on the town. We weren't planning on doing much that particular night, but Matt wanted to go out for a beer.

"Pockets?" he suggested. "Just one or two."

"I guess. I could slum it for a bit." I let myself get dragged out.

We got there, and I remembered why I didn't frequent places like this much anymore. The more I'd gotten out of Tallahassee, the less interested I became in sticking around.

We talked about our Vegas trip, and how we'd one day get out of town for good. Mid-conversation Matt saw someone he knew and went to say hi. I was left at the bar, daydreaming about the escape.

"Crack!"

I was woken by the sound of a cue ball breaking a rack on the table behind me. My mind was elsewhere. I wanted to go home. "Corona with lime please," I called to my buddy behind the bar. "We're heading out after this one. What do I owe you?"

"You know you don't owe anything. Why out so soon? It's only midnight!" In Tallahassee, there is always time for one more.

"I have a client in the morning."

He handed me my cervesa, and I squeezed the lime in it before taking my first sip.

Right as I placed my bottle back on the bar I felt a pair of cold, small hands, wet with the froth of a beer, cover my eyes from behind.

A familiar voice whispered in my ear...

"Guess who?"

HK

85

"All it takes is one bad day to reduce the sanest man to lunacy. That's how far the world is from where I am. Just one bad day. You had a bad day once. Am I right? I know I am. You had a bad day, and everything changed."

-Alan Moore

"You're staying at the Conrad Hotel in Indianapolis. If I keep this up I'm adding 'Josh Samman's secretary' to my resume," she texted as I got off the plane. She'd assumed full wifey duties, booking my flights and hotel for a quick weekend to Indianapolis. Because we hadn't gone to Boston, I was able to trade one flight for another. The UFC was holding tryouts for season 19 of *The Ultimate Fighter*, and I was accompanying two of my teammates to the tryouts, as I had Matt. Since he'd lost his bout to get on the previous season, Matt had accepted a regional fight, and stayed home to get ready for it.

The three of us sat down and made the schedule for the following week. I was going to drive to Tallahassee on Monday and fly from there to Indianapolis. Isabel was going to ride with Matt to Tallahassee on Friday, to help Stephanie with work for a week before the big doctor's appointment. We were going to share a car when Isabel got there, and she'd wanted to stay in South Florida while I was away. It would be her first time staying in our Hollywood home, alone. I asked her if she was sure that she didn't want to come to Tallahassee with me, before my flight to Indianapolis.

"I haven't felt good lately. I like it better here, and this is my home now too. I want to stay with Juice, and get used to having to be here when you're gone." She'd wanted to feel strong since the shower incident days ago. She lightened the mood. "Just don't go to Hopkins without me." I told her I wouldn't visit the sandwich spot without her. I wanted Isabel with me, but she needed to do whatever made her feel best.

Juice was getting old and slow, and every time Isabel and I left for a trip, we'd spend a good 20 minutes coddling him, wondering if this time would be our last. Instead of Isabel and I adorning him with kisses, it was me loving on the two of them. I gave them both a long embrace before leaving.

When I got to town, the first place I went was to dinner with friends. Everyone greeted me with the same question. *Where's Isabel?* I began to wonder if I shouldn't have put up more of a fight when asking her to come.

I got to Indianapolis the next day, and my suspicion of whether I should've brought her turned into certainty, as I tried to pleat my pants for the first time in longer than I could remember. I was failing miserably, and the hiss and hum of the iron as I tried to replicate her magic reminded me how much I'd grown to rely on her for everyday things.

We went to tryouts the following morning, and neither of my teammates made it. One didn't speak English well enough for American broadcast television. The other was Luis Palomino, the MMA Masters fighter from my Bellator locker room years ago. He was a natural featherweight, and was too small for the goliaths there.

There was a UFC event that night in Indianapolis that I took them to. Palomino's excitement at his first UFC was fun to watch and eased the disappointment of them not making it. I was anxious to get back to Tallahassee though, and for Isabel to be there.

I sat in the airport and waited at the gate for my plane to board. Isabel called while I was waiting.

"Hey! How were the fights?"

"They were alright. Kelvin won." The kid that beat me on TUF had fought the previous night. I always rooted for everyone from season 17 to win, especially Kelvin. It meant I didn't just shit the bed that day.

"Glory to God," she said, teasing me. She knew I thought it was silly when folks thanked God after winning, thinking He's up there, picking and choosing fist fights.

"Yeah, yeah. What are you doing?"

HK

"Watching *Ray*. Sorry, I know I was supposed to wait for you. I got a little bored." We'd bought the movie together weeks ago, at the little CD shop around the corner that she'd found.

She loved Ray Charles and was captivated by his tale. She was drawn to anyone's story whose conflicts included struggles with drugs, or needles. She liked Kurt Cobain, and Amy Winehouse, and had a natural affinity for those that died young.

I gave her a hard time for watching it without me. She promised she would bring it to Tallahassee. The flight attendant called for boarding, and I told her I had to go. As I was trying to explain, the phone cut out.

"I gotta go babe." No response on the other end. "Hello?"

Finally, I heard her voice. "Hello?"

"Hey, babe. I gotta go. I love you."

"Josh?"

"I said I love you. I'm boarding now."

"Josh?" She said again.

"I'll text you in a second."

"I can barely hear you."

I hung up in frustration. I'll never not regret hanging up.

My flight got in late that night, and I tried to call her, but she was asleep. She called me back in the morning, but then it was me that was asleep. When I woke up, she'd texted as well.

Isabel: 10:08 AM- Hey babe. I think I'm just gonna drive my car today. Matt says he wants to train and I don't wanna wait til this afternoon to leave.

Josh: 10:12 AM- You sure?

Isabel: 10:36 AM- Yeah. Plus Mitchell wants me to grab some Combat Night stuff on the way.

Josh: 10:42 AM- K. Lemme know when you leave.

Isabel: 2:30 PM- Ugh finally leaving

Josh: 2:32 PM- You waited on Matt?

Isabel: 2:35 PM- I tried. He was taking too long so I left

Josh: 2:36 PM- How you feeling?

Isabel: 2:55 PM- Tired. Ready to be there already

Josh: 2:56 PM- I'm sorry. Excited to see you.

Isabel: 2:59 PM- You too

Isabel: 4:50 PM- Fuck!

Josh: 4:50 PM- What??

Isabel: 4:51 PM- I just got a speeding ticket

Josh: 4:53 PM- You're supposed to be able to charm your way out of those things.

Isabel: 4:55 PM- He was an asshole

Josh: 4:57 PM- Shitty day, I'm sorry.

Isabel: 4:59 PM- I don't feel good at all

Isabel: 5:41 PM- What are you doing?

Josh: 6:38 PM- Laying around. How far are you?

Isabel: 6:41 PM- Three hours

Isabel: 6:41 PM- Are you going to meet me at Steph's?

Josh: 6:42 PM- Yeah of course

Isabel: 6:43 PM- :)

Isabel: 7:08 PM- [screenshot of Ray Charles Pandora station, song: "L-O-V-E" by Nat King Cole]

Josh: 7:11 PM- Aww :) They were playing it in the Atlanta airport yesterday and I thought of you

Isabel: 8:31 PM- Getting on I-10 now- meet me at 10 PM sharp!

Josh: 8:32 PM- Lol

Isabel: 8:36 PM- For real baby! I want you to be there when I get there

Josh: 8:56 PM- It's raining really hard here

Josh: 9:09 PM- What exit are you at?

Josh: 9:21 PM- Wtf

Josh: 9: 22 PM- Babe you're scaring me

86.

"Have you heard from Isabel?" I called Mitchell. He was the last person to have seen her.

"Not since she left a few hours ago. Why, what's up?"

"I'll call you back."

I got on the road, going east on I-10. I was panicking, nearing 100 MPH, as I headed towards I-75. I'd been driving for 20 minutes, calling her the whole time, before thinking to contact Florida Highway Patrol for crash reports.

"Florida Highway Patrol, how can I help you?"

"Hi, I'm looking to see if you have any reported crashes on I-10, specifically a black Honda Civic headed westbound on I-10."

A brief moment of silence, and the sound of typing on a keyboard.

"No sir, we don't currently have any accidents on I-10." I breathed a sigh of relief, reassured it was my imagination getting the best of me.

"Thank you." I hung up and turned around, headed back to Tallahassee.

I thought maybe she'd dropped her phone in a cup of water, or left it at a gas station. I was expecting to see her car in Stephanie's driveway as I pulled in. It wasn't.

My heart raced as I opened the door and rushed inside. Stephanie and Owen were sitting on the couch watching TV.

"What's wrong?" Stephanie said.

"Have you talked to Isabel?"

"Not in a while, she said she would be here around 10."

"I can't get ahold of her. I called FHP and they said there were no crashes, but she hasn't answered in a while."

"You know Isabel, she probably got sidetracked or something," Owen said, flipping through channels. I was the only one worried at the moment. Owen and Stephanie both tried calling. No answer. Worst case scenarios rushed through my mind. I did my best to quiet them. It was quarter til 10, and there wasn't much else we could do, so the three of us sat, and waited.

I was distraught by 10:30, and trudged outside to call Larry, our referee and local police officer. I wanted to see if he could contact any of the surrounding counties for accidents that may have happened off the interstate. He said he would get to the bottom of it. In the meantime, I called FHP again to see if any new reports had come in.

"Florida Highway Patrol, how can I help you?"

"Hi, I called about an hour ago. I still haven't heard back from the driver of the black Honda Civic."

"What's the driver's name?"

"Isabel Monroe."

"One moment sir."

I waited for what seemed like forever. There were muffled voices on the other end of the phone. Finally, the operator came back.

"Nothing on I-10 sir." Relief, again, though only momentarily. "I think you may want to try the other dispatch, for I-75." Something in the way she said it gave me a sharp pain in my stomach. "Please hold for transfer." Back inside I waited.

When I walked in, it was only Stephanie on the couch.

"What did they say?" She asked. I pointed at the phone, signaling I was on hold.

Finally, dispatch came back, a different one this time.

"What is your relationship to Ms. Monroe?"

Those fucking words.

The pain in my stomach grew worse, and I got dizzy.

"What do you mean what is my relation? What the fuck happened?" Any calmness I had was gone. My heart sank more with every hint.

"I don't want to panic you, but I need to know your relationship to Ms. Monroe to give you any more information."

My senses were nearing full meltdown when Stephanie's phone rang. She pointed at who was calling, and I dropped my phone in terror as she answered hers.

Cathy Monroe, Isabel's stepmom was the contact name on Stephanie's screen. Their conversation was short, and Stephanie just kept nodding, saying "okay" several times. Her demeanor gave me the last bit of comfort that I'd receive that night. Clearly something had happened, but it didn't seem catastrophic, or she would have reacted differently, I thought.

"We need to wake Owen up," she said.

"Wake up? When did he go to sleep, and what the hell did Cathy just say?"

"It's not good. We need to wake up Owen."

HK

She stood and walked up the stairs with an eerie calmness as I frantically grabbed Stephanie's phone to call Cathy back. I had never had a conversation with this woman in my life. She answered, sobbing, and chills ran down my spine.

"Cathy.." I uttered. She cried harder, trying to catch her breath.

"Oh honey, oh my God." The emotion in her voice made my life flash before my eyes. "I don't think I'm the person to tell you this."

Please, no, please, no, please, no, please.

"Something's happened." *Please, God, please God, no.* It was the only time I'd ever asked Him for anything with any conviction.

"There's been an accident," she tried again, knowing she was on the verge of delivering the news that would sink me to the depths of hell. She was sputtering and sniffling with every word. "There was an accident," she said for the last time. Her voice wailed as she got the final words out. "And Isabel didn't make it."

I screamed, a blood-curdling scream that I didn't know I had in me. I threw the phone across the room, as if separating myself from the device that gave the news would make it disappear. I ran across the room and picked it back up so she could tell me it was unreal.

"Please, no, please." My desperation verbalized as I begged for Cathy to tell me it was a misunderstanding.

"I'm so sorry Josh." She repeated herself. "I'm so sorry Josh."

I screamed again, harder than before. It was a sledgehammer to my senses. I collapsed to the floor. My ears rang sharply as if the words had driven a stake through my brain. Time slowed. I screamed so loudly and painfully I felt as if my vocal chords were going to burst. I screamed, and cried, and screamed more. It was involuntary. It was pure agony, immeasurable anguish, worse than any pain I'd ever imagined.

I laid there, crying on the kitchen floor, as Owen and Stephanie finally came downstairs. I will never forget him stepping over me as I laid curled on the tile. He didn't say a word, just walked to his car, opened the door, and sat in the driver seat with his face in his hands.

Everything in my head was immersed in a deafening silence, a ringing that took me off Earth. Time slowed worse. I was waiting to wake up at any moment.

It's not real.

I convinced myself it was another of the million Honda Civics on the road.

Not her.

I don't know how long it was before I picked myself off the floor. I kept telling myself it was a mistake, that she would pull up in the driveway any second. Alas, a pair of headlights made its way to the house.

They were accompanied by a set of sirens. I realized Larry had come to the address he had on file for Isabel. I knew why he was there. It became difficult to breathe. It was the final nail in the coffin.

Right behind him arrived Matt, in the car that Isabel should have been riding in, had we all stuck with the plan. That fact wasn't lost on anyone. I remained in the kitchen, planning on how I was going to talk Larry out of the pistol on his hip, to blow myself out of this nightmare. Owen sat outside, screaming at Matt that it wasn't his fault. *It's not your fault. It's not your fault.* He kept saying it. Matt was crying, apologizing, crying.

Anna was the last to arrive, speeding into the driveway, nearly hitting all the cars in the way. She screeched to a halt and ran straight towards me, inside.

"What is *he doing here?!*" She screamed, pointing at Matt. She cried and wailed with the same desperation I had.

"What is *he doing here without her?*" She screamed again and slapped me as hard as she could. I stood in brutal tears, just shaking my head. She kept repeating herself.

"She was *supposed* to *ride with him. Somebody fucking tell me why he's here without her.*"

I didn't know what to say. I tried to hug her. She slapped me again, and again. Finally she stilled, and we crumpled to the floor, together. The person I loved more than anything had just

HK

been taken from me, and hers too. We sat there on the cold kitchen tile, holding each other, broken, ripped apart.

I don't remember much else. Time was slow, then fast, ear piercingly loud, then quiet. It was sharp and painful, then dark and numb. Everything was not how it was supposed to be. I could write from now until the end of time and never be able to capture the despair.

It was the axis on which my whole life changed, and I knew only that things would never be the same.

87.

I woke up clutching a cold pillow instead of the warm, soft body I'd grown accustomed to. Crushed, defeated, heartbroken, shattered, destroyed; no words could ever describe what I felt as I woke up in the next morning. I continued where I left off the night before, screaming in terror, at what it was I was waking into. More than the immediate trauma of the night before, it was waking up Saturday morning that may have been the worst moment of my life. I have many of these moments from this point on, wondering which was truly the most painful.

Matt slept on the recliner next to me throughout the night. He did for several nights, and saw things no person should have to watch a friend go through. I laid on that couch for days, in a constant cycle of waking up, expecting to roll over and see Isabel's face, only to remember what had happened. I screamed and cried, and ate as many Xanax as I could swallow, before escaping back into my periodic coma away from reality. Rinse and repeat, until I lost count. I don't remember where they came from. I just remember making sure to go to sleep with them in my pocket so no one could take them from me.

Friends texted and came by. Strangers wrote letters of condolence. I wouldn't remember a thing any of them said until going back to read them, months later. I don't recall much from around this time. It was a dark and blurry whirlwind. I remember Owen and Stephanie coming in and out throughout the week to make sure I hadn't died on their couch. I vaguely remember my mom coming by, making me get off the couch for an inebriated trip to the grocery store, before forfeiting and letting me retire back to my resting place. I remember Lance bringing a bottle of Crown, with not a single word of comfort, because what could anyone really say?

The first bit of coherent memory I have was talking to one of her family members, although I couldn't say who. Wyatt, or Cathy maybe, telling me we'd all be meeting at her uncle's house to discuss funeral plans. Beth would be directing the memorial, I was told, and what an awful assignment that must have been for her.

I didn't know if it was two days after she died, three days, maybe a week. When I got the call, I didn't know the last time I'd eaten, or taken a shower, or what it was I was even sticking around for.

I made sure that I got to her uncle's house that day. It was the first place I'd taken the initiative to get up and drive to. He lived in a grand wooden cabin and had a circular group of chairs set up in the living room. I took the nearest seat that was open. Aunts, uncles, brothers, grandparents, they were all there, awaiting the details of how the dream queen had fallen.

I attempted not to stare too distantly into the next universe. I tried to focus on matching the faces of those I hadn't yet met to the stories I'd heard from Isabel about her family. *Everyone has favorites*, she used to say. Aunt Jo was one I'd heard about often, and was leading the meeting, with help from Landon's wife, Savannah, and Beth.

Isabel lost control of her vehicle in the rain, she explained, and had hydroplaned off the road into a tree. She felt it important for us to know that she was wearing her seatbelt, and tested negative for drugs and alcohol.

"What time did they police arrive at the accident?" It was the first thing I asked, and the only thing on my mind.

She looked at the papers... "8:41." I'm not sure if she realized why I was asking, or the implication an exact timeline

HK

provided. I immediately took my phone out. I should've waited. I simply couldn't. I had to know.

8:36, the last text I'd gotten from her.

This was the next passage in the *worst moment of my life* chronicles. The tragedy wasn't enough. It had to be layered with mountains of immense guilt. The powers that be had found the chink in my armor, and used it to pierce my soul to the core, not taking any pity, twisting and turning the knife in every way, until I was completely hollow.

I'd killed the thing I loved the most, the person I claimed to be my sun and moon. I'd promised her I would take care of her, and I failed, miserably. I couldn't have possibly failed any worse. I wanted to run out of the room and find the nearest tree to hang myself from. Those in the room who were paying any attention may have gathered the clues of what I'd just discovered. My face melted into my hands, and the whole world closed in around me.

Finally, Beth presented the question of who was going to speak at the funeral. Pastor Fran, whom Isabel had grown her whole life with, would speak. More were still needed to correctly celebrate her life, she said.

I waited for someone to say something, anything. All of us were shell-shocked, I'm not sure half of them even heard the question. It was the only thing I did hear, coming back from replaying the course of text messages back through my head.

"I'll do it," I said after a few moments of silence. My voice cracked as I tried to muster the courage to clear my throat and try again. "I'll speak."

The room looked around at each other, everyone waiting for someone else to give the first response. Finally, Aunt Jo spoke up.

"Okay, Josh. I think that would be good. Just send what you'd like to say to Beth and maybe she could print it out for you?" She wanted someone to vet what was being said. I didn't blame her. Anna was the only other to volunteer.

They discussed what the obituary would read, how they were to sum her up in a few short sentences. God first, mother and father, family, then lover. What a privilege, I remember thinking, to be included. Honored and mortified are two strange feelings to feel at once, for what it was we were having to do.

We wrapped up the rest of the formalities before hugging one another and going back to our own grieving places. Cathy suggested that I come visit, with just her and Dallas. Isabel's uncle and Dallas were neighbors, and I agreed to go. I wanted to, I was just terrified to have my first full conversation with the man who made Isabel. He was the one I'd made an unspoken agreement with to take care of her, and I'd let her slip through my fingers. I walked over to the house Isabel grew up in, the house I'd dropped her off at dozens of times, but was never allowed to enter.

Who Dallas was meeting at this point wasn't the man his daughter loved, or anything close. I was a shell of a human. I'd never felt so worthless and broken. I was the saddest man on Earth, I thought, and believed it, until I got there, and saw Dallas staring blankly across the kitchen. The room was dark, his hands fixed on the counter, eyes glaring at the dining room table where Cathy was sitting. She motioned for me to sit with her.

What were the details of the trip? Why didn't she ride with Matt as planned? What were some of the last things said? What were the final things she did? She asked all the questions, while he stood, still as water, gaze broken only to pick up his can of beer and take a long gulp. We all had our medicine.

I was having a hard time gathering my thoughts, let alone answering questions. I remember thinking how awful it was that this was Dallas' first impression of me. It was impossible to not feel like the bane of his existence. I told them we were texting. Cathy claimed they didn't think the accident was from that. They hadn't even gotten her phone yet, and I was being protected.

Finally, Dallas came to join us at the table. He remained quiet as he pulled out his bible. "I want to read you some words, Josh." He spoke slowly and softly, every bit the wise man I'd envisioned, just how she'd described him. He licked his fingers a bit to find the page and verse he was looking for.

I don't have a clue what he read to me. I'd pay any amount of money now to know what it was he shared at that moment. I wish so badly that I remembered, or had written down the verses.

HK

Instead, I nodded, and tried my hardest to find the right words to say back.

"I hurt like you hurt," I told him finally.

I have hundreds of regrets since August 30th, 2013, thousands of them, but of every mistake I've made since that date, this is the one I regret the most. I don't know why, but it haunts me, the memory of telling Dallas that I knew how he felt. I had no earthly idea how he felt, just like I expected no one to know how I felt. Every day I want so badly to go back and choose different words to say to him. I was only trying to convey that I, too, had lost my favorite person in the world.

She was my favorite person to do everything with. To dance with, to cook for, to cuddle with, and kiss on, to discuss ideas and plans for the future. She was my favorite person to argue with, and to be crazy about. My life felt instantly devalued, drastically. I'd the won the soulmate lottery, only to have my ticket fly out the window on I-75 on the way to cash it.

There wasn't much left to say, and I returned to Stephanie and Owen's for the final night before I felt it was time to burden someone else with the black cloud over my head. As I went to sleep, I remember being so afraid of what I'd signed up for, to speak at her funeral. I recall looking up fatal doses of alprazolam, to make sure I didn't die before completing my task at hand, to see just how far I could actually escape without teetering over the edge.

It was a tremendous responsibility. I didn't know how on Earth I was supposed to sum her up with words, without being reductive or diminishing. The undertaking was massive, but with it came objective, and objective kept me alive. If only for a few days, I again had purpose.

88.

I'd relocated to an extra bedroom in Lance's house. It was better than the couch at Stephanie's but made the mornings no less difficult. My life had been spun on its axis; my wildest dreams into worst nightmares, and I was reminded of it at the start of every day. It was the first thing I thought of as I opened my eyes, and I wondered if it would be like this forever.

My best friend, soulmate, motivation, inspiration, it all had been stolen from me, and it was time to say our final farewell. I was longing to see her once more, but now that the day had come, I was terrified. I asked Beth if she was sure it was a good idea. She told me I'd regret it if I didn't.

Isabel's mom asked if I wanted to go with her to see her daughter. We'd grow to rely on each other in the months ahead. This was just the beginning.

The funeral home was owned by a member of Dallas' family and bore the surname. We arrived at Monroe Funeral Home, and it took quite some time before I could bring myself to go inside. When we did, Beth was waiting. She warned us that Isabel wouldn't look as she did before, and that was natural. She told us to take our time.

I walked in first and saw the casket at the end of the room. It was open, but not to where I could see her from the entrance. I had to get closer. I knew what was in there. Sue was already crying behind me. I inched forward. There was a part of me that futilely told myself that it would be someone else in that casket, that this was still all a big misunderstanding.

Maybe that's why Beth said she'd look different. Maybe it's not her.

I was beginning to lose my mind.

Finally, there she was. It was her, but it wasn't. No flaring dimples, no impish grin, nothing that I remembered her by, when picturing her in my mind. She would sometimes make faces in her sleep as she dreamt, but now there was nothing.

She wore a tie-dye t-shirt and jeans, chosen by Anna, foregoing formality in the name of memorializing a teenage Isabel maybe. Gone already was the summer tan she'd earned with countless days at Hollywood Beach. Instead, she was pale gray, with more makeup than she'd ever wore while alive.

I sat in the chair next to the casket and let Sue approach first. She spoke to her daughter, in between an overflow of tears.

HK

Finally, she came back and sat down, clutching me, crying. It was my turn.

I drug myself to the casket. I don't remember if I said anything, or what I said if I did. Time went back to slow motion, the ringing in my head returned. The outside world darkened and disoriented itself, closing in and out of tunnel vision.

I touched her. It was the last time I ever would, and the idea made me want to stay there forever. I could stay until the funeral maybe, not leave her side like she hadn't mine in the hospital. I put my hands on hers. They were just as cold as they were that night at Pockets, where this whole thing started again. I asked Sue and Beth for a moment alone. They stepped out, and the barrage of tears really began.

How did we get here? What did we do to deserve this?

I was still thinking *we*. There was no more Josh and Isabel. No more we. It was me, and only me.

I put my hands on her face and ran my fingers through her hair one last time. I gave her a kiss on the forehead, and a final one on cold, hard lips. There was no warmth or passion to them, nothing that embodied the person who'd once been on the other side. This was truly the stuff nightmares were made of.

I wanted out of my body. I wanted so badly to not be there, to be wherever it was she'd gone. The best I could do was leave the room. I did, and Beth told me I could come back later in the day if I needed to.

I wouldn't be going back. I went to the local tattoo parlor and had my childhood friend from Christian summer camp tattoo her initials on my ribcage, right below my heart. If I did make it through this, I wanted a scar to show for it. More than anything, I wanted to remember how strongly I felt, how passionate she made me, as the realization that every day was a step further away from that. Sue joined me, and got a replica of Isabel's *Believe* tattoo on her wrist. We were all doing what we could to survive.

I retreated back to Lance's house to prepare for the memorial the following day. I'd already sedated myself before getting tattooed earlier, and was in the process of dosing back into comatose when I realized Isabel hadn't packed me anything to wear to her own funeral.

Is this real?

I stumbled back to my car to drive to the mall before Lance stopped me.

"Where you going, cowboy?"

"I gotta go. Clothes." I slurred as I talked, pointing at an invisible jacket. I was beyond coherence. He knew what I meant, or would gather it soon.

"Give me a second. We'll load up." I had no argue in me, every word was exhausting.

We got to the mall, and I wandered aimlessly. I was in a daze, successfully forgetting what it was I was there for. Lance dragged me through it. I felt like I was getting pulled around by everyone at this time, holding my hand through these steps as I rendered myself useless.

I guess I'd felt it appropriate to pick out a black suit, shirt, and tie, because I remember feeling very out of place when we arrived at the funeral home the next day. I saw the family outside waiting, dressed in khakis and sports coats, with white shirts, and dark Costa sunglasses.

Nice Johnny Cash impression, asshole.

I looked down at my odometer before getting out of the car. 200,000 miles, on the dot, and of course it was. Everything was a cruel joke at this point.

We'd be traveling as a group from the funeral home to the burial site. Once everyone arrived, the immediate family got in the arranged limousines, while some of them walked to their cars to drive themselves. I didn't know what to do. Matt and I walked towards my car to drive on our own.

"Josh, you guys are riding with them," Beth said, pointing to the vehicle holding Owen, Stephanie, Wyatt, and his fiancée.

"I.. Uhh.. Are you sure?"

"*Get in the car, Josh.*" She was trying to be polite. The tone in her voice said "For fuck's sake, today isn't easy on me either. Please don't make this harder."

H'K

We got in with the four of them and began the drive towards the cemetery. Owen and Stephanie had gone to the scene of the accident the day prior, to go through the wreckage for anything worth keeping. I don't know how they did it.

Stephanie handed me Isabel's phone. If they'd had it, they knew what I knew, that I was the last person to talk to her, and at what time. It was eating me alive, thinking I may have been the only person to know what happened. I wanted to bring it up somehow, to tell them why I felt so guilty. I wondered who else knew, who was keeping it, or sharing it, with each other.

Wyatt and Owen were both silent for the ride. Wyatt had gotten engaged and lost his sister within the same 48 hours. Owen had his own demons. The drive was short, and within a few minutes, we arrived at a large tent pitched over a gravesite.

We got out and walked towards the rows of chairs set up in front of a large hole dug for the coffin. A feeling of horror washed over me as we got closer, and I realized the casket was still in the hearse. We'd been told that it would be ready to be set into the ground, that none of us would have the burden of carrying her there.

One by one, all of us recognized what had happened, and what we had to do. I grabbed one side with Matt and Isabel's cousin while the brothers lifted the other. It was so much heavier than I thought it'd be. I looked at Matt, realizing he'd gone from being the best man in our wedding to a pallbearer at her funeral. I felt nauseous. This was not how it was supposed to be.

We placed the coffin on the crank-operated shaft that would lower her. I took a seat at the end and closed out the world around me, as I tried my best to hold the vomit in the pit of my stomach.

Don't throw up right now. Do not fucking throw up.

I failed, and my mouth filled with the acidic bile that had been waiting for the worst imaginable time to come out. I swallowed it, and tried to fight the sensation of it moving its way back upward. I threw up again, and gulped down one last time before it came back up immediately. I spit it on the ground next to me as quietly as I could.

I'd never been more mortified in my life. I remember thinking what a foul, vile person her family must have thought I was, sitting here at their daughter's burial, spitting on the ground of a cemetery. It still makes me sick, thinking of it now.

One of Isabel's closest friends from church played a hymn on his guitar as I tried to slow the spinning in my head. I wondered how he had such poise and composure. Further and further I slipped.

If I had any more of the old Josh Samman in me, this was the moment he withered and died. Gone was confidence and charisma. I'd been replaced by something else. I didn't know what I'd become, but it was hideous.

89.

"I carry death in my left pocket. Sometimes I take it out and talk to it: "Hello, baby, how you doing? When you coming for me? I'll be ready."

-Charles Bukowski

I was headed northbound on I-75. It was raining, and I was checking each mile marker, looking for 431. I hadn't yet found the crash site, but I had plans for when I did. Up and up the numbers went. 429...

Faster.

430...

You're not going fast enough, Josh.

431. Finally, I found it. I steered off the road and aimed for the tree with the black Honda Civic wreckage around it. I floated through the air towards the impact zone.

This was easier than I thought.

I woke up, naked, in a pile of my own vomit. The sheets had been torn off the bed, remnants of a broken liquor bottle on the ground. Pills were strewn about the room. There was a pistol on the pillow next to me.

HK

This won't hurt a bit.

I could feel my mental health deteriorating rapidly. The feeling of wanting to die wasn't subsiding. It was getting stronger. Sleep had once held the capacity to remove me from the immediate realm, but I was no longer able to escape into slumber. She'd learned to follow me there.

Just let her come back.

I bargained in my dreams.

I don't care about getting sick.

Taking a person and traumatizing the shit out of them can make them act strangely. I just wanted to know when the fucking crying was going to stop. I couldn't close my eyes without seeing her smile burning the back of my eyelids. I was scared to shut them, scared of my own thoughts. I couldn't discern between sleep and wake. Night terrors and reality mixed, blurred, melted into one another.

You killed the one you claimed to love most.

I was beginning to have hallucinations, visual and auditory. The face of every girl I saw melted into Isabel's, memories too. *Come closer,* I could still hear her say, *cuddle up.* I had visions of her on her tippy toes, arms draped around my neck. *You'll miss these kisses,* she whispers.

How did she know? How could she have known?

She would wake me with a phone call in my dreams before visiting. The number on the caller ID dictated which *her* I got. 509-5243 meant I got Izzi, feigning innocence, telling me how she felt only when no one was watching. She was out of reach, distant, toying with me. I ask her if it's real this time or just another dream. *What do you think?* She says, over a table of wasabi and sake.

Oh, I remember this one.

No, it's not real, but in my mind, I choose to believe it's genuine. If only one last time.

I can't believe this happened to us.

933-2189 meant I got Isabel, my Isabel. She was calling, asking what I was still doing here, why I hadn't done the things I promised I'd do, and just come home already. Cross your t's and dot your i's she tells me, stop wasting your time down there. Get it over with. Do what you're going to do and come home already.

There's no one waiting for you. You know better.

It was bizarre, the feeling of wanting it to all be over. It felt like the end of a long evening, wanting to just go to sleep and call it a night. My eyelids were heavy. I was delirious and vacant. Nothing mattered. I readied myself for the end, with the notion that my life had run its course.

What else is there to do?

Eulogy done. I'd said my words, and now it was over. I was barely alive anyway, the closest a soul could be to dead while still breathing. I was present only physically. My mind was elsewhere, itemizing all the ways it went wrong. Every waking moment was spent retracing the steps, a systematic calculation of each detail that could have gone differently. It consumed me, drove me insane. From the moment I woke, to the moment I went to sleep, the collective of my mistakes was the demon in my brain; picking, eating.

You're a shit person.

I felt like a detriment to those around me. The person I was, everything I'd become, all sane and rational thought had come to a swift end.

You're a careless, selfish, destructive shit of a person. You always have been.

I was disgusted. I hated looking in the mirror, or even passing by them. My self-loathing was comforted only by the feeling that I wouldn't be here much longer.

They were right about you. Everyone who said they had a bad feeling about you was right.

Appetite, inhibition, sleep function, decision making, everything was haywire. Reality was setting in, and I wanted to separate myself from it.

You did this, you fuck. Stop feeling sorry for yourself.

I was tortured, day and night, as my mind tried to make sense of the chaos. Thoughts of her in our earlier life, memories of her in our last throws, dreams of her being pregnant with our child. I had a recurring one, of me telling her the big

HK

misunderstanding, where we all thought she'd been in an accident.

It's all over.

I would leave Lance's for nights like these, and check into a hotel.

This is the end.

I don't remember where I got the pistol. Most mornings I woke up next to it I couldn't remember how close I'd gotten the night before. Some nights I did remember. I remember not being afraid. I remember dry firing into my temple, or pressing the cold steel against my forehead, trying to conceptualize my pain being gone in a single click. I was comforted by the availability of it.

Just do it, bitch.

Some nights the last thing I remember before dozing off is swallowing a cocktail of opiates and benzos. I was playing my own game of Russian Roulette, walking a fine line in the name of plausible deniability, should I drift off into a sleep I didn't wake from.

Plausible deniability.. That's the ticket.

I ate a few extra Vicodin for good measure before drifting into another nightmared sleep. Nice and numb, nice and numb. This won't hurt a bit.

90.

"Death steals everything but our stories."

-Jim Harrison

It came and went in waves. I'd given up and regained hope a dozen times over. I stayed heavily medicated, and journaled about what was happening as I did. Earth had turned into a desolate place, just a dustbowl to wander. I was on the brink and wanted to provide some sort of explanation as to what had happened if one of these things did roll in and kill me. I wrote, and wrote, and wrote. It started with her eulogy and never stopped.

I shared portions of things I'd put on paper. Some with just friends and family, some with the world. I wondered if what they were reading would be the last thing I'd ever write. It was raw, unpolished, and often repetitive, but if there were words to come out, it gave me temporary reprieve.

It was in this stage of the process that I started to actually remember what folks were saying to me. Much of it was just noise, but to this day, my feelings towards the people in my life are often based on these very conversations, when I was in such a dark place, when words were at the height of their importance.

Most of what everyone said was infuriating, but that was only because I was furious with everything. I had illogical rage, with myself, with my friends, with people that were moving on with their lives, being alive when she wasn't. I was angry with her for leaving me. My grief was evolving.

Some folks commented on the fragility of life. I wanted to bicker with them. Life isn't fragile. Life is resilient. Death is irreparable, the finality of it just gives life the facade of fragility.

She's still with you, some insisted. No, no. She was in a box on North Highway 27. I know, because I put her there. *What doesn't kill you makes you stronger*, they said. All around the world, people encounter things every day that make them less of a person than they were before. I rejected any bit of comfort or reasoning anyone tried to offer.

People told me I made them not take their lover for granted, as if I did. My situation reminded them to appreciate what they had. I'd never needed that reminder, not once. I knew what I had when I had it. It was the only thing I was ever sure of.

Many people told me to call them if ever I needed to talk. All but few kept that promise. Once things got heavy, people stopped answering their phones. That's why people pay grief counselors, I suppose.

Folks asked me the same question I'd heard the last eight years. *When's the next fight?* with an occasional *I'd sure hate to be that guy.* I felt as if I could barely keep my head above water, and they were asking when I was going to swim the Atlantic.

HK

It was many people's way of looking for an indication that I was ready to resume normal life, that I was willing to go back to old Josh. I wasn't ready, and I wasn't sure we'd ever be seeing old Josh again. It irked and confused me to no end that that's what people seemed to care about most. *When are you going to go psycho on some poor guy in a cage?* I knew the next fight would be an emotional and violent one. I could feel the rage, fucking and growing inside of me. I still had no idea how after I'd just dismantled my life and the lives of several others, that that's what people wanted to see; me destroy more shit.

There were few, who asked *if* I was going to fight again, rather than *when*. That was the more appropriate question. Gerard from TUF asked, and didn't tiptoe around other subjects either.

"Have you thought about killing yourself?" There was something grossly refreshing about the matter of factness in which someone finally asked that. I told him I had, and he shared a story of his uncle, who walked face first into an oncoming train. He'd become sick, he explained, and could no longer handle the effects of the treatment he was undergoing. The condition he was treating was Hepatitis C.

He hadn't known about Isabel being sick. I told him everything. He explained some members of his family never recovered from his uncle's death. He said we have a choice in which direction we move after tragedy and that the next few months would be important. "Have you watched The Fountain yet?" He asked. I couldn't even listen to the damn soundtrack. "One day," I told him.

Some of the advice was helpful. Chael reached out and gave me words about the path of defeat, and how time moves in only one direction. I remember my conversation with Theresa too, and the effect it had on me. "You have to live on for her, in the way she would want you to. You have to think of the things she loved most in you, and you have to do them for the rest of your life." I tried to look past my self-contempt, to remember what it was Isabel loved in me in the first place.

She liked when I was a gentleman, when I opened doors for people and tipped waitresses well. She liked when I wore my hair long, and when I played guitar. She liked when I gave to charities through Combat Night. She liked when I told stories about my past, when I was ambitious, and had goals to work towards. She liked when I recycled, and cleaned up after others that littered.

She liked when I was opinionated. She liked when I wasn't judgmental of people, as I had a habit of doing. That may have been why she loved me, because I didn't judge her. She liked when I went out of my way to help others, and when I told people "I love you." *You can never say that too much,* she'd say. Big things, small things, I remembered it all.

I often thought of her sentiments on being pitied, and how it applied to me now. When she was struggling, folks were always patting her on the back. She loathed it, and I was reminded of it several times a day. That was all anyone seemed to want to do, pat my back like I was a fucking dog.

It wasn't just the back pats. Everything reminded me of her. The triggers were endless, and I had to become calloused to them one by one. Every song on the radio corresponded with an image of her singing it. Black Honda Civics became the only car I saw on the road. Tire commercials made me want to throw my remote through the television. Beers we liked, dishes we loved, movies we watched, everything from my past life became something to avoid. It wasn't just the only thing on my mind, it was on the minds of everyone around me. Maybe my transparency was the reason they felt the need to address it, always asking how I was doing.

How does it look like I'm doing?

I grieved publicly, a lot, and used social media as a blog to share things about her, about us. I didn't know how to reach out effectively otherwise. It was unhealthy, having the same medium through which I was grieving also be the place where thousands of pictures and memories were housed. Everything was main-lined, streaming and cycling through itself.

HK

It was such a stark contrast to the way most of her family were dealing with the loss. They kept their feelings so private. It pained me each time I shared, thinking it may be causing someone else agony. It made me feel like I'd hijacked the grief train, like I thought I was the only one in pain. I just dealt with it differently. Sharing things about her was a strange little flame, the only one I had to keep me alive, and I couldn't let it go out.

Beth and I were at lunch, one of the few we had over the course of weeks. She needed to talk to me about something, she said. I was expecting her to tell me it was time to shut the fuck up about all of this. *That's enough. Time to be quiet. Stop picking the scab, you selfish prick.* I always thought it would be coming from someone sooner or later.

I always felt bad for Beth and the things that I'd put her through. I knew it was her that felt sorry for me now. I felt like it was just one more shitty chapter in her Josh Saga.

She was one of the only ones that would always answer her phone. She was kind to me, and admitted that this task had been the most difficult of her career. All of us were struggling to find any semblance of a silver lining.

"Have you thought about putting anything you've written into a larger body of work?" Her lunch wasn't to tell me to shut up. It was the opposite.

"What do you mean?"

"I mean that if you're comfortable sharing this stuff, then you should probably think about writing a memoir. I think it could be helpful to others."

"I don't think I'm in any position to help anyone. And I've got no ending."

"I'm confident you'll find one."

There was something about her insistence, her deliberation, her seriousness, that touched me. It felt like Isabel, urging me to go to *The Ultimate Fighter*. It was Isabel, in my mind. She was just speaking through Beth.

"I don't know that I can tell this story without divulging things people don't want revealed."

"I think you'd be surprised. I feel strongly about this."

I went home with a million more questions and objections in my mind that I wished I'd thought of at lunch.

Was this rational? Is any love rational? Was she really the most glorious thing ever, or was it just in my mind? Did that even matter? Did I owe it to her? Did I want to dig this deep, to immerse myself in this story for years to come? What would *she* want?

It felt like such a monumental endeavor, in the same vein as speaking at her funeral. It was impossible to fully capture and convey the beauty and complexity that was her, but I decided it would add to tragedy not to try. If the Shah of India could build the Taj Mahal, and Van Gogh could cut his ear off, the least I could do was try to write some words about a girl.

I had wind in my sails again. It wasn't much, and it was in a very different direction than I was sailing a month earlier, but I was still sailing.

91.

"You are beautiful, but you are empty," he went on. "One could not die for you. To be sure, an ordinary passerby would think that my rose looked just like you - the rose that belongs to me. But in herself alone she is more important than all the hundreds of other roses: because it is she that I have watered; because it is she that I have put under the glass globe; because it is she that I have sheltered behind the screen; because it is for her that I have killed the caterpillars (except the two or three that we saved to become butterflies); because it is she that I have listened to, when she grumbled, or boasted, or ever sometimes when she said nothing. Because she is my rose. And now here is my secret, a very simple secret: It is only with the heart that one can see rightly; what is essential is invisible to the eye." "What is essential is invisible to the eye," the little prince repeated, so that he would be sure to remember.

-Antoine de Saint-Exupery

Talking and spending time with Isabel's family became my favorite thing to do. I loved learning about where she came from, seeing a piece of her in all of them. "You stick around as long as

HK

you need to," Cathy told me. *As long as you need to* told me I was on a timeline. They were patient with me, and forgiving. They had a damaged person clinging to them for any last shred of Isabel that I could find. We all get things we don't ask for.

There were so many of them, all with their own special memories of her. They were the most remarkable group of people I'd ever met. I could see a piece of her in all of them. I saw how she was shaped to be the person she was, and why the acceptance and validation of her family was so important.

Sue Monroe was a spitting image of her daughter. They moved the same, scurried with the same cute stride as they walked. They said the same things, the product of a lifetime of Isabel stealing her mother's quips and quotes. They hugged the same, and latched onto arms with the same affectionate touch.

Sue lived right down the road from the gravesite and had to drive past it every time she went to and from work. We visited it together often. We'd go there, and she'd ask questions for hours about Isabel, about us, and I did the same.

I relied on Sue for so many things. To see glimpses of Isabel when I needed her, to answer late night calls and texts because I did the same for her. I relied on her to see Isabel as a young woman, as I did.

She invited me over often, wanting someone to go through Isabel's journals with. I didn't know what to think of it, or why she did it, but I knew I wanted every last morsel of Isabel that was left around, and would take it however it came. I broke my promise to Isabel about never reading her diaries.

There were no dark secrets I hadn't known about, nothing I hadn't heard. Instead, it was books full of art I'd never even known she was capable of. Volumes and chapters lined the pages, filled with even more reasons to fall in love with her. Short stories, sketches, and poems, about everything. About her brothers, about her drug use, about lust, and self-reflection. She was powerful, far beyond her years in mind and soul.

Besides Sue, I relied heavily on Cathy. She reached out often, and was instrumental in keeping me connected to the Monroes. She made sure to invite me to family functions, and served as a buffer between Dallas and I. He and I never knew what to say to each other. She answered her fair share of late night phone calls too, and left me with a bit of wisdom each time we spoke. It had to have been difficult for her, having to console the two saddest men on Earth. She did it with grace.

Cathy made sure to get me a locket of Isabel's hair, and I wanted to do something special with it, something besides having it sit in a dresser drawer with countless other relics. Isabel's hair was something so special to her. No one had seen her cry as I had, as she lost it in the shower, or tried to hold herself together as she brushed it.

I read of a practice in which kings made jewelry of their queens' and princesses' hair, like the opening scene in The Fountain. I found a jeweler that specialized in it. I took the locket Cathy gave me and made a ring for Dallas, one for myself, and an amulet for Sue.

Sue told me it was the best gift anyone had ever given her. The ring became my most prized possession, too. It was my talisman, my proof of having once been in love and being loved in return. It was the most acceptable manner in which I could still carry a piece of her with me.

To most of them, she was still with us anyway. When folks dreamt about her, they took it as her visiting them. They saw butterflies, birds, and sunsets, felt gusts of wind, and swore it was her. Cathy and I talked about religion, and I told her I was an atheist. She suggested I switch that word to Agnostic if I wanted any sympathy from a family of Southern Baptists.

Tragedy, as I was learning, was a bleak time to be an atheist. We were all accepting of each other's beliefs, but the implications were enormous if fundamental; them thinking that she's up in heaven, and I'd be going to burn in hell.

I wished that I could've believed how they believed. What bliss it must've been, imagining being able to see her again, and what comfort it would've brought, knowing there's a grand order and plan for everything; not random, cruel, chaos. I listened to all the scripture and bible verses and advice that any of them had. I wanted so badly to believe. Thinking everything happened for a

HK

reason was so challenging for me. I couldn't wrap my brain around believing that what had happened could be constructed into anything better than her being here.

I battled my own notions of natural selection, that partner choosing was part of evolution, and that she'd chosen a terrible one. I began to assess our lives thus far, wondered how many times we'd both put ourselves in harm's way. I wrestled with Isabel being on borrowed time already. What was our life expectancy anyway? My life hadn't been any safer. *Why not me?*

I grew close again to my hometown, and the people in it. I'd been holing myself up in Tallahassee, still at Lance's. Leaving Tallahassee meant leaving my support system, and my comfort zone. Leaving Tallahassee meant leaving her there. Leaving town meant going home to her stuff, *our* stuff. Going home felt like putting the casket in the grave felt, another symbol of finality. I felt like a coward the longer I waited, and I let it eat at me until I could no longer stand it.

I had to do one last thing before leaving town. I had to talk to Landon. We both knew it. At this point, I'd stopped being so sedated around her family so that I could remember our interactions, and this was one I wanted to remember. I was sober, shaking with nervousness as I drove to his house. His approval was important, but more than anything I just wanted him to tell me what he really thought of me.

I expected resentment, because how could I not? Someone had to be held accountable for all of this, and I was convinced we'd agreed I was the one to fill that role. With each and every family member, I expected resentment, and with each, I felt none.

Landon greeted me warmly, with a hug and a smile, and invited me on his back porch. He was a much bigger part of my life than I was his, and may have been realized it lately. I knew the feeling, being looked up to without being entirely comfortable with it.

We sat and exchanged stories. He addressed earlier times in our life and joked about my lack of approachability. He told me anecdotes of their family growing up, that only he remembered. He told me stories of how Isabel would hide as a child, getting the boys worried sick, before revealing herself and telling them to stop crying because she was okay. We all had our memories turned into nightmares, it seemed.

He explained that while all the grandparents had a hand in raising them, Dallas' parents were the ones to drive home that everything happens for a reason. Landon knew I didn't believe in that. He admitted that sometimes he wondered, too. I wanted to tell him it was okay to not believe, but I just kept listening.

He told me I'd find another. He was the first person to have brought it up. We both cried when he said that. The notion that there was one person for all of us was an illogical one, but one I subscribed to. I'd have liked to think that he, of all people, knew what it was like for his heart to beat only for one.

His eyes teared as he spoke. He had Sue's eyes, the only other one in the family whose weren't dark and piercing. He told me that life would never be the same, but that things would eventually normalize, and I'd find a new level of that word, normalcy.

He stopped himself midway, wondering aloud to himself if he was the one to be giving me advice. He didn't know what it meant to me. He was the one I truly needed it from.

"I have a good feeling about you," he said. "And I think a lot of us do. That church wasn't just full of our people, they were there for you too. Our people are your people. You are our family now." He told me what I needed to hear, and it was the last thing I'd do in Tallahassee before leaving. It was time to face the music.

92.

"What the hell are you doing there?" Gerard asked. The date was October 30th, exactly a year after I was celebrating my first Ultimate Fighter victory in Vegas.

Trying to turn back time.

"I had to see." I'd sent him a picture of the wreckage. There was still some there. I was at the crash site, trying to visualize where it all went wrong. Up until then, I'd constructed it only in

HK

my mind, based on what Owen had told me. I was standing right in front of the tree. That was my crash site as much as it was hers. That was the place I died too.

Fuck that tree. I wanted to cut it down, burn it, find the person who planted it and curse their existence. I never realized how many miles of guardrails there were on the interstate until my world was turned upside down by a lack of one. It was a matter of inches to safety, fucking *inches*, and it was one more thing to drive me insane.

It was horrifically ironic, the culmination of things that killed her. It wasn't the Hepatitis. It wasn't the drug overdose. It was things she was drawn to that were her demise. Trees were symbolic of life to her. She wore the one on her bracelet from Venice Beach, from the day I bought it for her, until the day she died. She loved the rain. She embraced it. And she was always texting me, telling me things on her wandering mind. Together, the three of us were her downfall.

The tragic irony was everywhere, like the pieces of her car around me. The last place Sue wanted to eat lunch before I left town was Hopkins. On the way to the crash site, I'd bought Isabel a bouquet of roses to lay. "Must be a lucky girl," the lady at the register said as I was checking out. I couldn't even answer her.

One of our friends was an inspector for Department of Transportation and had told the state, months before the accident, that the area where she crashed was problematic. I was so angry with her for even letting me know that. Everything piled atop one another until my insides collapsed.

The rest of the way home was awful. Driving in itself became an arduous task. I had four more hours before I'd be home. Many times I'd let go of the wheel, veering off the road a bit, hitting the gas. I don't know what I was doing. I was playing Russian roulette again, trying to wrap my mind around what her last thoughts may have been.

I got home and sat in the driveway for over 20 minutes before dragging myself in the house. It felt like a negative magnet, pushing me away as I tried to muster the strength to walk in. When I finally did, memories overwhelmed me.

Everything was exactly as she had left it. I tiptoed through the house, as to not disturb a single speck of dust. At the entrance was a pair of her tiny red Indian shoes, she called them. In the fridge, the single coconut water she'd promised to leave me. In the DVD player, the copy of *Ray* that she'd forgotten.

I moved into the bedroom. Recently hung pictures of us decorated the walls and dressers everywhere. The bed was perfectly made, her laundry still on the couch, and a bottle of hot sauce on the dresser that she'd bought for us but forgot to bring. Her clothes dominated the dresser, bathing suit drawer still slightly open. The ironing board was left out, as if she couldn't wait one more moment, gotten fed up mid-pleat while waiting for Matt, and left for Tallahassee.

Senses sent my emotions into overdrive as I opened the bathroom door and became flooded with the scent of her shampoos, lotions, and bath gels; all those fragrances that companies made sure to douse their products in to make sure shmucks like me never forgot the girl who wore it. Her thin pink robe still hung on the bathroom door.

I sat carefully on the edge of the couch and cried. I felt the urgency to preserve everything exactly the way she left it, knowing it was among the last things she did on her final day. Any time I unfolded something, or moved a bit of her jewelry back into her box, or lit a candle she had left, it was as if I felt a piece of her melting away with it.

Her clothes still hung in the closet. Weeks later, a friend would ask why I still had them there. I was so hurt at the question. "That's her closet too," I said, without thinking. It begged the question, of if the deceased could own things. I supposed they could, as I still felt like I belonged to Isabel. I wondered if there would ever be a time when I didn't feel like that.

I went through the series of night terrors again; sleeping in our bed brought them all back. For weeks, I tried and couldn't do it, sleeping on the couch instead. I woke up countless times, tossing and turning, drenched in sweat. Many nights resembled the ones I had in the hotel room in Tallahassee.

HK

When I finally began sleeping in the bed again, I couldn't bring myself to even lay on her side. I didn't even face it. I could still smell her there. I left her half of the bed untouched, pillows and all. I realized it was the pillow talk I missed the most, the feeling of having the world in between my arms, telling her things I'd never told anyone. If ever I was dreaming of her and woke up, I would lay there for hours with my eyes closed, trying to recreate whatever world I was just in.

Juice spent much of his time in the bathroom. I think he missed her scents, too. It was there that I struggled most, because it was there that the most morbid took root. Under the sink was a hazardous waste basket for discarded interferon needles. In the shower was her hair, all collected at my feet, waiting for me. I was paralyzed by it.

I thought this moment would pass, that I would be able to kneel down and clean it up one day soon. I had about as much of a chance of reaching down there as I did taking the pictures off the wall, or removing her clothes. It was the most confusing thing I'd ever gone through. I'd always thought I was a strong person, but there I was, haunted by a clump of hair at the bottom of a shower.

93.

It was December, nearing Isabel's birthday, and I did not want to spend it alone. It wasn't long before I was on my way back to Tallahassee. For all my apprehensiveness about going to our house, I had just as much difficulty leaving it.

Cathy had invited me to join them for the day. When I got there, it was only her, Sue, and Aunt Jo. They lit candles, and sang happy birthday, and it was the most depressing scene I've ever been a part of.

My life had split into two worlds; the one I was living in, and the parallel universe I desired, the one where she still makes it to Tallahassee that day. Particularly painful were times when I would ponder what we'd be doing, only to have no doubt. Combat Nights became insufferable, times when I would know details, down to the very place she'd be sitting, right next to me. Never was her loss more present than in the company of Mitchell and Brandi, and our relationships suffered because of it. All of mine did. The tribulations of the time did not make me closer with the people around me, it was the opposite. I had jealousy, disdain, resentment, all sorts of negative feelings, directed everywhere.

Being around couples was worst of all. There was a succession of our friends getting married and babies being born, and I found it impossible to not be loathsome towards those who still had their lovers. Every display of affection was another stab to the heart; every kiss, every stroke of hair, every embrace. There were boiling points where I just could not take it anymore and I would go to my car, to scream and cry.

I didn't feel like socializing, I didn't feel like being in crowds, and most of all I didn't feel like being with anyone else. I had zero energy to pursue women, and I didn't have to. Girls threw themselves at me, in attempts at being the one to bring me out of my funk. I slept with many to satisfy physical needs. I would sometimes wake up, and not remember who I was in bed with. Many times I left them in the middle of the night. I never brought girls to our home. I suffered from episodes of crippling guilt. I'd never been a forgiving person, and that character flaw extended to self-forgiveness as well.

I didn't want people to think I was moving on already. I didn't think I deserved to. A girl I met out one night asked me if I had a girlfriend. "It's complicated," I told her. "Oh, one of those guys, huh?" "No. She's just dead." I realized how crazy I sounded. I tried to convince myself that it was a noble thing to be committed to one person my whole life, no matter the circumstances. I gave feeble attempts at dating. None were fruitful. They were all the same. They were all not Isabel.

I didn't want to be responsible for anyone again. I wasn't equipped to. I was emotionally bankrupt. I didn't want to care for someone again. I wasn't just grieving the loss of Isabel, but the loss of my old self. Grief intertwined my every aspect of being, taking root and leaving nothing untouched. My attention span became weak, my irritability through the roof. It was a ball and chain that

HK

dragged me down everywhere I went, and I saw myself no different than the countless weak people I'd exiled from my life.

I felt old. When I looked back, I could see the moment that my youth ended. I could look at pictures of myself and could tell in an instant whether it was before or after August 30, 2013. I drove around Tallahassee, relishing in nostalgia.

I visited Isabel almost daily. I contributed towards her gravestone, the last birthday present I may ever be able to purchase for her. It adorned a picture of her face, on a bronze plate, the same photo used for her funeral programs. Beside that, an image of a beach photo that she'd taken near our house. The base of the plate was lined with bible verses that Dallas had chosen.

I played music for her on my phone and talked to her about things I was struggling with. It was the only place I felt remotely whole. Sometimes the Florida fire ants would bite me as I sat with her. They came from where she laid though, and may have been down there with her, before coming up to nip at my ankles and calves, so I let them bite as they pleased.

It occurred to me a strange comfort as I sat there one day, a revelation if it could be called that. I realized that a successful relationship could be defined by one thing, and that thing may be *until death do us part*. On a long enough timeline, someone has to pass away first. Part of me was jealous of her having the easy way out, leaving me here suffering. Part of me was glad that it wasn't her left here in pain. I wondered how she'd have handled it, had it been the other way around. Probably with the same fortitude and determination she'd had her whole life. It was bizarre, and morbid, and boggling, but I took a comfort in knowing that we had plans to spend the rest of our days together, and that's what she got to do.

94.

"Words are the weight that hold histories in place."
-Beth Kephart

I began to heal, one breakthrough at a time. I was learning to compartmentalize, on an enormous scale, but it was a step in the right direction. More importantly, I was becoming able to use different outlets to express myself, when I didn't feel like hiding.

I kept writing, as Beth encouraged. I didn't want Isabel's story to just boil down to a *don't text and drive* ad. I wrote small things, and long. I wrote about recent times, and old. I dug deep, to memories I didn't know I still had; repressed resentment, rejection, bitterness, things I swore I'd never think about again.

I wrote to make sense of death. I wrote to immortalize her. I wrote because I could feel her as I did. It was love, still radiating out of Isabel, if I tracked it to the source. I navigated grief, mapped through it with painstaking detail.

I harbored a great cognitive dissonance regarding the need in which I had to tell our story, and how certain loved ones would feel about her tale being told. I was still waiting for them to tell me to shut up. I tried to be quiet. The frequency of my internet sharings subsided. I focused more on the words you're reading now. I realized I had to tell a lot of stories that didn't have anything to do with Isabel, in order to properly convey just how much she changed me. I had to put things into context as to what was at stake. At times, I wondered if I should even be doing it, exposing myself to glorify her.

I had a recurring dream where Cathy would call me and tell me they found her, that she was still alive. In my dream, she'd relapsed and forgotten about us, and I had to write a book as a love letter to remind her. I would wake up in the middle of the night and type as fast as my fingers could move.

I'm writing. I'm writing, Isabel. I'll get it done. I swear.

I picked back up my guitar. *Play for me,* she'd whisper, nodding towards the instrument in its stand. I wish I would have more. Now there was only Juice to play for. He would look at me and wag his tail and smile, and I would close my eyes and pretend she was in the room with us.

I wrote songs, and learned to play others'. I practiced things I hadn't in over a decade. Music was a way for me to make something constructive out of being a drunk. It didn't matter if it was good or not, I could worry about that later. I felt the catharsis I got from it earlier in life, and I wondered why I ever stopped in the first place. I needed every tool at my disposal to get the empty feeling out of me. As long as I was expressing, I was surviving.

For all the instant and delayed gratification that writing provided, there was still a hollow desperation in it. Part of me was terrified that I was already delegated to telling stories about the glory days, at 25 years old. I wanted to be in the phase of my life where I was getting married and starting a family, not staring into a computer, reminiscing about nostalgic memories of what could have been.

My pivotal turning point came at the expense of another. I was at a bar, and had a bumbling drunk stumble into me, and pat me on the back. I'd known him most my life, and never particularly liked him. He was six inches from my face, slurring his words, spitting as he talked, and spilling his drink on me. I felt my temper flaring, anxiety rising, and I got up to leave. He asked me to wait. He was trying to explain to me that I was an inspiration to him, how he wished he'd done more with his life.

I couldn't name one thing the guy had ever accomplished. I was aggravated that he used my tragedy, or hard work, or whatever the hell it was he was even referring to, as a drunk talking point. I was frustrated that he was a talker and not a doer. I wondered what the point was to proclaim inspiration by something or someone and not act on it. Motivation is empty, without action.

I told Matt about the incident.

"Aw, give the kid a break," he said. "You ain't never had anyone inspire you?"

The question baffled me. It infuriated me. Had he not been paying attention this whole time? How could he be such a fool, to ask me if I'd ever been inspired by someone?

It was in that moment I realized I was the fool. I was the drunk bumbling idiot. I was the one claiming inspiration and not acting on it. I had been wallowing, feeling sorry for myself, and spilling my fair share of drinks.

I realized that inspiration itself is meaningless, if not used for actions that by nature pay it forward to others. I knew that I'd never be the same after what happened, but I also realized that if I wanted to reclaim any of my past identity I'd worked so hard for, I had to get back to competition, back to fighting.

I felt as if I were walking in the dark with my hand on the wall, searching for the switch, and had just found it. I needed something to fill the void. I did not just want to survive. I wanted to thrive. And deep down, I knew what I had to do.

I was ready for the bright lights again.

95.

It's a beautiful thing; sports, and the capacity it has to remove someone from the world around them. Even more enchanting is to be the thing that folks rally behind, that people cheer for. Athletes provide experiences for people, they share moments with them, most of whom they've never even met. The best way for me to pull myself out of my nightmare was to chase an old dream, to deliver those moments for people, for myself.

One by one I watched my all my friends get wins and dedicate them to Isabel. I appreciated the sentiment but was jealous. I needed an ending to the story if I wanted any hope of moving forward.

I was going to get the chance on April 19th, 2014. I was finally scheduled to fight, against a Brazilian, Caio Magalhaes, in my home state of Florida. The event was to be held at the Amway Center, in Orlando.

I began putting the hours in, getting into the routine of fight life once more. It was a stark contrast to the lifestyle I'd been living. I came out of the haze and delegated my medicinal escapes to evenings only. The ringing in my ears had subsided, the shell

HK

shock dissipated. I had survived the blast and was taking steps to a better life again, a happier one. Coming to terms with Isabel's death meant accepting a more ordinary existence, one without the depth and color I'd once felt. Still, I had a UFC contract. I'd built the largest MMA promotion in Florida. There was much to be grateful for, things to make my life not so ordinary.

I began doing media again, opening up to the press about what had happened. In many interviews, I realized I was still using the term *we*, in the same way I was when standing over her coffin. I wondered how long that was going to last, speaking for both myself and the girl in my head.

A powerful bond formed between Master Cesar and myself over that camp at MMA Masters. Months before Isabel died, Cesar had lost his 16 year-old son. Shortly before that, his sister passed away suddenly, in a case of hospital negligence.

We had many emotional days. We grieved together. There were times when we would be hitting mits, and one of us would burst into tears. We didn't stop. We hit harder, faster, and more intensely. We were both in a bad place, but we were in a bad place together, and it made it more bearable for us.

I'd once been forced to pose the question; that of either Isabel or fighting. I thought I'd chosen the right one. I know I chose the one I wanted most. Fate doesn't always see eye to eye with our plans. Life made the decision for me, and a life with neither love nor career was a desolate one, so fighting it was.

There was a security that I found in going back to it. It was with a comfort that I knew the worst was over. No matter what happened, I'd walked through the fire and made it out alive. It couldn't get worse. That's what I thought.

96.

"When doubt seeps in you got two roads and you can take either one. You can go to the left, or you can go to the right, and believe me, they'll tell you failure is not an option. That is ridiculous. Failure is always an option. Failure is the most readily available option at all times, but it's a choice. You can choose to fail or you can choose to succeed."

-Chael Sonnen

There was crying on the other end of the phone. It wasn't a visceral, agonizing cry. It was a soft whimper, someone trying to fight it, sniffling and shaky.

"I didn't mean to." It was Matt. Something had happened.

"You didn't mean to what?"

"I didn't see it. I don't remember."

Someone else grabbed the phone. "Y'all gotta come to the hospital, man." My heart dropped.

"Shit's real serious. He hit a line, man. It knocked him out real good and he fell out the tree. He done pissed himself and some of his fingers are gone." Matt had been trying to make ends meet with a part-time job down south, and hit a power line with his saw. Brian and I rushed to the hospital.

When we got there, Matt was in the emergency room. His eyes were bloodshot and wet, his hand above his head. Two of his fingers had been burnt to a crisp, as if they were hot dogs left in the microwave for an hour. He couldn't string together a sentence, and he had monitors hooked up all over his body.

The doctor said he was lucky to be alive. I'd always struggled with that concept, calling someone lucky in light of a terrible accident. If he was lucky, he wouldn't have hit the power line. The point was moot. He was suffering, early signs of neuropathy already cramping parts of his body. More than anything, he was terrified at his brush with death, and it showed.

After several nights of monitoring, he was able to come home. Brian and I helped him around the house, cooked for him and fetched things so he wouldn't have to get up.

HK

Matt and I had been going through a training camp together, and when he got in the accident, it motivated me more. It was one more person to fight for, one who wanted to fight but wouldn't be able to for a long time. I was full steam ahead, and it was just when I was feeling optimistic again that the planes circled around to drop more bombs.

I was optimistic, but I was still angry with everything, including myself. I found solace in daily self-punishment at the gym. I pushed the limits, as I always had, and in the end, the same destructive behavior that I was trying to rid myself of came back to cripple me once more.

"One more round. One more. Just one more." I was sparring with Clint, my teammate from TUF. That time in my life seemed like forever ago.

I was so close to the finish line. It was two weeks before the fight. Master Cesar urged me to stop. "You've done enough today, brother."

"Last one." Last day of sparring. Last round. I should have listened.

I was tired. I don't recall the sequence of events well. I remember the end, and the noise it made when my hamstring tore off my hip bone. I remember the feeling of not being able to stand, and the muscle coiling up on the opposite side of my knee. I remember the alarm and dread my mind went through as I realized what had happened.

I fell to the mat, and Master Cesar rushed in. I stayed on the cage floor for 30 minutes, the back of my leg in shreds. I couldn't support my own body weight. I fell back down and stared at the ceiling.

I finally got up, and let Clint and Cesar carry me to my car. Clint drove to the hospital. I got an MRI, and they told me they'd send the results to the doctor immediately. He called shortly thereafter. A tear at my left ischial tuberosity. The light at the end of the tunnel had been pushed back. Another surgery. More darkness. I'd made it several days, weeks perhaps, with dry cheeks. Immediately, it all changed. I was back to dejection, back to despair.

They slit my leg open and pulled my hamstring back to my hip. They reattached it with bone screws, and sewed me shut. The doctor tried to show me pictures of the surgery as I came to. I waved him off and asked the nurse to call in my prescription so I could leave.

The rattle of the pill bottle made me cringe as I left the pharmacy. I'd spent so much time at the end of bottles in the last eight months. There were all kinds of bottles, but none so vile as one filled with opiates. I didn't mind sedation, I just loathed that particular kind. I'd been conditioned to believe they were the worst, and they were. They reminded me of a different her, my least favorite her.

I relied on other drugs to take me out of that world. I left the pharmacy and went to a liquor store. I stopped at a dealer's house. I swan dived head first back into the rabbit hole. The binge began.

I ate codeine because my ass hurt. I drank because the taste comforted me. I snorted cocaine because I wanted dopamine, and because the opiates made me lethargic. And I ate Xanax, because Xanax was my most trusted and reliable escape.

I was miserable. I couldn't sit. I couldn't lay on my back. I couldn't take a shit without having to shower because the incision was so close to my ass. It was impossible to have good body language, impossible to try to have grace or posture as I clinked and clanked around the house, refusing to let anyone help me. Worst of all, Juice was scared of me because of my crutches.

We were both cooped up in the same house, Matt and I, pitiful, wondering what we'd done to deserve this. The pain and grief compounded, and we fed off each other's misery. She wasn't there when I went into surgery, or waiting with a Gatorade when I got out. No nurse, no housekeeper, no lover, none of any roles I needed her so badly for. It was an overwhelming contrast between this surgery and the last, and her absence was glaring. It crept its way back into my thoughts, all day.

I made the mistake of still going to the UFC event in Orlando, seething with jealousy at all the athletes that had made it to their bouts that night. "No excuses next time," Caio remarked

$\mathcal{HK}$

when he saw me after his win. I felt pathetic, crutching around the arena, having to readjust my seat every few seconds on account of the stitches in my ass.

I watched fights on TV and battled feelings of deflation as I saw the sport passing me by. I was in a much different kind of pain than before. Still, I had no doubt about competing again. It kept me alive. It was something concrete on the bucket list.

Get back in there. I had to, at least one last time.

97.

I shouldn't have been climbing. It was only four months after a career-threatening injury, and I was on the side of a mountain in Colorado. Maroon Bells was the name, and the summit was nearly three miles in the air.

It was a trip Wyatt and I planned before I'd gotten hurt, and I didn't want to miss the opportunity. I'd learned that my gratitude for her family was best shown from afar, so when I got to spend time with them it was cherished.

He was in Colorado doing an internship before opening his chiropractic office in Tallahassee. Over the course of Isabel's death, funeral, and whirlwind after, Wyatt had been driving back and forth between Atlanta and Tallahassee, and managed to graduate at the top of his class. He earned the title of valedictorian, and it was the most awe-inspiring feat I'd ever seen.

His graduation was beyond moving. He spoke about his sister and the things she'd taught him about living life to the fullest. He used a line from something I'd written about her, and I got goosebumps. When he was done, a pianist played Ray Charles' "Georgia." It was a gripping moment, and one I'd never forget.

Wyatt filled in the cracks of family history I'd never heard. Sometimes I'd ask him the same questions I'd asked her, to hear the stories again. He gave me the deepest insight into how the family saw Isabel, and all the ways she'd changed them. He was the most socially intelligent person I'd ever met, always observing, never saying as much as he knew.

He'd been more patient than any of them with my grieving. He spoke with me at length about subjects I suspected he never wanted to talk about. He acknowledged gestures that others didn't, and thanked me for the things I did for Isabel.

The trip was all I'd had to look forward to in a while. I'd paid for tons of physical therapy to try to prepare my leg for it. It would not be an easy climb. In fact, when we arrived, there was an Apache helicopter rescue mission taking place. Wyatt gave me a look. While the ascent was difficult, there was more than just that. There was elevation, and gear, and camping on the side of a mountain. I hadn't been in the wilderness in 15 years.

We were on the second day, halfway to the top. We'd been climbing for around 12 hours total, and gotten lost early in the day, before retracing our steps and getting back on track. We were headed for the peak when I peered up and something caught my eye. There, 30 feet above us, stood a pack of horned mountain goats, dead in our path. They did not stay for long, trekking down the steep cliffside, straight towards us.

Wyatt had his risk aversion alarm turned on for the whole trip anyway, and became uncomfortable when they aimed their horns in our direction. They had the body language of a territorial animal threatened. I'm not sure if I was scared at him being frightened, or the other way around, but we both decided retreat was the best option, and our slow trek upwards became a quick descent downwards.

We'd dedicated the whole trip to getting to the top of that mountain, and were now getting thwarted by a pack of wild goats. We were running out of daylight, and wouldn't have enough hours left to make the trip back up by the time they'd cleared the way. We would not be reaching the summit.

We laughed it off after the scare was over, but Wyatt said on the way down that he felt the goats were Isabel's way of speaking to him. He said he'd never be doing anything like that again. I felt ashamed for even suggesting to take another member

HK

of this family on something remotely dangerous. I told him I'd come back next year and get to the top for both of us.

We packed our tent and finally made it back to our car. His phone received signal before mine, and rang the noise of a dozen messages, as they came through all at once.

"Hey Wyatt. Please have Josh call me as soon as he can." He read it aloud as he looked at his phone. It was from a 941 area code, my grandmother. I didn't know how she'd gotten his number. I didn't have time to ask, or explain. There was only one reason why she'd ever call him, and I knew that. Someone else was gone.

98.

"...Be at peace with God, whatever you conceive Him to be."
-Desiderata

Jeff Grove was 62 years old when he died. He suffered a fatal heart attack in the middle of the night while my mother was lying next to him. She was crying violently when she answered the phone. Memories of crumbling under the weight of the news in Stephanie's kitchen hit me with a fierceness.

I told her I loved her. I told her I was sorry. I told her I loved her again, and that we knew he was sick. I tried to think of words that people said to me that comforted me and found none.

I thought of my time by the gravesite, coming to the realization that someone had to die first. I told her we took the brunt of pain for our partners, to be grateful it was not them that had to endure. My mom taught me to love wildly and deeply, and now we were both feeling the calamity of having those that we loved taken from us.

Jeff and my mom had been residing in Arizona, at Lake Powell, traveling the country seasonally as planned, living the life she'd dreamed of. Now she was on the other end of the phone, broken, wondering how she was going to continue. I was in Colorado, flying back to South Florida the next day, and would drive to Tallahassee to meet her as soon as she got there. Mom still had the RV that she and Jeff had bought, except he was the only one of them that knew how to drive it. My uncle flew to Arizona to be with his sister, and to bring her back with the mobile home that Jeff had died in.

Feelings of helplessness revisited me. I felt I should've been stronger for her. I was there for her as much as I could be, but I wasn't healed yet either. I wasn't in a position to provide comfort, in part because I never felt much good at it anyway. Instead, we grieved together, from close and afar.

Jeff was cremated, and his ashes buried in the plot that my mother owned. My grandmother had bought it for her when she was diagnosed with cancer. I'd never known about the plot, and realized I was probably sheltered as to how sick she'd really been. Mom had made it through that, and she'd make it through this, but it was heartbreaking, watching her go from wife to widow.

She planned his memorial service, with the help of few friends and family members. I didn't want to see another burial. I dreaded it. Couples poured into the funeral home, hand in hand, showing displays of affection in front of a woman who'd just lost her husband. It wasn't their fault. They didn't know better. That didn't make it any less painful to see.

My mom asked me to say some things. I thought she'd might. I felt terrible for not offering, for making her ask in the first place. Unlike Isabel's eulogy, I had just minutes to prepare for Jeff and what I thought represented him. I took to the table of his things that my mom had laid out, and scribbled notes on his memorial program as I tried to keep it together, fighting tears and memories of the last time I'd had to do this.

I spoke about the first time I met Jeff, and how I grilled him on matters of religion and politics. I told how he took it in stride, gracefully telling me that what matters most is only how we treat people.

Dallas and Cathy came to the funeral, making the moment all the more heavy. The four of us were all in one place, mourning the loss of another of our loved ones, and while they weren't close

𝓗𝓚

with Jeff, their presence crystallized the loss of both Isabel and Jeff together.

A slideshow played of Jeff, in all his youth and glory. It moved chronologically through his life, significant moments that his family and my mother had chosen to speak for him. My heart strings were yanked and tugged as The Beatles' "Let it Be" played in the background. I realized it was the same one chosen for Isabel's slideshow not even a year prior.

The final stake through the heart was the very last picture shown; Isabel, Jeff, my mom, and myself, at our post weigh-in dinner in Las Vegas, before the Kevin Casey fight. We all had our arms draped around each other in love and bliss, ignorant to our future. It was as much as I could handle.

I left the funeral on a mission. I had to do something, anything. I was out of money, my mom was in shambles, and I could feel myself going back into a bad place. My leg still bothered me, but I didn't know how much longer I could wait. I had to get a fight.

Gary told me to find a card that I wanted to fight on. I was hoping the UFC would come back to Florida, and I started looking at the schedule on the website, pressing the refresh button incessantly, waiting for new announcements.

Finally, one of those times I pressed the button, and I saw it.

December 6th, 2014.

Isabel's birthday.

The room got cold, and goosebumps covered my body.

Location: TBA.

I called my manager. I called Joe Silva. I called Dana White. I called anyone and everyone that I thought would listen. Within days, I got a call back, and an opponent.

I'd be going up against TUF season 19 champion Eddie Gordon. He was one of the goliaths from the season I'd accompanied Palomino to tryout in, on that stupid fucking trip to Indianapolis. Eddie had ended up winning the whole thing.

The fight was scheduled for what would have been Isabel's 24th birthday, in the location I'd last fought, where she'd curled her hair, and whispered in my ear how proud she was. Mandalay Bay Event Center. *Montauk.* Fate had a funny way of coming around.

I spent the last few days that I could with my mom in Tallahassee and said my final goodbyes to the rest of those around town. Wyatt and I brought a lawn mower to Sue's house and cut her grass. I told her about the fight on Isabel's birthday. She cried, and hugged me, and told me that she knew that Isabel would be with me that day, that it would be a good day.

She told me to make sure that I *believed*, pointing to her tattoo she'd gotten to match Isabel's. She told me she loved me, to train hard, and to "sleep with the angels."

It would be the last time I'd ever see Sue Monroe.

99.

Sue Monroe died at 59 years old, slipping away in her sleep exactly 13 months after her daughter died. Some of her health problems were self-inflicted. Many she couldn't help.

I'd been back in Miami only a couple weeks. After practice one morning, I picked up my phone to see a single missed call from Landon. Just as when Grandma had called Wyatt, I knew that something was wrong. Landon never just *called*.

He texted me as I dialed him back.

"Mom passed away this morning."

I didn't react. I sat there, staring at the phone. I felt numb. I felt as if the last string had been cut, the final piece of Isabel that I could touch, and grab onto, and love, gone.

Training camp stopped as I drove back to Tallahassee for another burial, another funeral. There was no grave bought for Sue, and her ashes were buried with her daughter, as Jeff's had been preemptively buried with his wife.

Once more I was asked to speak, this time not by family, or by choice, but by Pastor Fran, of the Monroe's church. It was the same that Isabel's funeral was in, the same chapel that Dallas and

HK

Sue walked down the aisle in. I wondered how any of them still went there.

No one but Landon and Wyatt saw Pastor Fran ask me to speak. I wished it had been more people making that decision. I wished he'd have run it by others before asking me. Passivity was high in the family, and there was no patriarch, no one to make those decisions. I wasn't sure of my place, but I wasn't sure of a lot of things, and I said yes, as he'd figured I'd might.

I spoke on what I learned from Sue, about the value of parenthood. I think we all have paths to greatness. Some paths may be through art, or creativity, or civil duties, but some paths of greatness are through one's children, by creating people who change the world. Any of the ways Isabel moved me, or her brothers for their lovers, or their children and so on, could all be traced back to Sue and Dallas Monroe. Just as Isabel had a hand in anything I ended up contributing to the world, the same could be said for Sue, and that, to me, was her greatness. If the people we create are a person's measure of success, then Sue was the most prosperous I'd ever met.

There's no way to describe speaking at three funerals in a year. I wondered if Isabel dying and Sue dying were even separate instances, or just one with a 13-month shelf life. I felt responsible for Isabel, and it made me feel responsible for Sue too, and how she died. I wondered if I'd been the wind to blow over the dominoes, the catalyst for the demise of a family.

One of Isabel's aunts had lived with Sue, and asked me to come by. She'd watched me sit with Sue as she went through her daughter's things, and now she wanted me to do the same for her. There were notes Sue had written about me, about seeing her daughter in love. She had the same potency for words that she'd passed on to Isabel. She still had all of Isabel's journals too. We sometimes couldn't decipher which of them had written what.

At her house was also the amulet of Isabel's hair I'd made for Sue the previous year. Landon asked me to retrieve it for him. I was happy for him to have it.

My reality had become a series of tragedies that I wasn't sure was ever going to stop. Nothing seemed out of the realm of possibility anymore. Every conversation I had with friends and family became a potential last. I didn't know who was going to get picked off next, who else would fall victim to something I'd done.

I spent much of the camp in Tallahassee. Joey created a makeshift training area in the attic of Gold's to accommodate us, and we trained every morning. It was just he and I, like the old days. The routine of a past life brought comfort. War brought peace in a way I'd never experienced. It was unlike any other fight I'd had, in that I never grew tired of the question that had irked me for years.

When's the next fight?

The fight was on December 6th, and I was reminded of its gravity each time someone asked. Purpose. Purpose. Purpose. I had it in spades for months.

Training for Eddie was easy, mentally. He had children, a family, and title of *The Ultimate Fighter* tournament champion. He represented everything I wanted in life and didn't have. The fight was a platform to elevate Isabel, and the things our families had went through. To win became my only focus. Every time I trained, I trained for all of us. Accomplishment made struggle more meaningful. Success was never more delectable than in the wake of collapse.

Physically, it was anything but easy. It was the most painful training camp I'd ever gone through. During each massage a therapist kneaded at my incision point where my ass met my hamstring, grinding out scar tissue from the surgery with every session.

It hurt my leg to wrestle. It hurt to grapple. It hurt to run, and to lift heavy. I skipped those things, and half the other movements I was accustomed to practicing. I made damn sure to not get injured. Being ill prepared and making it to the fight was better in my mind than not showing up at all. Anything besides another injury. So I hit mits. I lifted light. And I trained my left high kick.

I drilled it over and over again. We repped it hundreds of times a day. It was the only thing that didn't hurt, it seemed. I wondered if I had nerve damage. I didn't care. Every day I woke

HK

up, looked at her initials on my ribs, and practiced my head kick. It spoke to me as if I had no other choice.

I added to her initials, a Phoenix bird to honor my mother, and to symbolize my return to the cage. My tattoos became a way for me to wear the pain of my journey, to not forget the places I came from. It was my way to bring the things I valued most with me, as I tried to catapult into another life, one where my best days were not behind me.

I donned the fight name *Anqa,* an Arab firebird, to strengthen the notion of rebirth. To be reborn, I had to win. I had to do something with the stage I'd set. I romanticized about battering Eddie with my left leg, the same one that had crippled me, the one that had stolen my opportunity last time I'd tried to turn things around. Time after time in my dreams I saw my shin land on his jaw, and him crumpling to the ground.

I would soon be in Las Vegas, to see if my vision would become reality.

100.

"There is love in me the likes of which you've never seen. There is rage in me the likes of which should never escape. If I am not satisfied in the one, I will indulge the other."

-Mary Shelley

And so here I am.

612 days.

That's how long it's been since I've last seen the inside of the Octagon. I've reached my threshold of all the death I can take, and it is now do or die myself. I'm half asleep, wondering to myself whether I'm in the exact locker room as before, or a next door replica. The familiarity helps. It comforts me knowing the last time I made this walk in the Mandalay Bay Arena, I returned victorious.

I've been in plenty of cages since the one on April 13th, 2013, but none so consequential. I've wrestled in my mind with far larger monsters than the one I'll face tonight, just none so public. The locker room is eerily quiet. An occasional smack of a kick on a pad interrupts my pre-fight nap.

Eyes open, go time. As soon as I wake, movement begins. Movement relieves tension, and as long as my body is in motion, my mind is at peace.

"Slow down," my coaches say. "We've got plenty of time." They don't know how I feel. No one could.

I start to think of them one by one, the people I draw courage from. I begin with those that are no longer here to watch. I suspend my disbelief in afterlives, convincing myself that the three of them are looking down on me, surrounding and enveloping me, guiding my every movement. They've been on my mind every second of every training session for the last year, and I feel their presence now more than ever.

I move next to the most important people that I know with certainty are watching, the folks who've seen me at my worst. I think of my mother and Isabel's family in Tallahassee. I know that it's not enough to have just made it here. I have to do something truly special with the opportunity.

I think about my corner, the men in the room with me. I think about how exhilarating and frightening it is to be mere feet away from one of your best friends in a fist fight, not being able to do anything but yell from the outside. I think of how all of us will be celebrating wildly in a few minutes; if only I can just find that off button on my opponent. They all have one. I know I'll find his. It may take some digging, but I'll find it.

Lastly, I think about all the random folks along the way. All the coaches, the training partners, the fans, people I know, people I don't. They've all been a part of my experience, part of this journey.

I use all these people and I paint a picture in my mind that fills me with such determination and moxie that I know no matter what happens, the one thing I can rely on with overwhelming conviction, is that I won't be broken. Not in there. I may win, I may lose, but I will bare all from start to finish, never having to explain

HK

to a single person as to why I gave up. There will not be any letdowns on this day. Today is meant for celebration.

I step out of my locker room and look to my left to see my opponent and his coaches already waiting. I'm set to walk first, led by a production team of cameramen and UFC employees in black t-shirts, logo emblazoned on the front. Hyper focus begins, minor details become apparent and abundant. I'm stopped at the curtain, able to see only a fraction of the thousands awaiting my entrance. I'm afforded one last moment of self-reflection before the show really begins.

My lover's got humor..

I hear the opening lyrics of my walkout music blasting through the arena, and everything changes. I'm overcome with emotion and scream in anticipation as I sidestep the security guard ushering me in.

Knows everybody's disapproval..

I've walked out to this song a million times before in my head, so many that it feels unreal to be actually doing it in real life. This is the last bit of outcome that I'm 100% sure of, the last thing that I know will happen how it did in my mind, before the bedlam begins.

I should've worshipped her sooner..

I reach the end of my walk, and remove my shirt first, then my most prized possession, my piece of her draped around my neck. I place it over the head of Joey, and take solace in the fact that it will be there waiting for me when I return.

If the heavens ever did speak, she's the last true mouthpiece..

I hug my corners, get inspected by the referee, and make the final few steps up the stairs into the cage. I take one last look down at my body, and tattoos, and remind myself what it took for me to get here. I feel the soft give of the canvas underneath my feet. It's been too long.

I take the center of the cage, my way of claiming my territory from the onset. My coaches are behind me, screaming pre-fight instructions, but their words are drowned out by Eddie's walkout music. I'm waiting desperately for the moment I can lay my eyes on him.

Finally, he enters, followed by his coaches. He clenches his jaw and slaps hands with fans as he walks in the arena. He looks mean, and crawls into the cage before circling me as I continue to stand in the center.

I'm looking for any indication that he's uncertain of himself, any misstep in his behavior, and I've found one already. He stops 90 degrees short of 360, setting up shop in the neutral corner. I point at his coaches in the red corner, directing him as to where he should be standing. He looks a bit confused, before realizing his mistake. I'm pleased by this. Confusion is good.

We stand across from each other for what feels like an eternity. Bruce Buffer takes the center of the cage and I can feel my heartbeat in my chest for the first time in the night. I let out one last scream before he begins, and do my best to take it all in.

"Fighting out of Tallahassee, Florida!" Those words sound so damn sweet.

I know the ensuing moments will determine how I feel about myself and what people think of me for a long time to come. I take a final look at the face on my banner. The same picture used on Isabel's funeral program and gravestone is now behind me, standing over my shoulder, watching. Sue was right. She's with me, as much as she ever will be again. They all are.

Buffer introduces my opponent, and Eddie looks away. Another misstep on his part and my confidence is further strengthened. Referee Herb Dean asks if I'm ready. I nod, and the bell rings. My fate awaits me.

Eddie motions to touch gloves. This isn't a glove touch kind of fight. He knows that. It's his last and final misstep, and I know now that it's just a matter of time. I oblige him, and the violence begins.

A kick, a punch, a takedown attempt, and I finally feel his strength.

This is not going to be easy.

An accidental eye poke on his part, an inadvertent knee to the groin on my part. The action is halted. The ref gives him a moment to recover, and I look down at my corners as they urge me to calm down. I try to.

HK

Another glove touch, more kicks and punches. He throws me on the ground and lands on top. He's stronger than anyone I've ever faced. I try to be active on the ground but he gives me no room to work. I opt instead to hold on for a referee standup. After a couple minutes of inactivity, the referee obliges.

Kick, kick, kick, another takedown. I'm on my back again. My corner tells me he's getting tired. Another lull in the action, and it becomes apparent that Eddie is there only to win rounds. He's content being on top, not doing damage. I'll keep trading those kicks for these takedowns, as long as he keeps reaching down to catch that body kick.

The round ends and my corner rushes in the with the stool. They aren't happy. "Set your kicks up," they plead. I'm staring across the cage, trying to gauge how tired he really is. I look outside the Octagon and find Joe Rogan watching me. His face depicts confusion, eyebrows scrunched low. I stare back at him, and we lock eyes briefly. I pretend for a moment I have telepathy. "I'm still here," I tell him. "I know that last round wasn't pretty." The referee interrupts my whimsical conversation, and it's time to fight again.

The round begins with more kicks and punches. He falls to a leg kick, I follow, and end up on my back again. Smother, smother, attempted sweep, more smothering. He has his head in the center of my chest, nullifying any movement from bottom. I am losing the fight. The crowd boos, and I feel another referee standup imminent.

We're back to our feet again. We reset and his hands are low, his breathing labored. I know it's time.

Ding, ding, wop.

My punches are landing, and he is a step behind now.

Believe.

I fake a body kick, the same one I've thrown dozens of times in the last few minutes, and change trajectories at the final moment. I feel my shin land with brutal momentum, perfectly nestled in the crevice where his jaw and neck meet.

I did it.

He falls below my line of vision, and I know he won't be getting up. I throw my hands up. The crowd roars. I fall to my knees. It's everything I thought it would be, and more.

A high kick for The Housekeeper.

If I never do another thing, I've become the hero, at least one final time. I have no control of my emotions as I circle the cage, uncertain of just what to do next with my life. I find the nearest camera, my imaginary medium to the heavens.

I love you Isabel. I love you Jeff, I love you Sue.

My coaches come rushing in, raging with excitement. Joey places my chain back around my neck. Everything is back to happening how I imagined it in my mind. Rogan comes in, microphone in hand.

"Doubt and uncertainty be damned, never give up," I tell him, in more words than that. "I love you, mom. I love you, Tallahassee."

Eddie is finally up and walking, and I jump out of the cage to apologize to him. The people have gotten what they wanted, more destruction, and Eddie is just a victim of circumstance.

We make our way back to the physicians that await post-fight combatants. There is a thin curtain separating our camps. A doctor shines his light in my eyes and asks me if anything hurts. Nothing hurts, and everything hurts. I burst into tears. One of my cornermen cries flowingly with me. Cesar chokes up but holds it back. Joey is wearing a huge smile.

I'm ushered towards a photographer with a large tarp behind him, asking me to pose in a victory stance, tears still rolling down my face. Everything is a blur, and I'm escorted next to the press. Folks I recognize, folks I don't, all congratulating me. Cameras flash, and more microphones in my face, asking me to explain the miracle that just occurred. I relish in the moment, while simultaneously wanting nothing more than to get back to my locker room and digest the act in solitude.

I make my way back to the room I warmed up in, and sit with my coaches, reliving the moment several times over. Finally, I head to the showers. I lean my head against the tile wall, and enjoy the silence and seclusion. I decide it is indeed the same

HK

locker room and shower as it had been nearly two years ago. Life is much different now though.

I wash off my sweat, and the sweat of my opponent. Down the drain it goes. With it, the regrets and tears amassed over a tumultuous 612 days. I'm not rid of it all yet, but it's a start. I cry more, realizing that it is all finally over.

"Walk with the dreamers, the believers, the courageous, the cheerful, the planners, the doers, the successful people with their heads in the clouds and their feet on the ground. Let their spirit ignite a fire within you to leave this world better than when you found it."
                                                                    -Wilfred Peterson

Love, Isabel once told me, while in a particularly cerebral mood, is all the little memories we share with someone that no one else has. Love doesn't always have to be romantic, she said. It could be with a friend, or a pet, and by her standards, love was everywhere. Some of my favorite memories of her were when she was in these moods, when she was feeling talkative about abstract ideas and beliefs, being spiritual.

I suggested that maybe love was exclusive to only good memories, to which she asked who in my life did I love that I had only good memories with. Bad times add depth and give context to love, she explained, in more words than that. She'd seen family members suffer from Alzheimer's, and they forget who they loved, she said, because they'd lost their memories of that person.

It was one of the more profound things she ever told me, that memories and love are one and the same. It was a mentality I ended up adopting. She was right, after all. The interactions among one another are what we love most, and remember.

I'd already suspected in my mind that love was the meaning of life. All the weddings, the arts, the sciences, the religions and drugs, those are the things the human experience is made of, but love will always be king.

History is littered with remarkable folks that people feel the need to tell the world about; through books, poems, songs, and other arts. I've always known that Isabel was one of these, one that could not be left unremembered. At the end of the day, we are vessels, I think, for whatever emotions it is we're carrying. Isabel, at her best, was a vessel for pure bliss, with an infectious smile that would make you want to go conquer the whole world. She was a

HK

supernova, and this was my attempt at crystallizing her star, and what it was like to be next to her when it burnt out. After she died, many told me that she would live on through me. I didn't know what that meant at the time, but I do now.

Most relationships damaged in the wake of her loss were reconciled. Some were not. Many were reduced, or left out of writing entirely, because this story wasn't about them. It was about a girl and the things she taught me. It was about her, living after death.

Time has come and gone since December 6th, 2014. Juice died before the end of the year. I got another dog, one born on the same night. I named him after the doctor that delivered Juice to the other side. I still do that sometimes, actions to remind me of a time that is ever fleeting. My grandmother died days before completing this. I sang at her funeral, tired of speaking at them.

I got to the top of Maroon Bells as promised, and got the hair out of the drain. I was a groomsman in a Monroe wedding. I rewatched The Fountain, and removed most her clothes from the closet. I fought more, winning, and losing, which is all life is; a series of victories and defeats. It's chaos, both beautiful and cruel. We must do our best to embrace the beauty when it comes, and take the cruel in stride.

When I embarked on this years ago, my purpose was not to just tell the story of Isabel, but to include all the things I never got the chance to say to her. These words encompassed only part of her life, but over the course of writing, I inventoried all of mine, to identify the things I learned from her.

She taught me what it's like to have someone more important to me than myself. She taught me that success is easier when we believe. She taught me that there are consequences for our actions, every single one of them. Sometimes life lessons are merely consolation prizes, at having to learn things the hard way. If I can bestow that knowledge on at least one person without them having to go through what I went through, then I am satisfied.

There's still a piece of me left on I-75, still things I'll never forgive myself for. There are things one kick cannot atone for, nor a whole book. All the small triumphs, the colossal failures, they all become a part of the equation. **I've learned to live with them.** I push forward, hoping my accomplishments define me more than my character flaws; that if I'm talented enough at things, people will forgive me for my defects.

I continue my pattern of thinking that began once Isabel died, always looking for my next purpose. Wasted potential is my only fear now. I do better when I'm sharing my stories, when I'm explaining why it is I act the way I do, why I love the things I've loved.

Happiness to me now is attempting to create more than I've destroyed. **It is a tall order. Teaching, sharing, giving; I try to use anything at my disposal as a way to inject positivity into my life. I realized eventually there's no removing the darkness. There is only outweighing it.**

I've learned to trust the journey, because in the end we have no choice but to. I trust, not because I think things are predetermined, but because I believe in my ability to make the best of them. The world may bring us to our knees, but what matters most is how well we walk through the fire.

I still don't fear dying nowadays. Everyone has a birthday and a death day, and it's the singularity of life that makes it so special. We're marching towards the end from day one. As we march, ask yourself, if your end were to come today, what seeds did you plant?

What will you be a vessel for?

What will your verse be?

HK

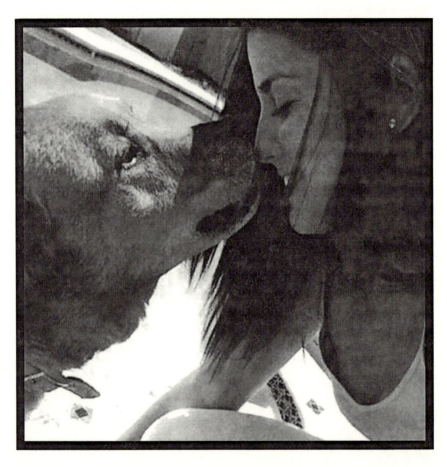

December 6, 1990 – August 30, 2013

To Gerard, for his faith and encouragement. To Sophia, for her patience. To Taylor, Hunter, Chad, and everyone else not mentioned. To those who were included, that understood the need to paint the picture. To the readers who've followed along, and the fans who have always supported me. Thank you all.

HK

O. 1/17
B 7/17
W 2/18
H 8/18

CPSIA information can be obtained
at www.ICGtesting.com
Printed in the USA
LVOW12s1510040117
519724LV00006B/977/P